IMAGES
of America

EASTLAND GARDENS

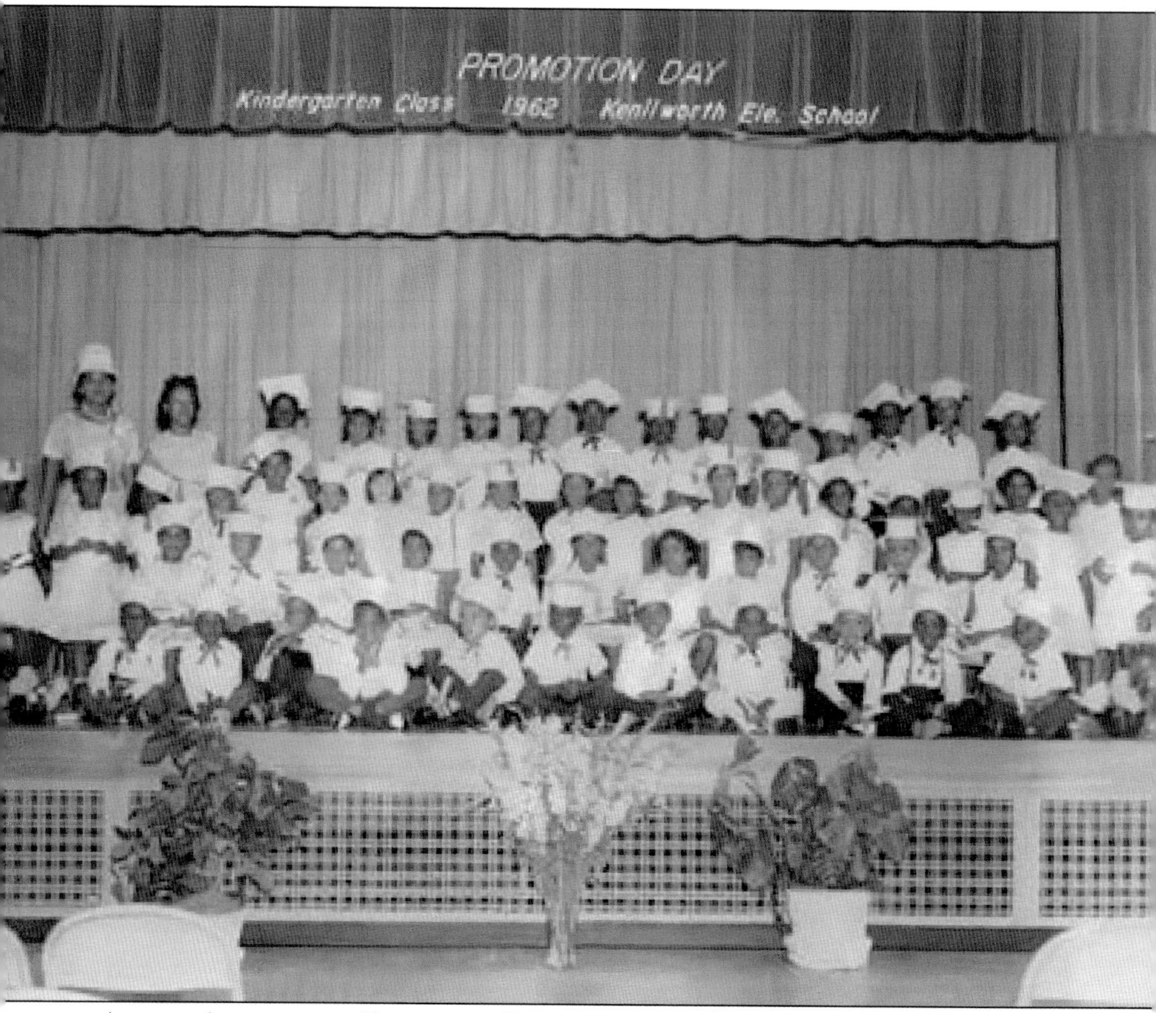

AFRICAN AMERICANS AT KENILWORTH SCHOOL IN 1962. The students in this class photograph attended the neighborhood public school, which at one time was closed to children of African American descent. In 1953, after white enrollment fell to 40, the District of Columbia Board of Education turned the school over to accommodate black students, most of whom lived in the neighborhood. And, for the first time, black teachers were hired to teach at Kenilworth, several of whom already lived in Eastland Gardens. (Justina Wilkins.)

ON THE COVER: LITTLE OASIS OF THE CITY. By 1960, the Eastland Gardens development had expanded to encompass areas beyond its original boundaries. That year, William Wood, a US Department of Navy employee, his wife, Frances Wood, and their three children moved to Ord Street into the community they felt was an urban oasis. Frances, who worked as a library technician at the US Information Agency, is pictured here with their children, Timothy, Francine, and Larry. (Frances Wood.)

IMAGES
of America

EASTLAND GARDENS

Eastland Gardens Flower Club

ARCADIA
PUBLISHING

ISBN 978-0-7385-9202-2

Published by Arcadia Publishing
Charleston, South Carolina

Printed in the United States of America

Library of Congress Control Number: 2011930903

For all general information, please contact Arcadia Publishing:
Telephone 843-853-2070
Fax 843-853-0044
E-mail sales@arcadiapublishing.com
For customer service and orders:
Toll-Free 1-888-313-2665

Visit us on the Internet at www.arcadiapublishing.com

This book is dedicated to all past and present residents of the Eastland Gardens community—members who made this work possible. It is because of their unselfish love of their neighborhood that they provided materials, oral histories, personal and family information, and photographs that brought this book to fruition.

Contents

Acknowledgments

The authors are Javier Barker, Althia Harris, Regina King, and Zerline Hughes, officers and webmaster of the Eastland Gardens Flower Club. Patsy Fletcher of the District of Columbia Historic Preservation Office assisted in the research and writing.

We wish to express our utmost gratitude for the existence of the photographic and documentary collection of Owen Davis and Rhuedine Davis. Without the Davis family collection—and the activism of the Davises—this book would have been almost impossible.

Many thanks go to the following Eastland Gardens Flower Club members who provided encouragement, history, and photographs: Portia Allen, Delores Crim-Neal, Alan Davis, Helen Haynes, Geraldyne Jackson, and Gregory "Koolgalou" Williams. The generosity of the following Eastland Gardens neighbors and family, past and present, who understand and value the preservation of this community, is very much appreciated: Hobson Bowser Jr., Wilhelmina Burdette, Michael Chinn, Erman T. Clay, Lunetta Cromer, Jackie Edwards, Bernetta Matthews Francis, Christine Glover, Duwayne Glover, Siraaj Hasan Family, Herndon Family, Elaine Overall Hymes, Mary Lincoln, Frank Matthews, Charlita McMillan, Saundra Oyewale, Maxine Rosborough, Willie Stewart, Edwin B. Washington Jr., Ethel White, Lucille White, Justina Wilkins, Theresa Williams, Frances Wood, and Zion Baptist Church of Eastland Gardens.

The special efforts of the following local historians, local history repositories, and their staffs and other experts made the quest to put this book together so much easier: District of Columbia Office of Planning; Timothy Dennee, Ruth Trocolli, and Brian Kraft of the District of Columbia Historic Preservation Office; Dianne Dale; the Eastland Gardens Civic Association; the Black Studies Division of the Martin Luther King Jr. Public Library; Marya Annette McQuirter, PhD; Kay Peterson of the National Museum of American History; Faye Haskins of the Washingtoniana Division of the Martin Luther King Jr. Public Library; Stephen Syphax of the National Park Service National Capitol Region East; and Kimberly Springle of the Charles Sumner Museum and Archives.

Very special thanks go to the Frederick Douglass Garden Club, the District of Columbia Historic Preservation Office, and, especially, the Humanities Council of Washington, DC, for its support and funding of this project.

CONTRIBUTORS

Most of the images used in this book were graciously and lovingly offered by residents of Eastland Gardens. The initials at the end of each caption indicate the source of each image, and a key to the initials is presented below.

AA—*Afro-American* Newspaper
BK—Brian Kraft
CM—Charlita McMillan
CSSMA—Charles Sumner School Museum and Archives
CTDC—Cultural Tourism DC
DCHPO—District of Columbia Historic Preservation Office
DCN—Delores Crim-Neal
DF—Rhuedine and Owen Davis family collection
EBW—Edwin B. Washington Jr.
EC—Erman T. Clay
EOH—Elaine Overall Hymes
EW—Ethel White
FM—Frank Matthews
FW—Frances Wood
GF—Glover family collection
GJ—Geraldyne Jackson
GW—Gregory Williams
HF—Herndon family collection
HH—Helen Haynes
HSW—Historical Society of Washington, DC
JB—Javier Barker
JW—Justina Wilkins
KL—Kencell Logan
LC—Lunetta Cromer
LOC—Library of Congress
LW—Lucille White
MC—Michael Chinn
ML—Mary Lincoln
MLK-B—Martin Luther King Jr. Library, Black Studies Division
MLK-W—Martin Luther King Jr. Library, Washingtoniana Division
MSRC—Moorland-Spingarn Research Center
NMAH—National Museum of American History Smithsonian Institution
NPC—National Park Service National Capitol Region East
PA—Portia Allen
WB—Wilhelmina Burdette
WS—Willie Stewart
ZBC—Zion Baptist Church

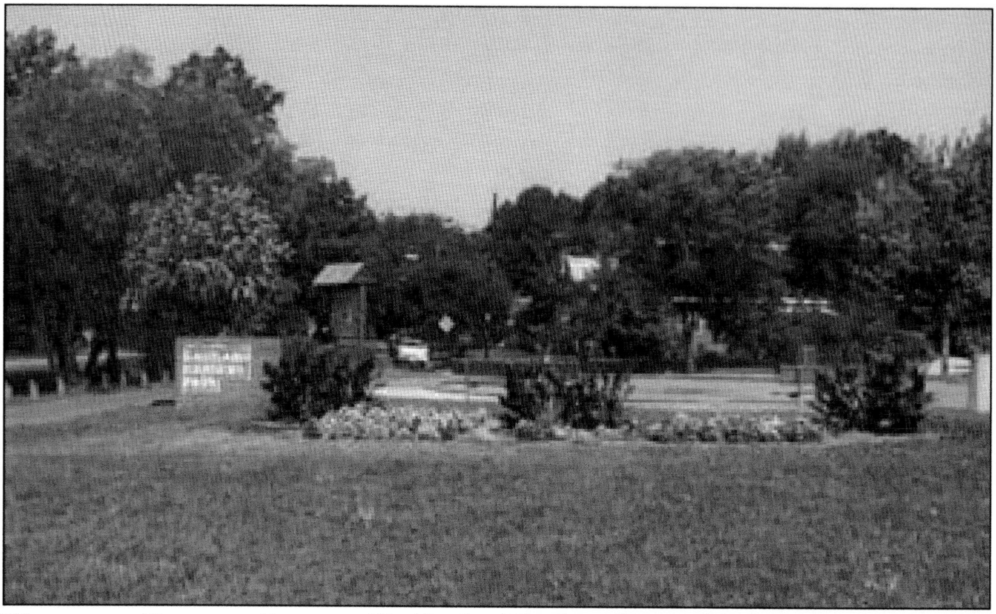

Welcome to Eastland Gardens. The Eastland Gardens Flower Club, formed in 1957, took on the responsibility decades ago to create and maintain this inviting entry to a slice of suburbia in Northeast Washington, DC. Each year, the flower club tends the plot of land on Lee Street. In 1957, Rhuedine Davis, the flower club's founder and first president, negotiated with the National Park Service to share management of the small triangular park, a section of US Reservation 523. One of her goals was to ensure that there would be citizen participation in maintaining an attractive entrance to Eastland Gardens. (JB.)

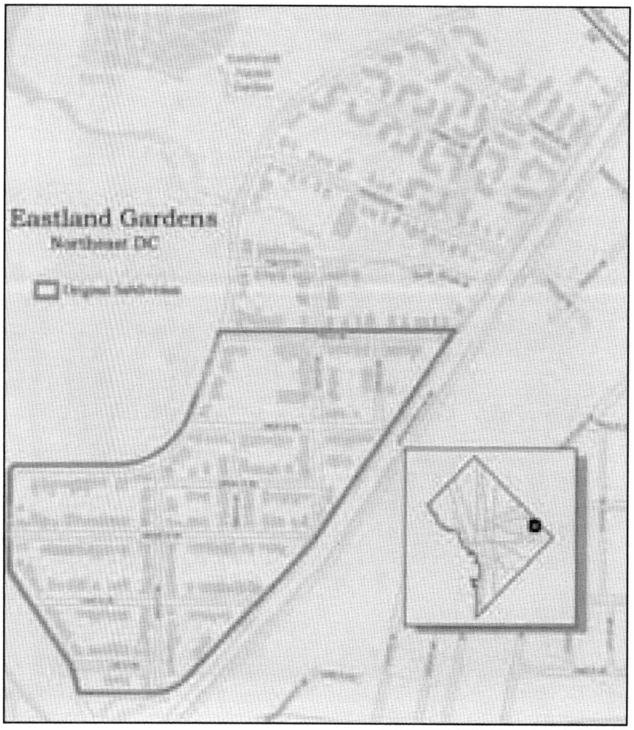

Location of Eastland Gardens. This map shows the boundaries of the original Eastland Gardens in Northeast Washington, DC. Within these boundaries, many of the homes were designed by African American architects or constructed by African American builders. While several communities in Washington, DC, have examples of projects of black designers and craftsmen, Eastland Gardens is significant particularly for the concentration and proportion of black-originated buildings. (BK.)

INTRODUCTION

Eastland Gardens is a unique community in Northeast Washington, DC, situated on the southern shore of the Anacostia River adjacent to aquatic gardens of lotus, water lilies, and other exuberant flora. It is a suburban development of 300 single-family, mostly brick, houses designed primarily by African American architects and builders. The homes are surrounded by spacious yards, lush gardens, and broad streets. Sandwiched between two primarily apartment communities, Kenilworth-Parkside and Mayfair Mansions, and bordered on the southeast by a busy freeway, Eastland Gardens is a safely guarded treasure.

Around 400 years ago, the Algonkian Nacotchtank Indians found ample fish and game, particularly beaver, in the Anacostia Valley, as well as fertile ground for cultivation. They were able to parlay those resources into developing a powerful fur trade industry with markets as far north as New York.

During the Colonial period, seagoing ships navigated the river to Bladensburg, which had become a busy tobacco port by the mid-1700s. Fishing remained a thriving industry. Over the years, however, the clearing of land for agriculture caused erosion and sedimentation of the waterway and the death of the upriver ports. The 19th-century Anacostia River, filled with mud flats and sand bars, became a repository for much of the sewage of Washington, DC. Muddy pools bred malarial mosquitoes, and the river, deemed noxious, was largely avoided.

A one-armed, white Civil War veteran, nonetheless, saw potential in this stretch of bottomland that bordered what became Eastland Gardens. In the 1880s, Walter Shaw purchased 30 acres from the Fowler family, who contributed seven free acres of "worthless" marshland. Shaw decided that these wetlands might be a good place for a water garden and he sent for a few wild water lilies from his native state of Maine. They flourished, and he began making more ponds and adding new varieties of flowers. When he died in 1921, Shaw Gardens was a successful commercial enterprise and popular summer attraction run by his widowed daughter Helen Shaw Fowler.

When the Shaw enterprise was threatened by congressionally mandated improvements to the Anacostia River, Helen lobbied vigorously to preserve the gardens that she and her father had worked so hard to develop. With the support of congressmen and US presidents, the renamed Kenilworth Aquatic Gardens was purchased by the federal government in 1938 and incorporated into the National Park Service system.

Eastland Gardens was also close to the Benning Racetrack, which had been operating at least since the 1870s and was considered to have the best mile track in the country. In fact, the property on which Eastland Gardens was built was purchased from track owners. In 1890, the track changed hands, becoming part of the newly reorganized Washington Jockey Club, one of the nation's oldest racing clubs. In 1902, when the track was being renovated, workers found more than 25 human skeletons. George Sheriff, great-grandson of Joshua Beall, the original owner of land grant, came forward to explain that the property over which the track had been built had been a burial ground for people enslaved by the Bealls and Sheriffs. The last interment occurred in 1860.

Horse, bicycle, and automobile racing were popular events at the Benning track, patronized by socialites and ruffians alike. They traveled to the track by train to the east in Deanwood, by streetcar along Kenilworth Avenue, or by carriage and automobile along Anacostia Road (now Minnesota and Kenilworth Avenues). On Sundays, an outing to the track may have included a stroll to or tea at the aquatic gardens or lily ponds. By the end of the first decade in 1900 though, gambling was illegal, effectively ending some of the allure of the racetrack. Although racing continued, other attractions, such as circuses and fairs, were also presented. Eventually, the Benning became a training track for jockeys and race car drivers until its final closure in the 1940s. As early as 1927, however, the Jockey Club began selling sections of its land. One buyer was Howard Gott, a white developer who was central in building Eastland Gardens.

Eastland Gardens, Inc., (EGI) was formed in 1927 to purchase and develop property at the intersections of Ord Street between Kenilworth Avenue, Lee Street, Fortieth Street, and the Anacostia River. EGI's subdivision plat from 1927 revealed the company's intention to construct row houses. But, as its parcel was far from the highly urbanized sections of the city, there was insufficient demand for that density of development. The company sold many more unimproved lots than completed homes. These factors kept the land prices fairly low and enabled most buyers to purchase double lots upon which to build.

Interestingly, Eastland Gardens was established without the restrictive racial and religious covenants that were popular among white developers. Further, Gott seemed to prefer African American architects and builders, as did the principally African American buyers. This was because, it was speculated, African Americans were hungry for work and for homeownership. By 1955, a total of 166 structures had been built in Eastland Gardens—Colonials, bungalows, ranches, and ramblers—and 16 black architects and seven black builders constructed more than 120 of them. For new owners and their architects, Eastland Gardens was a site of considerable opportunity.

Like the white Shaws and Fowlers before them, current residents work hard to preserve their enclave of beauty and peace. The Eastland Gardens Flower Club, for example, ensures the neighborhood has a proliferation of flower gardens in this beautiful suburb-in-the-city. Indeed, a spaciously developed area within the city's boundaries amidst endless row houses and apartment buildings is truly rare.

One

There Were Always Gardens

The area that became Eastland Gardens was a floodplain of the Anacostia River, formerly called the Eastern Branch. Along the river, there once were fish camps of the first inhabitants, the Nacotchtank Indians. Their settlements dotted the southern side of the Eastern Branch from Giesboro Point as it made its way to the head of the river at what became, in 1742, Bladensburg, Maryland. The Nacotchtank were known for their trading prowess. However, they also hunted and raised crops. Thus, it could be said that they were the first gardeners of Eastland Gardens—newer inhabitants merely carried on the tradition.

By the early 19th century, overdevelopment and clearing of the natural ground cover caused the river to become silted and sluggish. Navigation became difficult. Walter Shaw saw an opportunity in the undesirable marshes to develop and create gardens for water lilies and other exotic water-based plants. He was successful, and the area became known as the Lily Ponds or Shaw Gardens.

In the 1920s, Shaw Gardens was almost lost. Once efforts began to dredge and clean the river, there were attempts by the Army Corps of Engineers to take the gardens to improve the navigation of the river. Shaw's daughter Helen Fowler vigorously promoted the contribution of the gardens to the restoration of nature. Ultimately, Congress authorized payment in 1938 of $15,000 for eight acres. The gardens, saved from being filled, were added to Anacostia Park where they could be enjoyed by successive generations. It would be many decades before the social and environmental value of wetlands was recognized.

A later challenge to the area came in the form of a city dump. Established in 1942, the site was a noxious presence and the source of endless hazards, such as fumes and smoke from the burning of the trash. Garbage trucks rumbling through the community and rats came with the city dump, and feral dogs roamed in packs terrorizing local residents. The civic association complained vociferously until finally the dump was closed and covered in layers of dirt in 1968. In 1969, it was converted to parkland, which offered garden-like open space. Now Kenilworth Park, the "garden" is a site for sports activities, picnics, and various celebrations.

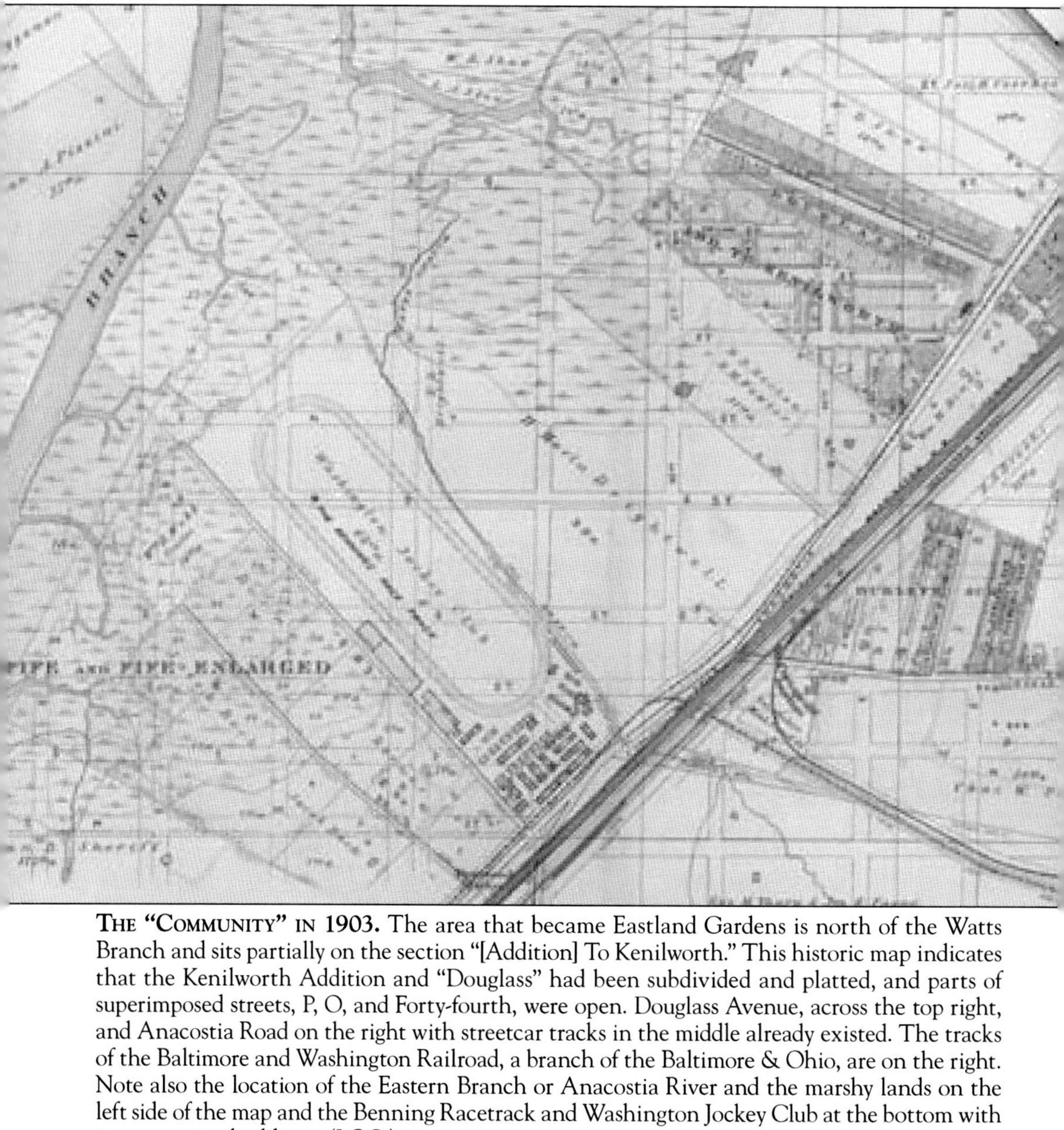

THE "COMMUNITY" IN 1903. The area that became Eastland Gardens is north of the Watts Branch and sits partially on the section "[Addition] To Kenilworth." This historic map indicates that the Kenilworth Addition and "Douglass" had been subdivided and platted, and parts of superimposed streets, P, O, and Forty-fourth, were open. Douglass Avenue, across the top right, and Anacostia Road on the right with streetcar tracks in the middle already existed. The tracks of the Baltimore and Washington Railroad, a branch of the Baltimore & Ohio, are on the right. Note also the location of the Eastern Branch or Anacostia River and the marshy lands on the left side of the map and the Benning Racetrack and Washington Jockey Club at the bottom with its supporting buildings. (LOC.)

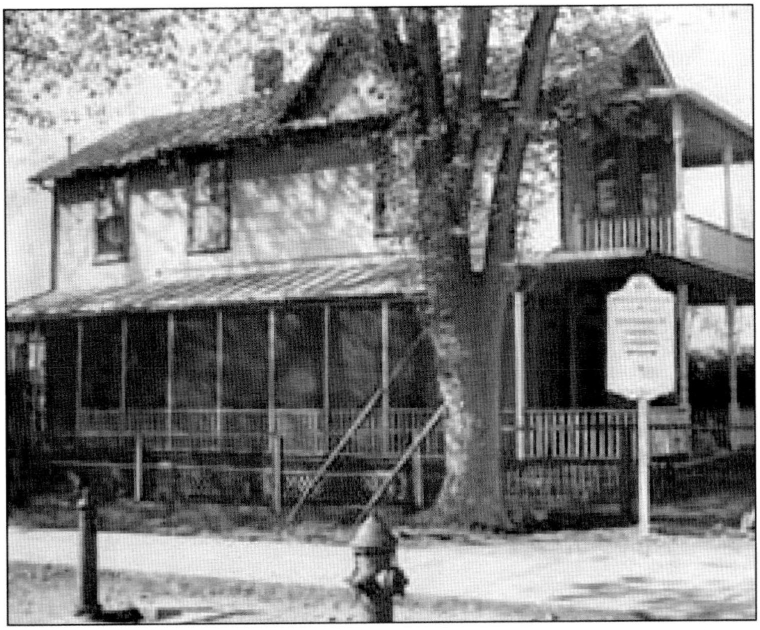

Nestled Amidst A National Park. Congress authorized Kenilworth Aquatic Gardens as a national park in 1938. However, the gardens, with their extensive lily ponds, had been in operation at least since 1908 as a private enterprise selling water plants and aquarium fish. (MLK-W.)

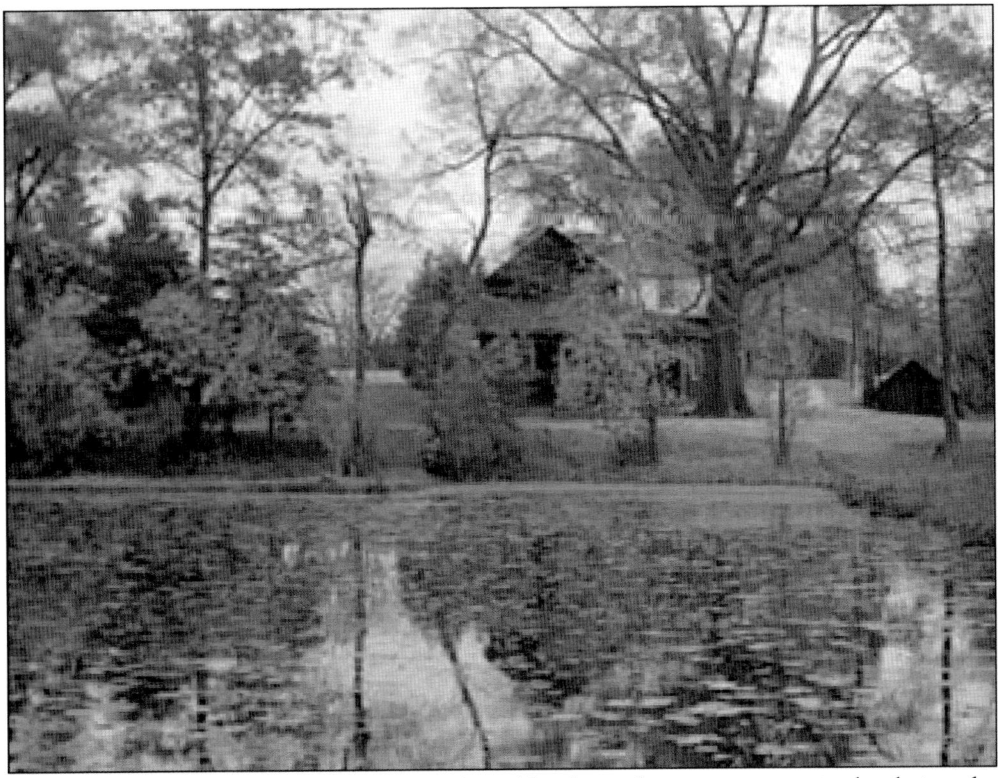

Lily Ponds. In 1879, Walter B. Shaw purchased land in a farming community bordering the Anacostia River. He began growing water lilies in artificial bogs cut from the tidal marshes. He experimented successfully with new varieties of lilies and named two after his wife and his daughter. His wife, Lucy, insisted that one new variety be named after him. Here are the old farmstead and the "lily ponds" in 1953. (DF.)

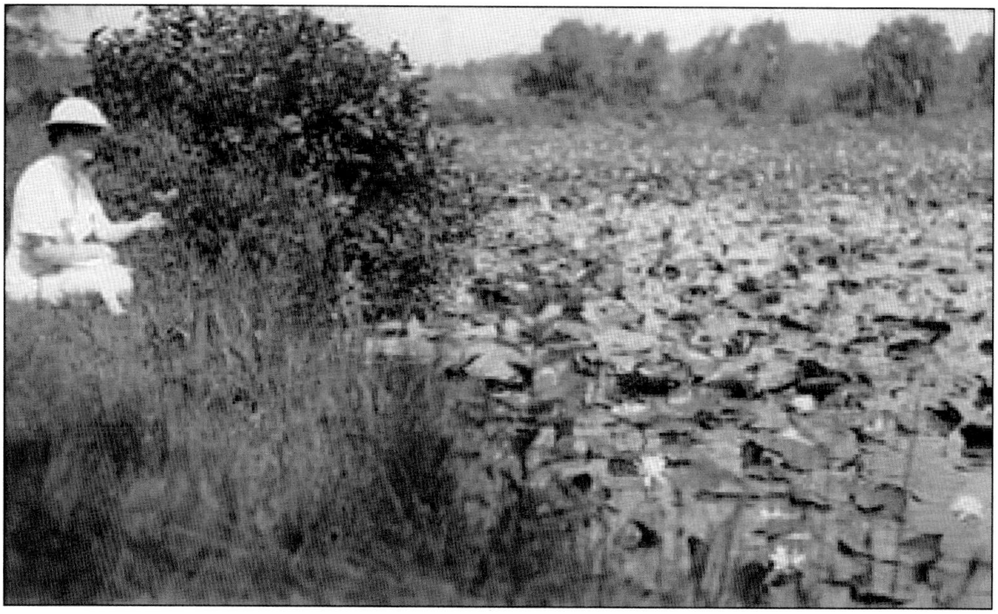

Helen Shaw Fowler. Shaw's daughter Helen Fowler, after losing her husband and child, took over her father's water gardens in 1912. She shipped flowers to high-end hotels and traveled extensively collecting more exotic species of flowers to add to the garden inventory. She also developed beautiful catalogs for water gardeners, illustrating them with her own renditions of the lilies. (Both, DF.)

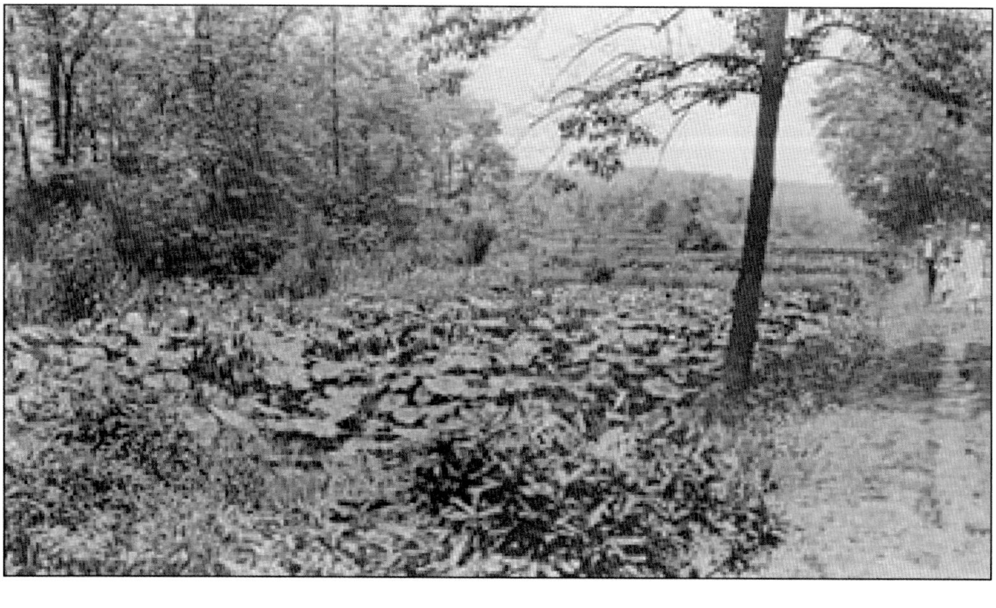

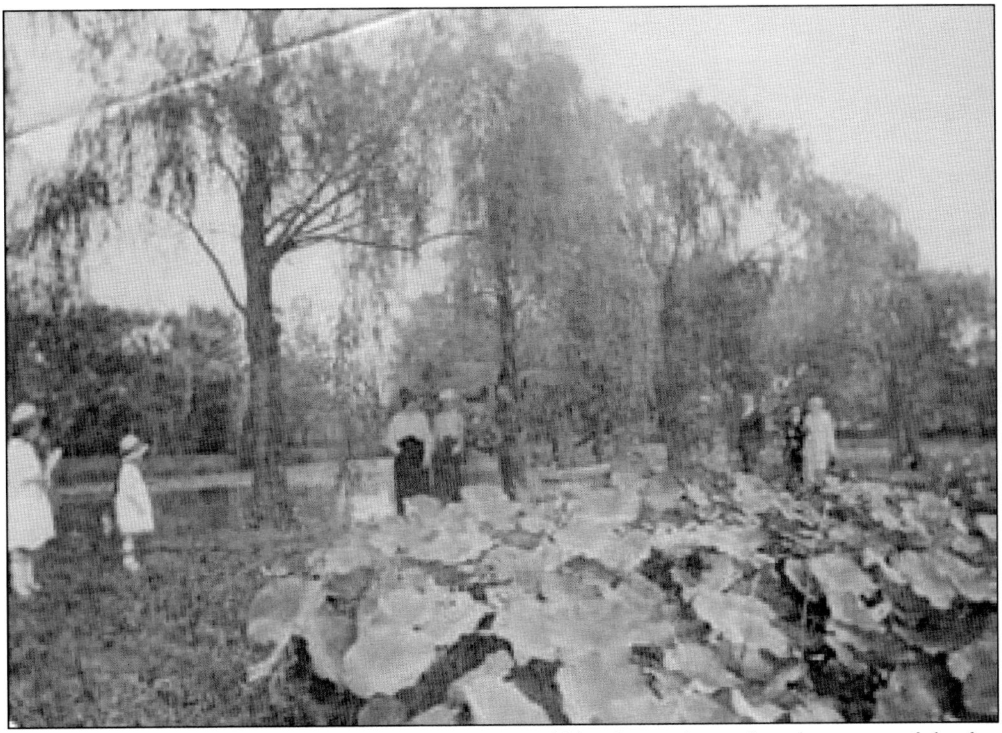

A Local Attraction. Noted for its exotic lotus and lily plants, the park today is one of the few natural remaining estuarine habitats along the river left for flora and fauna. However, Shaw's water gardens had already become a local attraction, visited by Presidents Wilson, Coolidge, and Harding, and their wives and friends, and by local socialites who frequented the nearby racetrack, seen above. Female drivers were considered as rare as the flowers at the lily ponds. (Above, DF; below, LOC.)

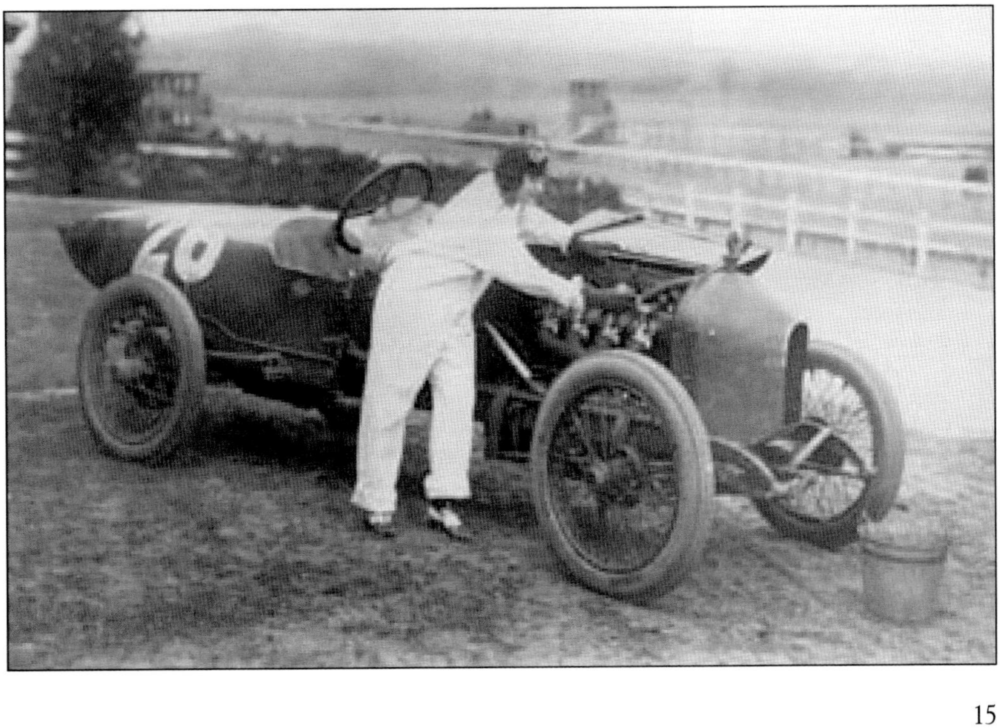

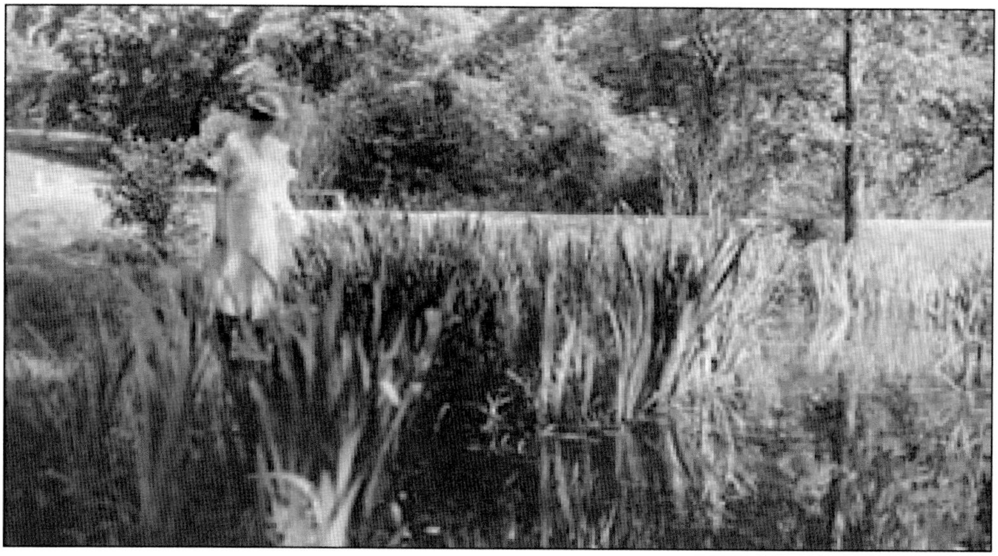

Saving the Lily Ponds. In the early 1900s, the Army Corps of Engineers began to dredge the Anacostia River, using the dredged material to build up the river shores. Some of the fill became the Anacostia National Park. The corps also believed that the marshy wetlands hosted waste and disease and sought to take the property to fill all lowlands along the river including the lily ponds. In the mid-1930s, Helen Shaw Fowler successfully fought to retain ownership of the family property. (DF.)

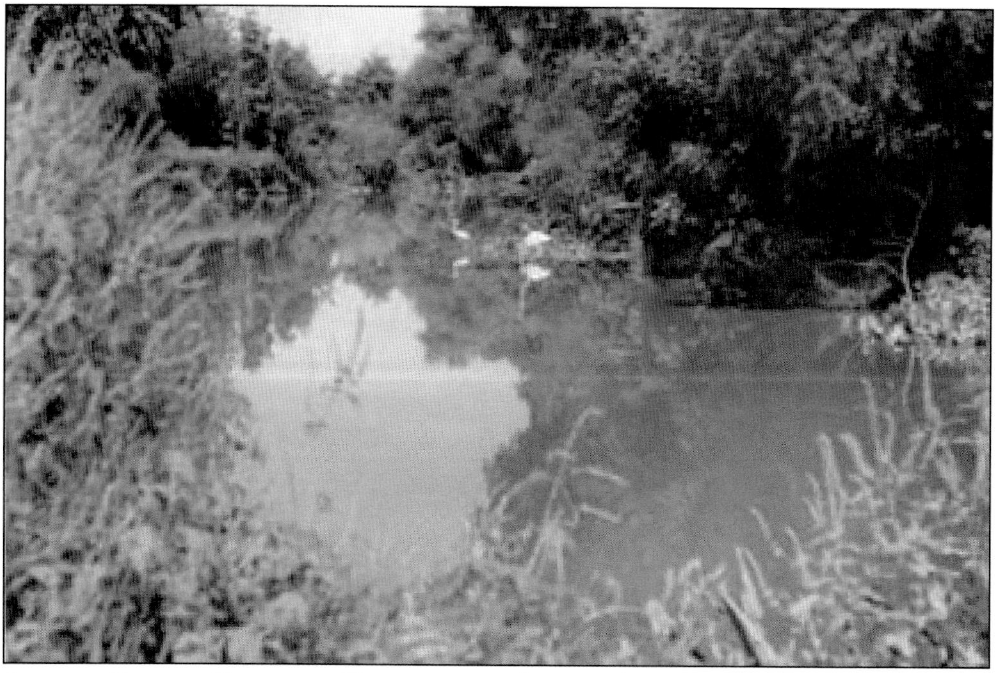

Aquatic Gardens Providing Nourishment. Aquatic plants provide oxygen, food for the inhabitants, and shelter, and they also protect shorelines and stream banks from eroding. In the park, one may expect to see waterfowl, such as geese, ducks, and swans, maneuvering in water. Blue herons also enjoy the water with their long necks, legs, and spear-like bills. Deer, fox, and other wild creatures feast along the shore and in the forest as well. (DF.)

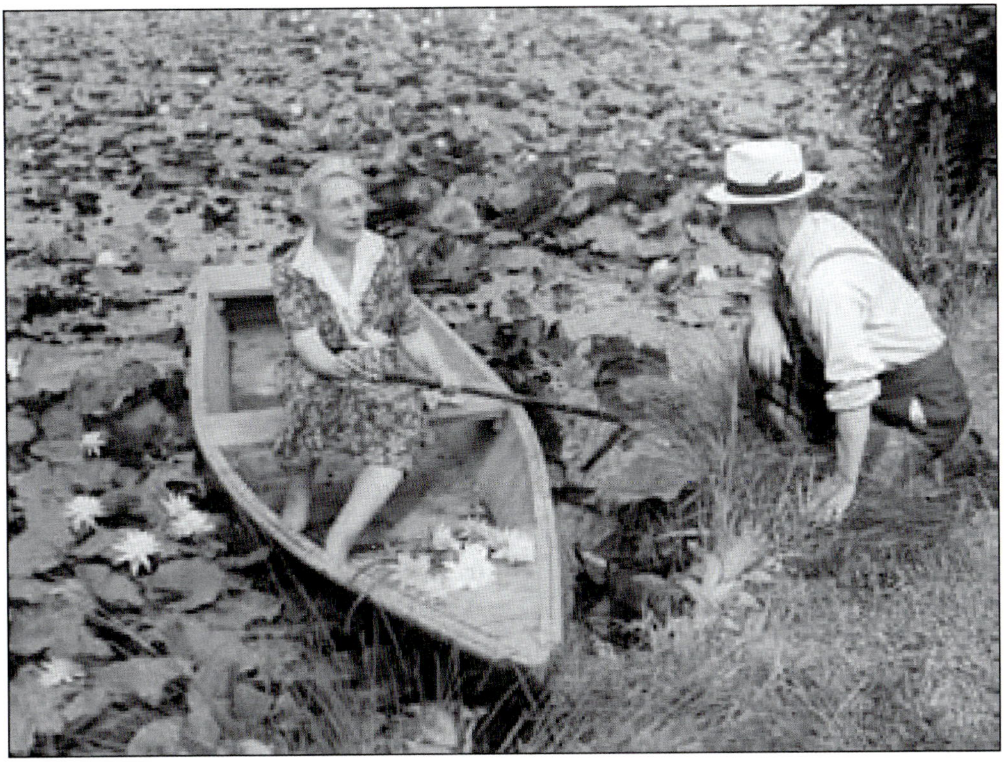

"A Biological and Cultural Resource." In 1938, Fowler sold her gardens to the federal government, which in turn established the attraction to the Anacostia Park system. Contrary to the corps's earlier misconception about the value of marshes, it was learned that the wetlands and bogs filter water, reduce flood damage, and they preserve the biological and cultural resources of the area. (Above, MLK-W; below, DF.)

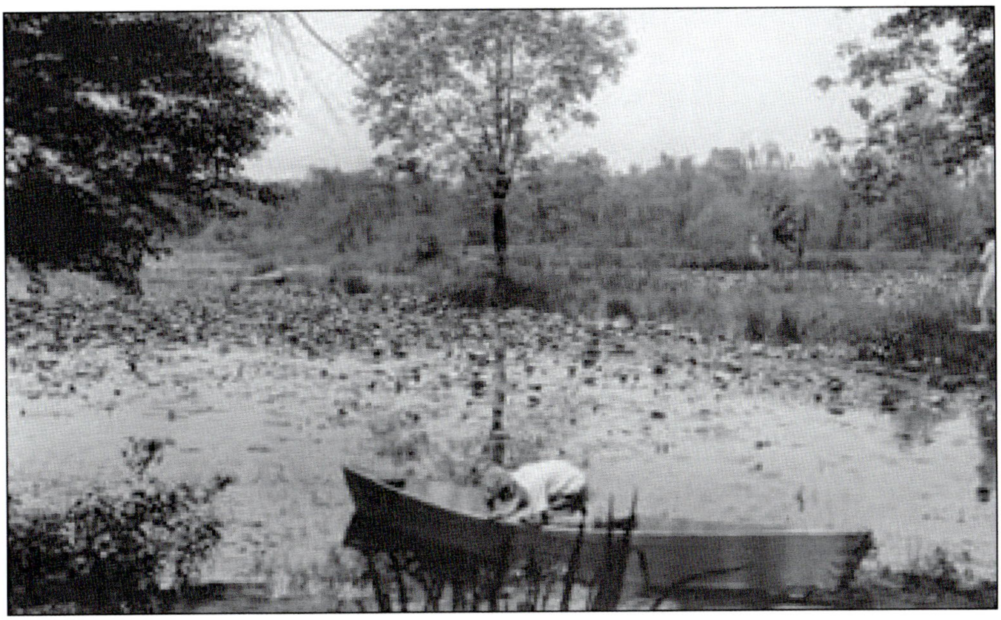

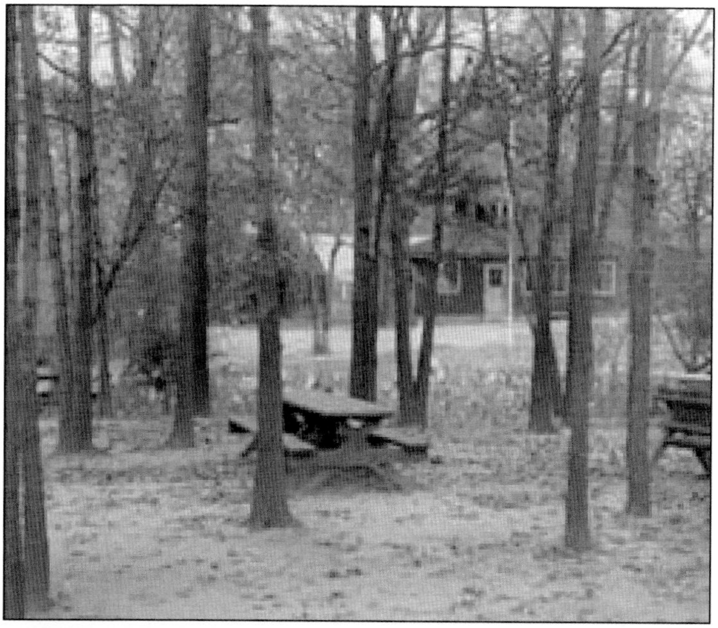

National and Unique Destination. Today, the water gardens are known as Kenilworth Park and Aquatic Gardens, the only national park to display cultivated aquatic plants. The old Shaw-Fowler homestead from which the water gardens enterprise was hatched serves as the park's headquarters. (DF.)

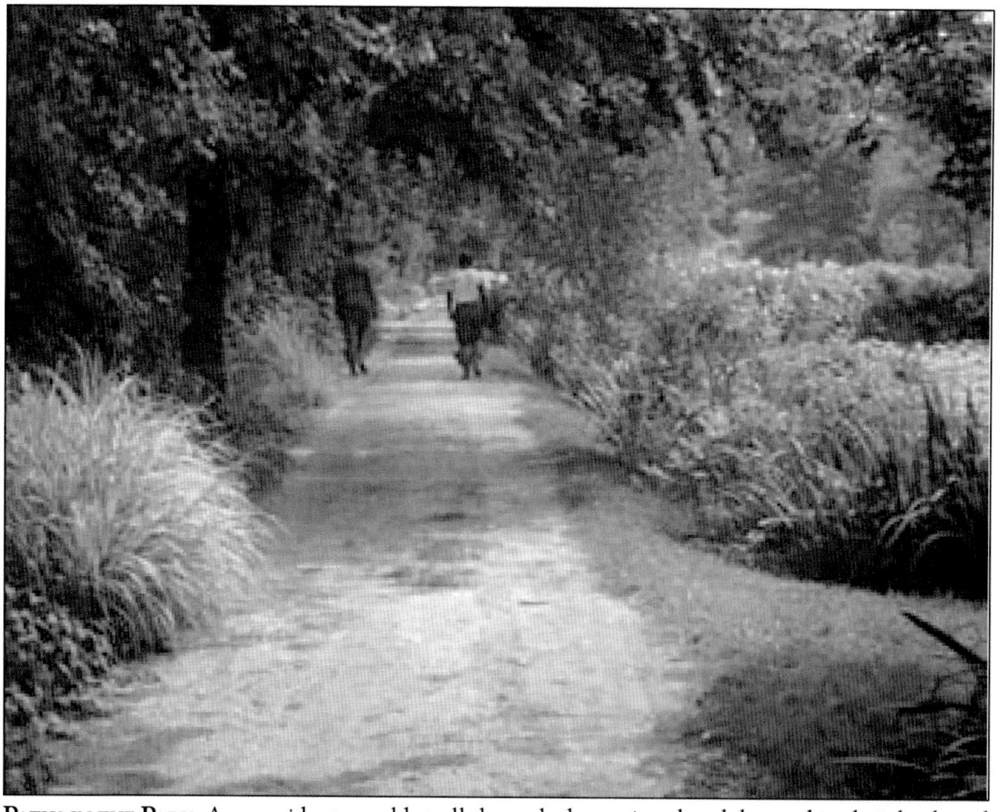

Paths in the Park. Area residents could stroll through the national park located in their backyard to visit the ponds filled with colorful water plants and flowers. This dirt path winds under a tree canopy through a portion of the 12 acres overflowing with ornamental grasses. It is not unusual to see unique species of birds, like bald eagles. (DF.)

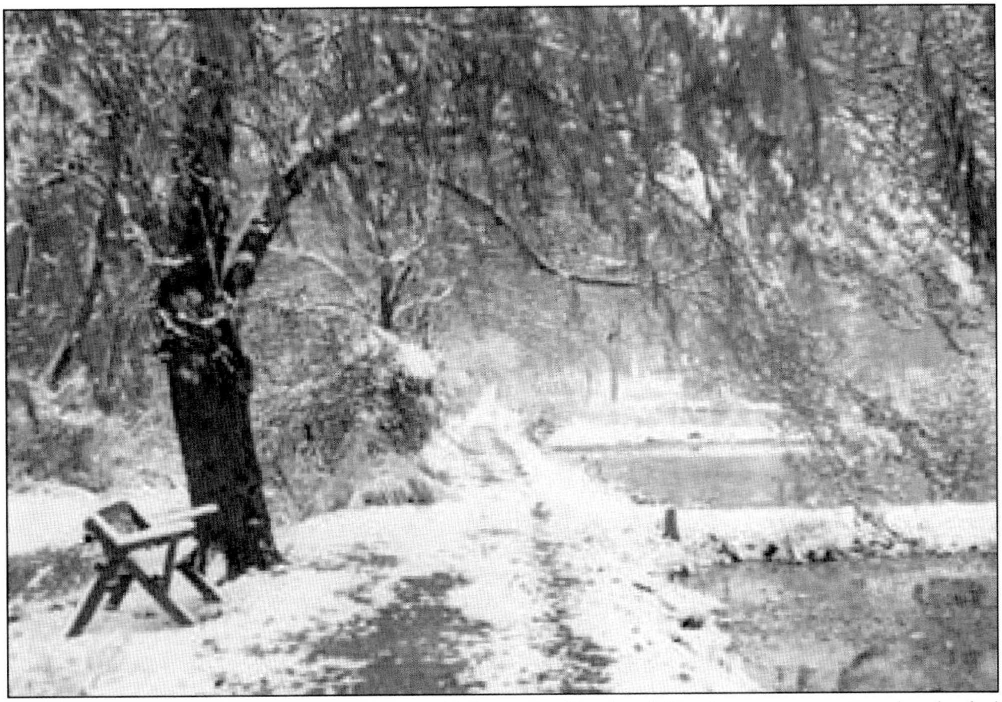

Wildlife Sharing the Park. A short walk from the Eastland Gardens community, the shaded pathways and beauteous scenery of the lily ponds provide immense peace and tranquility to residents, even on a cold snowy day. Mink, fox, and otter are sometimes sighted in the winter months, as the park is their home. (DF.)

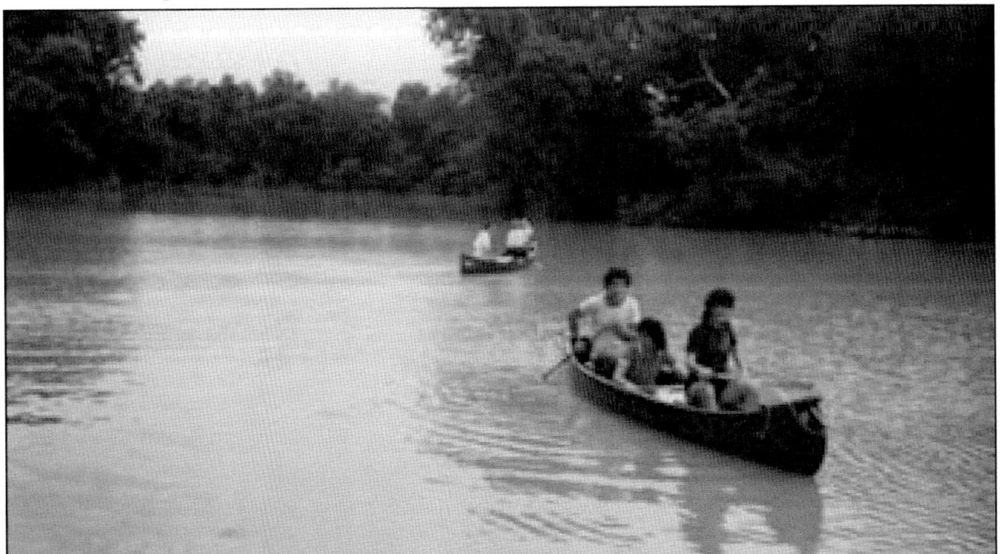

Canoeing on the Anacostia River. Eastland Gardens residents also enjoy the river at the shore of the Kenilworth Aquatic Gardens, an attraction bordering the Kenilworth neighborhood as well. One may also sight exotic butterflies and blue herons, as well as the lush lilies, while canoeing on lazy summer days. Eastland Gardens youth participating in summer camp activities would frequently take in the river sights. (DF.)

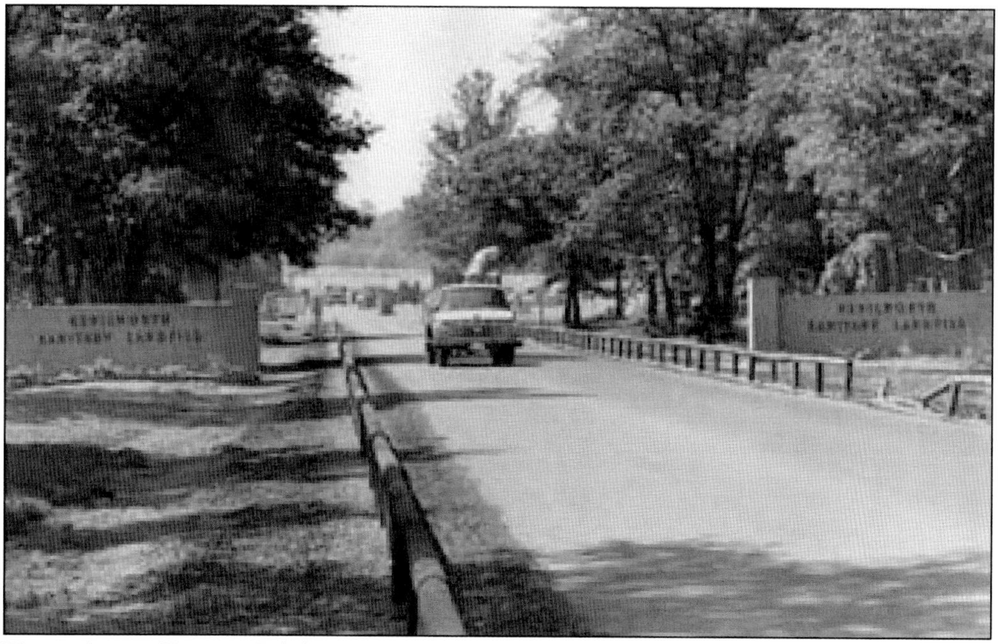

Trash Amidst Beauty. While a portion of the filled marshland became a national park, another portion was selected to become a city dump. Nearly adjacent to Eastland Gardens, this noxious neighbor, known as the Kenilworth Dump, was both a boon and a plague. Some people from nearby neighborhoods made a living sifting through the debris for salvageable items for resale. Others, children and adults, enjoyed hunting for treasures among the discarded materials for their own use. Toys, books, and furniture were among the great finds. Opened in 1942, as an alleged temporary measure, the dump accepted trash from all over the city. Eastland Gardens and the surrounding communities were burdened with a steady stream of trucks hauling refuse along their streets. The incinerated trash brought smoke and toxic fumes, as well as soot and general poor air quality. (Both, MLK-W.)

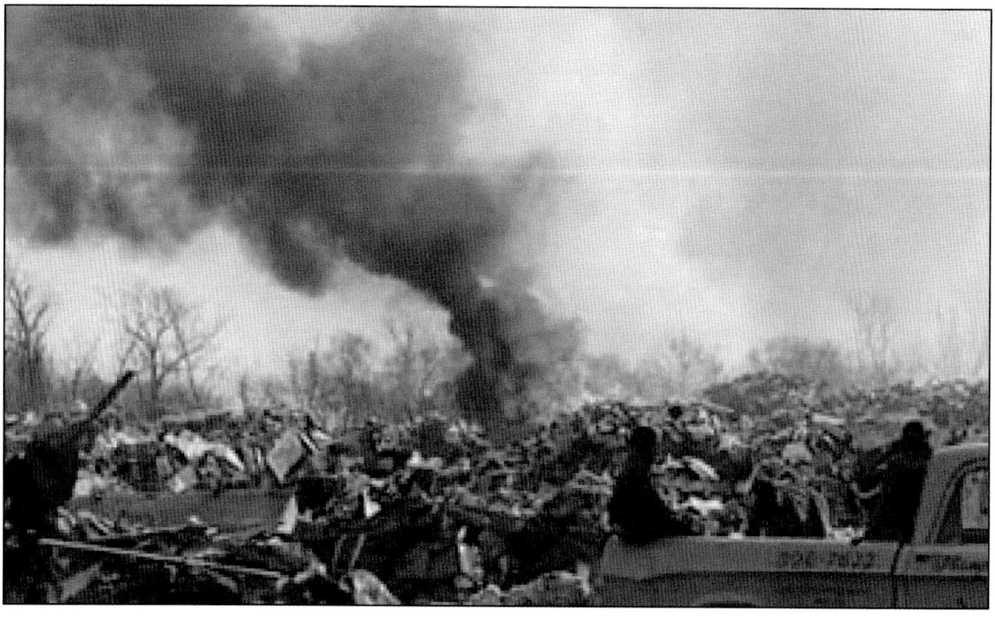

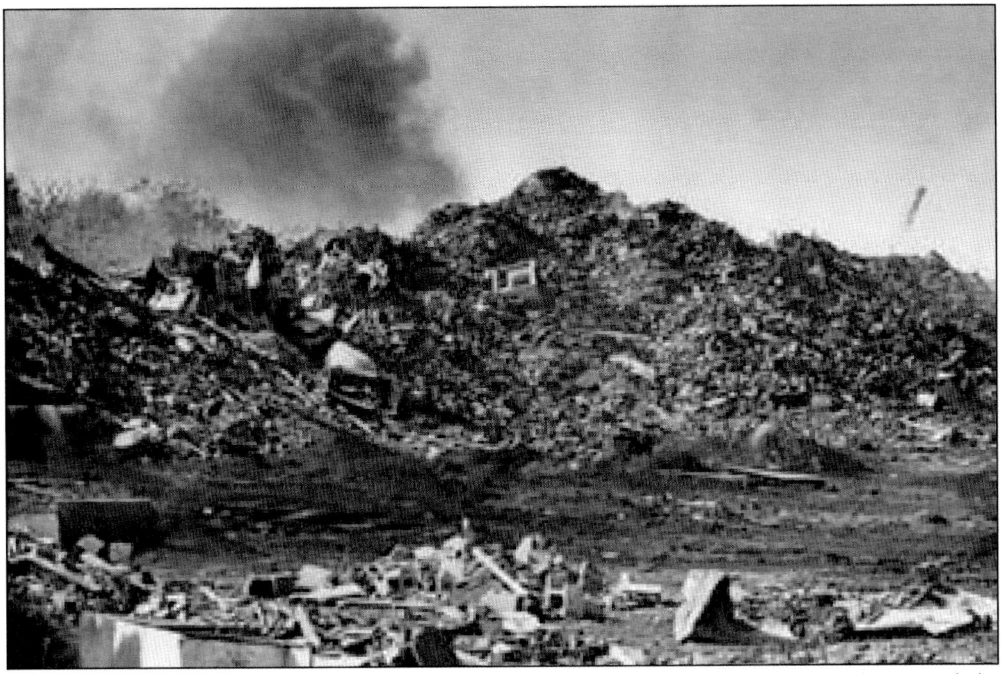

Landfill Becomes Deadly. Eastland Gardens residents began complaining about the "unsightly, nuisance-causing open dump," as described in the local newspaper. More than 1,000 tons of garbage were said to have been burned daily, which contributed to the District of Columbia's ranking in the 1960s as having the 18th-most polluted air in the nation. The city had been seeking incinerators to halt the open burning taking place, but funding and site selection were delayed. The burning was ultimately scheduled to stop at the start of 1968, and the site was to be converted to a "sanitary landfill" operation. This involved compressing the garbage and covering it with a layer of dirt. Once the 125-acre landfill reached sufficient elevation, the entire area was to be covered with about three feet of soil and converted to a recreation area for the community. The open burning of trash did finally end in 1968 when seven-year-old Kelvin Tyrone Mock, playing near the dump, was killed by the fires shifting and trapping him. (Both, MLK-W.)

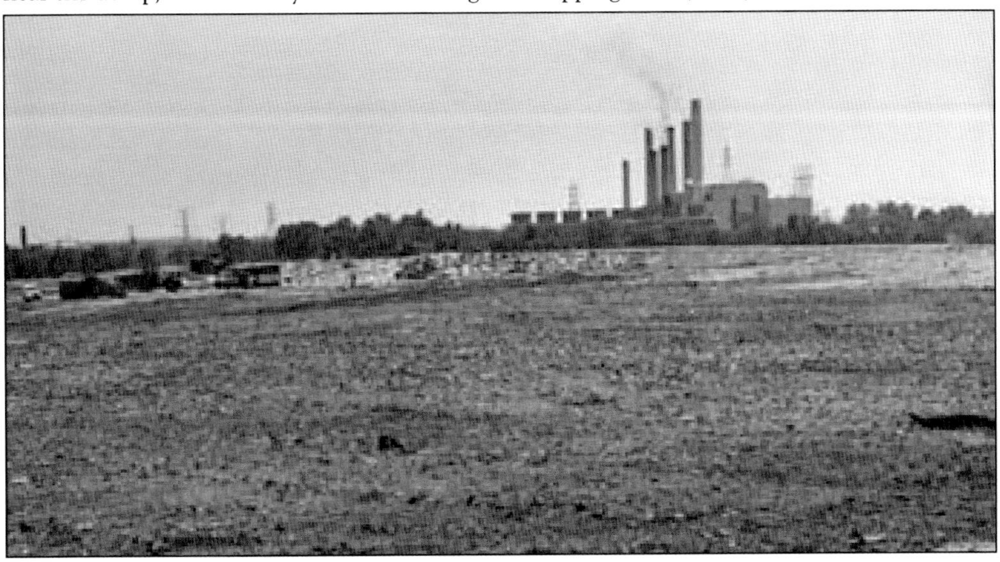

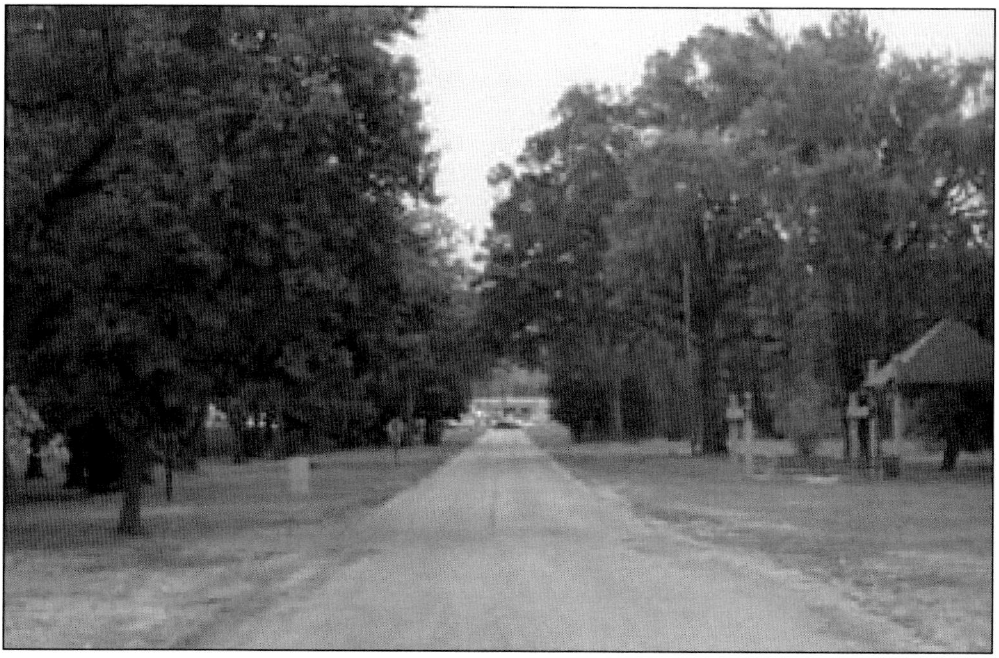

Metamorphosis to Parkland. When the dump closed and the land was reclaimed Eastland Gardens, residents in the area had a beautiful and vast setting for their communities and events. Because of its location and lush greenness, Kenilworth Park was popular not just with Eastland Gardens residents but also with black leisure-seekers from all over the city. The park became the scene of many local family picnics, sporting and recreational events, and church and fraternal organization functions. (Above, JB; below, DF.)

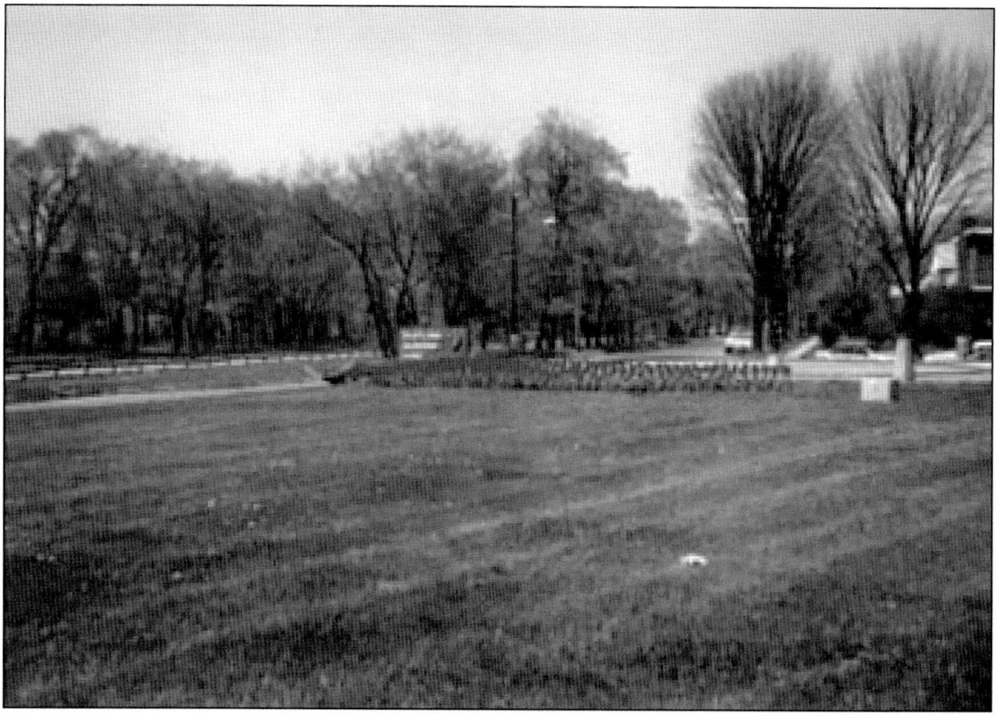

Two

A Place of Our Own

The J-shaped community of owner-occupants in Ward Seven displays a variety of styles and works by African American architects and builders. As a result, Eastland Gardens residents have consistently exhibited pride in their homes and tidy neighborhood.

Howard S. Gott, the white principal of Eastland Gardens, Inc. (EGI), had already developed property in other parts of Northeast Washington, including in the nearby Deanwood neighborhood. He frequently teamed with African American builder Randolph Dodd, who, with his brother Jacob, was responsible for the construction of a sizable number of buildings in Northeast.

The residential work of African American architects is found throughout Washington, DC; however, Eastland Gardens provided a unique opportunity, from the 1930s to 1950s, to showcase their modest designs. It is probable that Eastland Gardens has the greatest concentration of works by early professional black architects. In addition, some homes were designed by Howard University architecture students working with a master architect. In other instances, residents acted as designers and builders of their own homes; *Ebony* magazine featured four families in its December 1951 issue.

Through 1955, the most prolific Eastland Gardens architects were Lewis W. Giles Sr. (1894–1974) with 45 homes and J. Alonzo Plater (1908–1965) with 20. Architects with five to 10 designs included Romulus C. Archer, Augustus N. Bull, John B. Holloway Jr., and Roscoe I. Vaughn. Other designers included Leslie Branson, Howard H. Mackey Sr., Lewis K. Downing, Clyde M. Drayton, Cyril G. Bow, George Alonzo Ferguson, and J.L. Turner. Styles ranged from Georgian, Colonial, and Tudor Revival to Foursquare, bungalow, and ranch. Many of these architects were "homegrown;" they had attended African American Armstrong Technical High School in Washington, DC, where they received a superb education in mechanical arts and drafting. Although several Armstrong graduates left Washington, DC, to attend college elsewhere, many stayed home to attend Howard University because they were attracted to its architecture and engineering degree program.

Besides the Dodd brothers, other African American builders included H.M. Griffin, R.A. Froe, Harry Entzminger, W.H. Lewis, and Oliver B. Cassell. They ran their own companies and were retained to construct buildings, purchase lots, develop properties, and even design homes. These artisans, and many others, continued a long tradition of contributing to the architectural landscape of Eastland Gardens. Indeed, the last home built in the neighborhood, in 2005, was designed and built by African Americans.

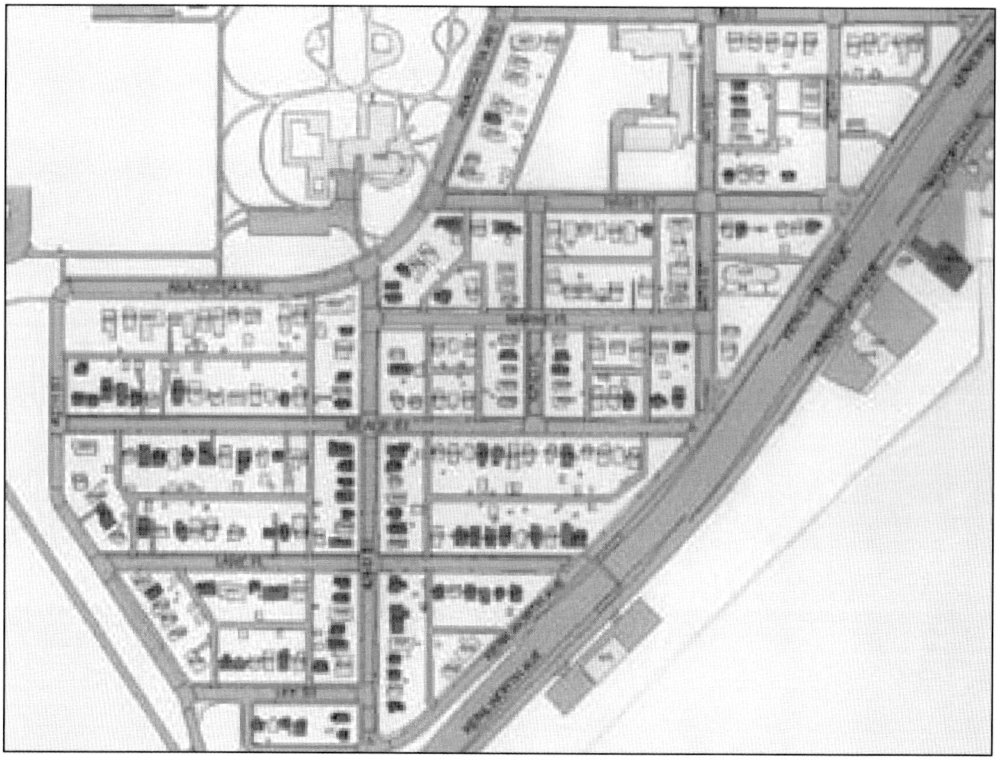

Work of Black Architects from 1927 to 1955. The filled marks represent houses designed by African American architects between 1927 and 1955. The map shows where Interstate 295 divided the community and created two Kenilworth Avenues, one on each side of the interstate. More than 20 buildings designed and constructed by African Americans were razed to make way for the freeway. One spared building, a warehouse erected in the 1920s, can be seen on the right side of the interstate when headed north. It was designed through a partnership of Roscoe Vaughn, George Ferguson, and Howard Woodson, prominent black professionals during that fertile period. (Both, JB.)

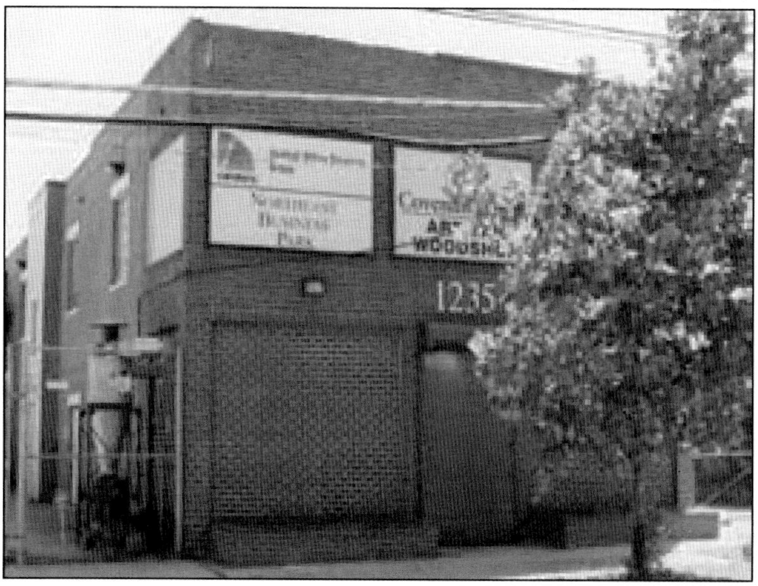

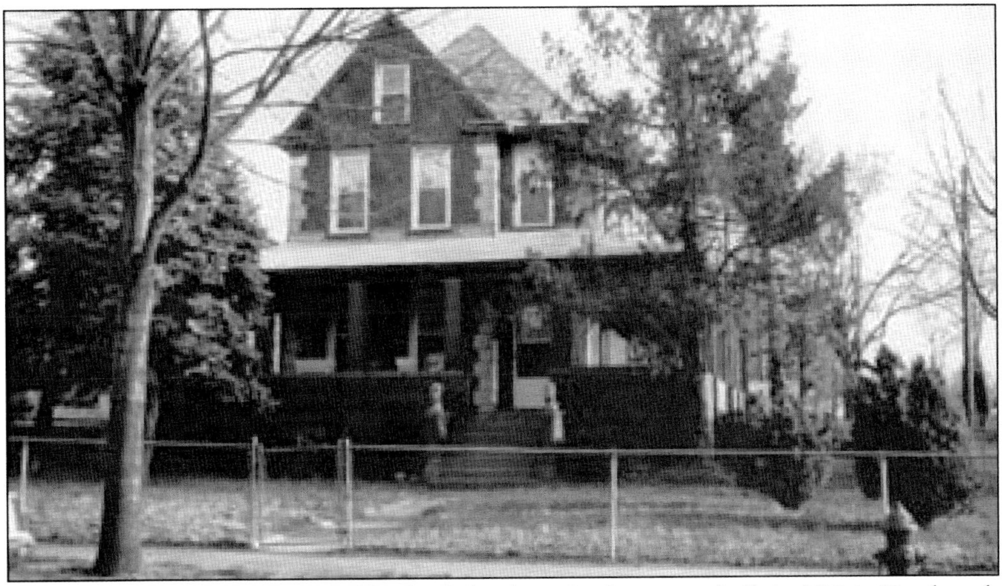

4415 ORD STREET. Now a part of Eastland Gardens, this home was built in 1911 in Kenilworth Addition, an all-white subdivision developed by Allen W. Mallery, a white developer. It was one of several homes already built when Eastland Gardens development began in 1927. In newspaper advertisements, Mallery offered "lots for a dollar down and a dollar a week." In addition, he advertised that his company would provide assistance to parties interested in building on a purchased lot. In 1927, the area was still sparsely populated. (DF.)

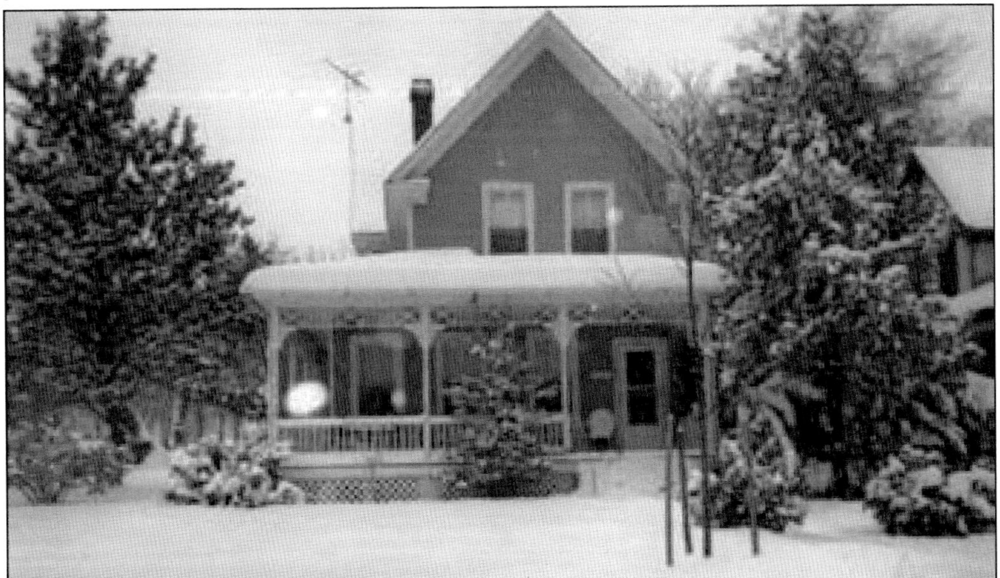

ONCE ORD WAS O STREET. This 1909 house, at 4409 Ord Street, was part of the Allen Mallery Kenilworth development. The house is occupied by the Wood family, who are longtime active residents. At the turn of the 20th century, street names in more than 100 of the District of Columbia's subdivisions were changed to conform to a permanent road and highway system. Thus, for example, N, O, and P Streets became Nash, Ord, and Polk, respectively. Anacostia Road was renamed Kenilworth Avenue. (FW.)

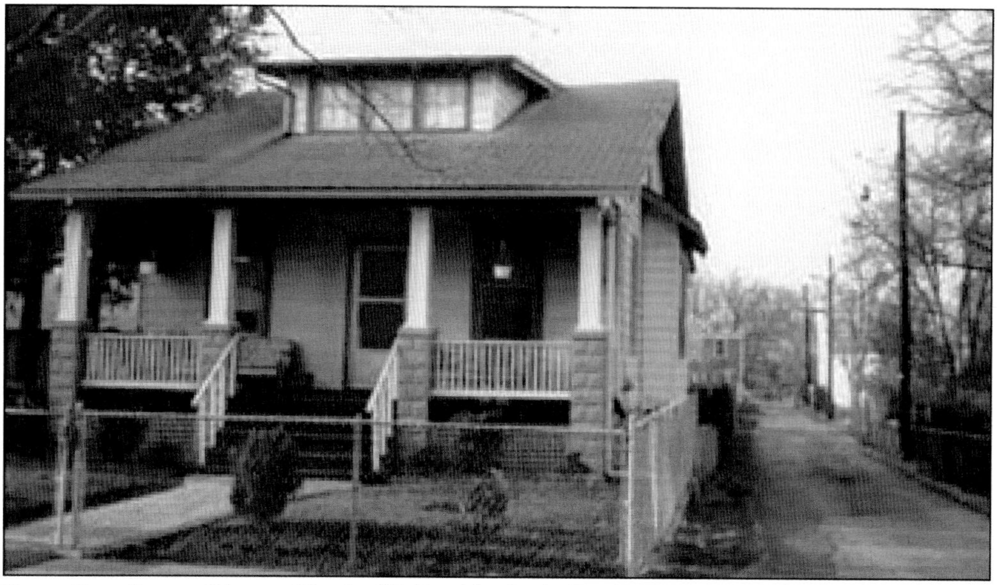

Early Ord Street House. Charles W. Dunkley built this Craftsman-style house on Ord Street in 1925 and retained ownership. Located at 4404 Ord Street, it was eventually engulfed by the new development that slowly spread south and west over the next three decades. The house is now part of an eclectic row of single-family homes for which Eastland Gardens is known. (DF.)

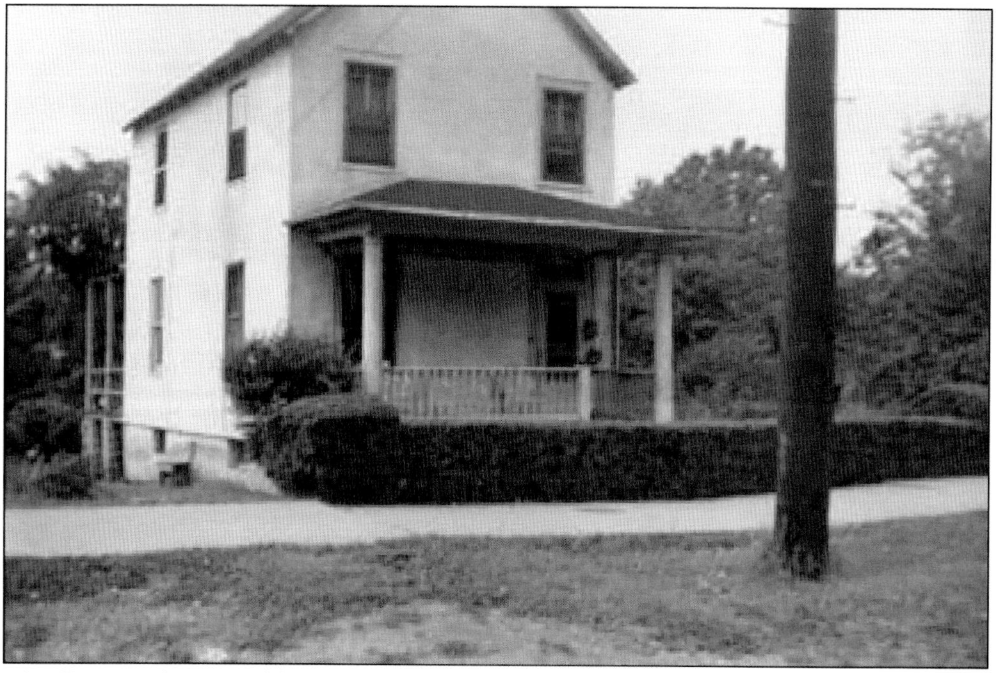

4529 Douglas Street. Although Douglas Street is not part of the Eastland Gardens development, the two communities have long enjoyed common interests and concerns, largely because black residents almost exclusively populated Douglas Street. Douglas was one of the earliest streets developed in the Kenilworth subdivision, as evidenced by this 1899 house that still remains today. Frank and Sadie Matthews and their family are said to have moved into this house in 1907, and their descendants have continued as owner-occupants. (FM.)

4440 Douglas Street. This 1907 house was designed by Owen Fowler, a white developer, who was related to the owners of the Fowler farms, which became the Kenilworth neighborhood, the Kenilworth Aquatic Gardens, and Eastland Gardens. In his numerous projects between 1907 and 1927 in nearby Deanwood and Kenilworth, Fowler frequently acted as owner-investor, architect, and builder. He also collaborated with builder Thomas Stokes and architect W. Sidney Pittman, both African Americans. (DF.)

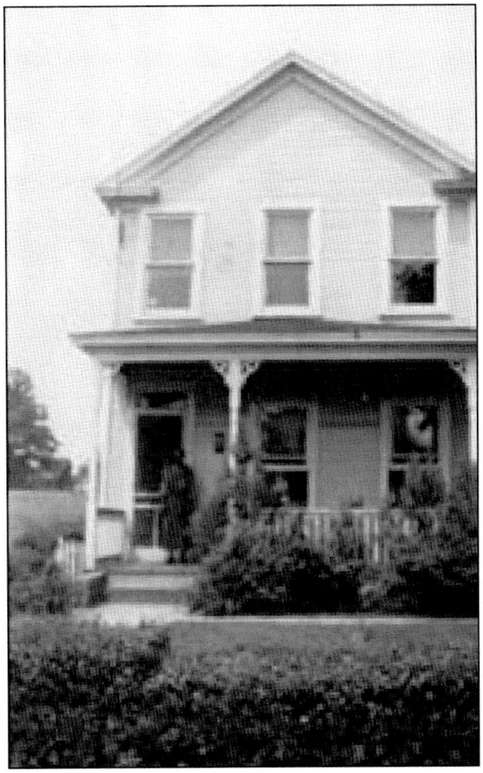

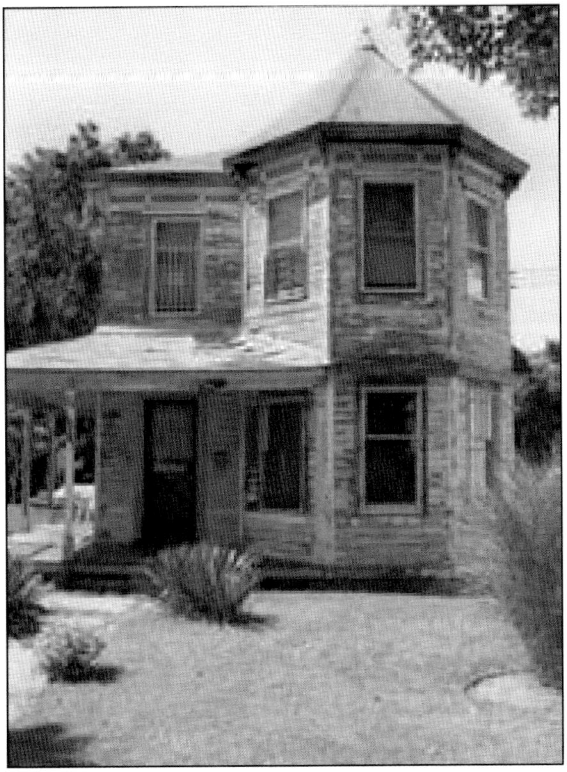

A Street of Homeowners. Formerly located at 4409 Douglas Street, this beautiful house was razed in 2009, almost 100 years after it was built. The Douglas Street residents during the early 1900s were mostly black homeowners. They worked as laborers, laundresses, messengers, gardeners, waiters, barbers, and teachers. William Pannell, a doorman during Pres. William Howard Taft's administration, lived on Douglas Street. Pannell started as a messenger in the War Department during Pres. Grover Cleveland's administration and worked his way up to superintendent of the White House Executive Offices, where he served for more than 20 years. (JB.)

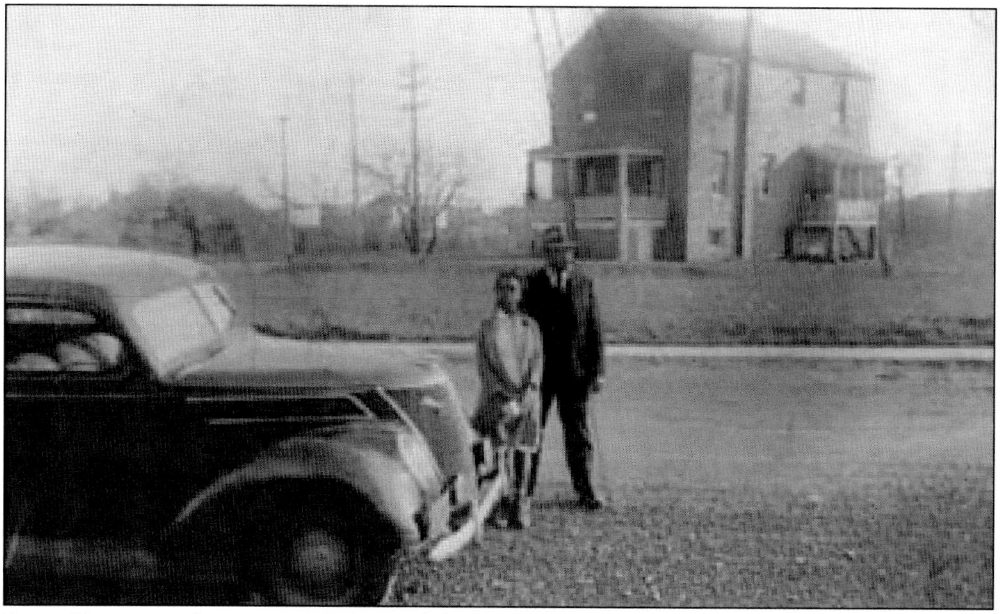

Early Eastland Gardens. A father and daughter look over lots for sale on Kenilworth Avenue in Eastland Gardens in the early 1930s. Still underdeveloped, Eastland Gardens offered African Americans the opportunity to buy land and build a home, which was rare during this period in both Washington, DC, and the nation. In 1955, homes and buildings along this street were razed for the construction of Interstate 295; the remaining community responded by strengthening its civic pride and committing to activism. (DF.)

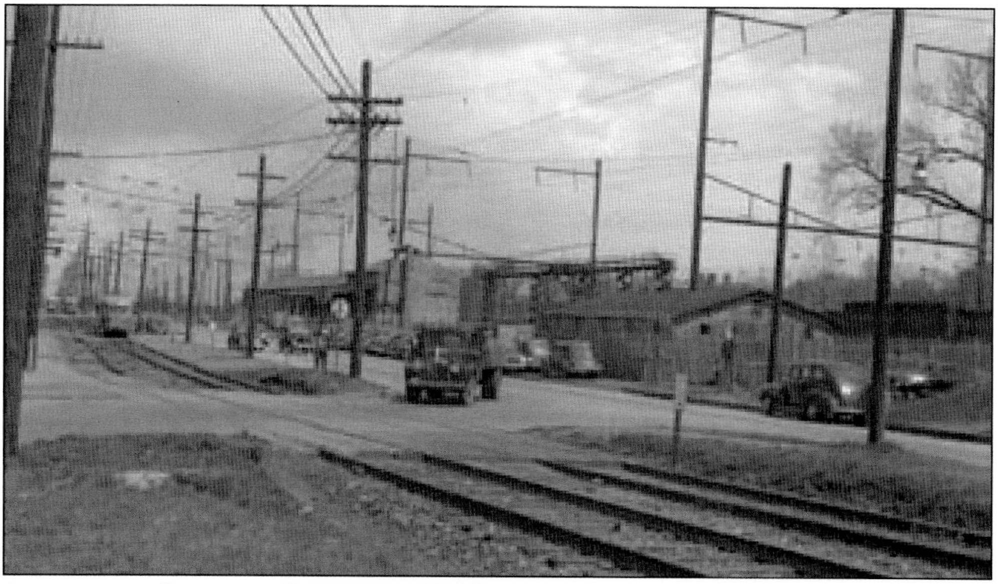

Accessible by Streetcar Since 1900. Unlike many communities in Northeast Washington, Eastland Gardens and Kenilworth were served by what became known as the Kenilworth Streetcar. Both neighborhoods bordered the streetcar line, which ran up Kenilworth Avenue to the District line. Early photographs of the first Kenilworth School, built in 1901, show the streetcar tracks running along the front of the school. This photograph shows a 1940s north-facing view toward Maryland. (HSW.)

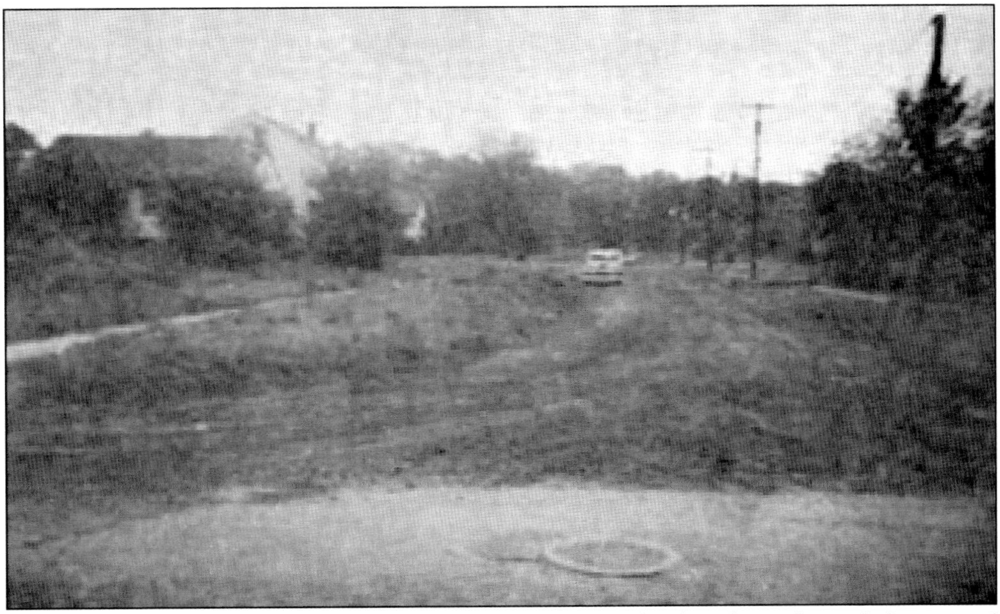

EASTLAND GARDENS, 1928. Eastland Gardens is a community that has always demanded municipal services and stressed self-reliance. Many early homeowners raised chickens and planted vegetable gardens in their backyards. Amidst the challenges of segregation and racism, homeowners did not allow discriminatory laws and social practices to lessen their demands for services made possible by the taxes they paid. (PA.)

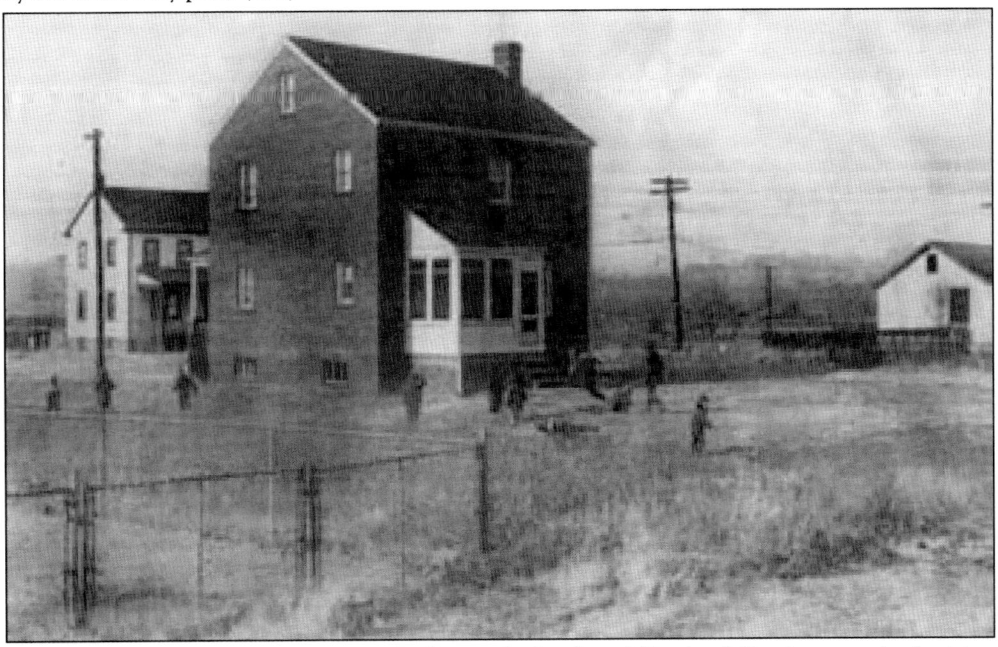

FORTY-SECOND STREET IN THE 1930S. Still sparsely developed, Eastland Gardens was slowly rising from the flatlands recently purchased from the Washington Jockey Club. On Anacostia Avenue, for example, in the 1930s, there were only five houses, although their water and mailboxes were located at Forty-second Street and Marne Place. This photograph illustrates the freedom of movement youth enjoyed while roaming the wide open spaces and making discoveries. (CTDC.)

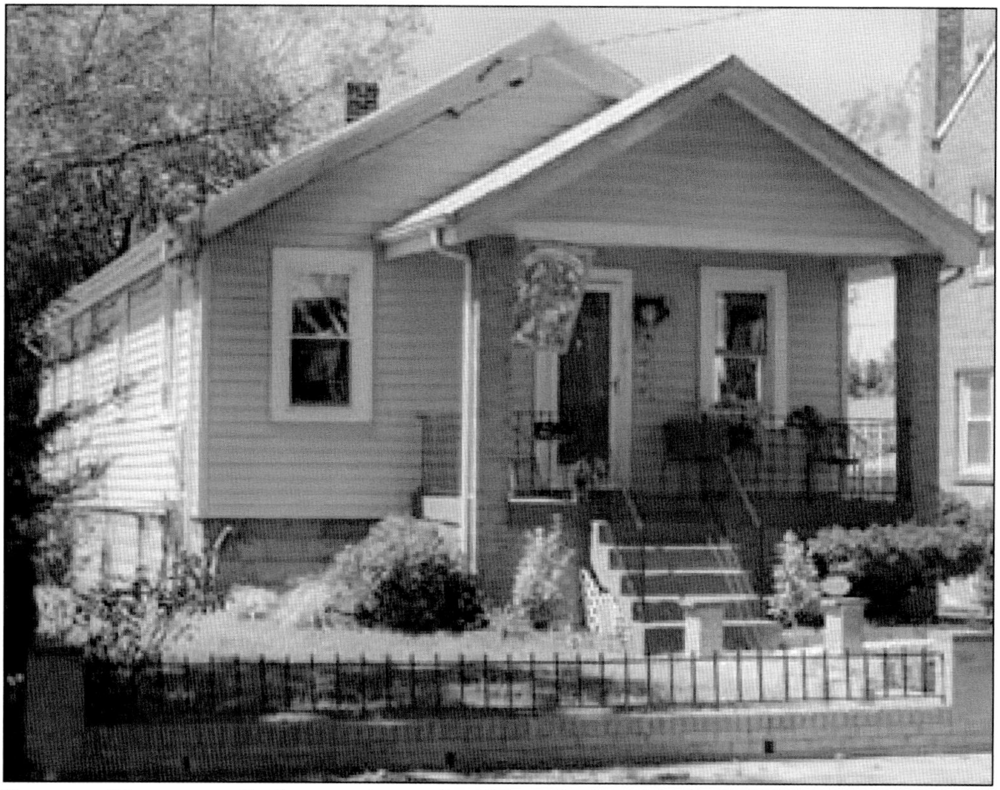

Earliest Designers. Still attractive and well-kept hallmarks of this community today, the Craftsman and bungalow houses, respectively, at 1204 Forty-second Place (above) and 4244 Meade Street (below), are among Eastland Gardens's earliest homes. In 1928, they were designed by the original developer, Howard S. Gott, and Kenneth Vieth, also a white developer. Vieth, who built similar houses in the Woodridge neighborhood, also in Northeast Washington, died tragically in 1932 in an automobile fire. Although the permits list EGI as the builder, it was probably Randolph Dodd, who worked on numerous Gott projects. Other early houses were either razed during interstate construction or replaced with newer ones. (Both, JB.)

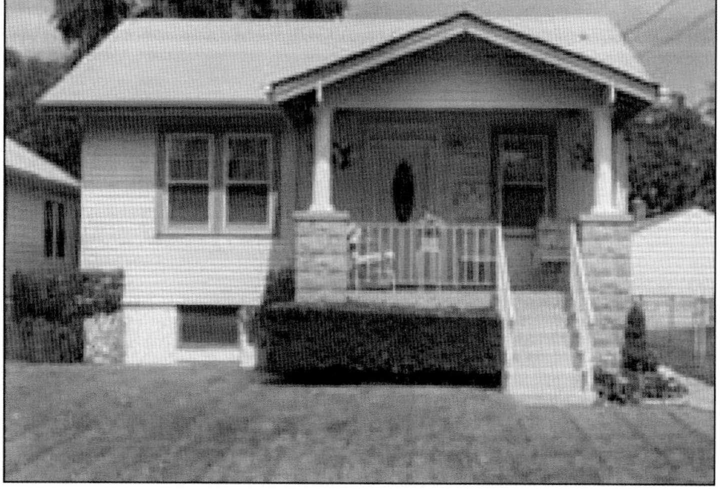

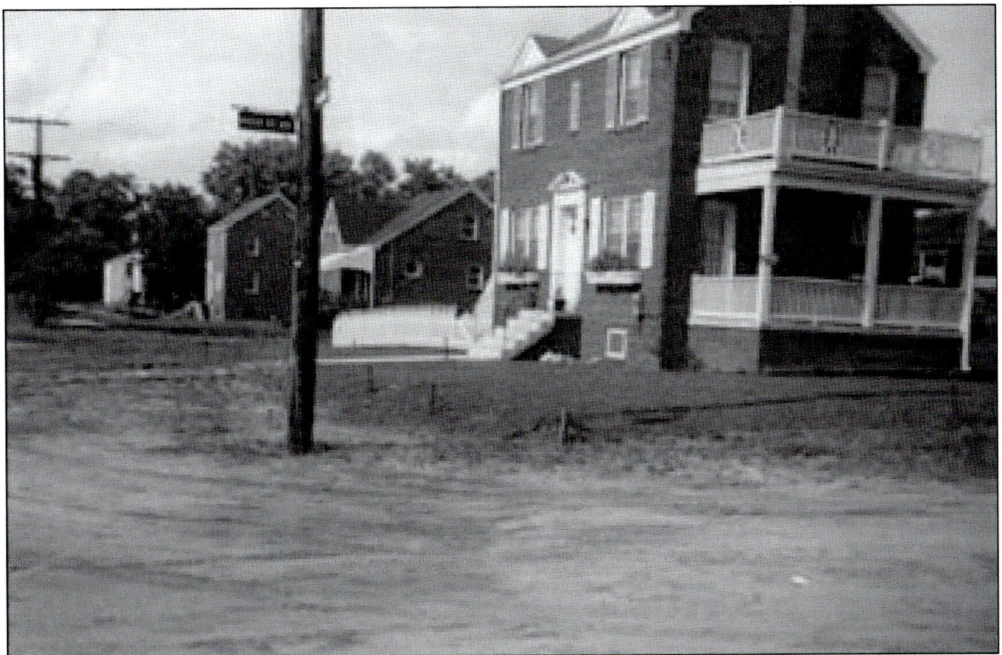

A Community of Class. In Eastland Gardens and other nearby African American communities, lot buyers commonly constructed a home themselves after purchasing a design from an architect. Laurence Herndon built the Georgia Revival home pictured above, designed by J.L. Turner. The Herndons moved into their home at 4400 Nash Street in 1948, joining a row of classically styled homes. Above, the lawn is staked off for the coming sidewalk and street paving. Turner (1901–?), a graduate of Armstrong High School and the Pratt Institute in New York, was the architect for the old Matthews Memorial Church (1932) in Southeast Washington. He was also one of several Washington, DC, architects granted registration in 1952 by exemption for practicing architecture for at least five years. (Above, HF; below, JB.)

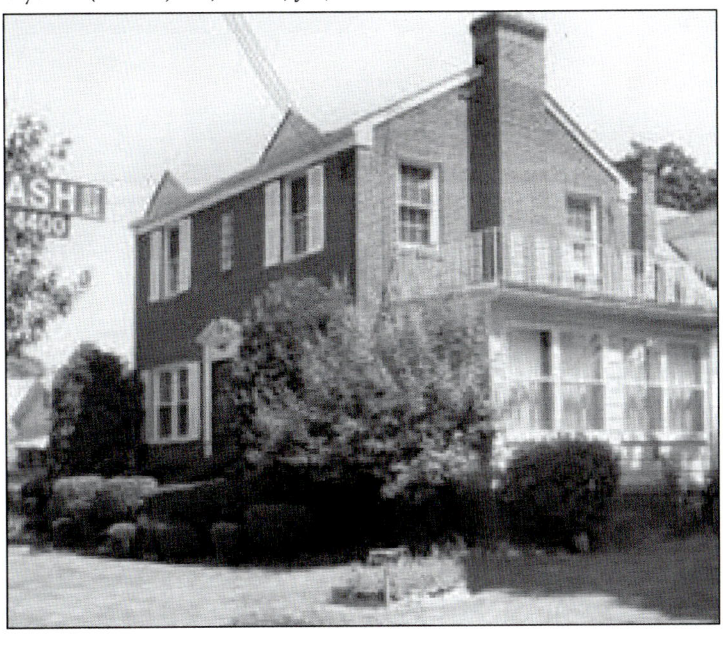

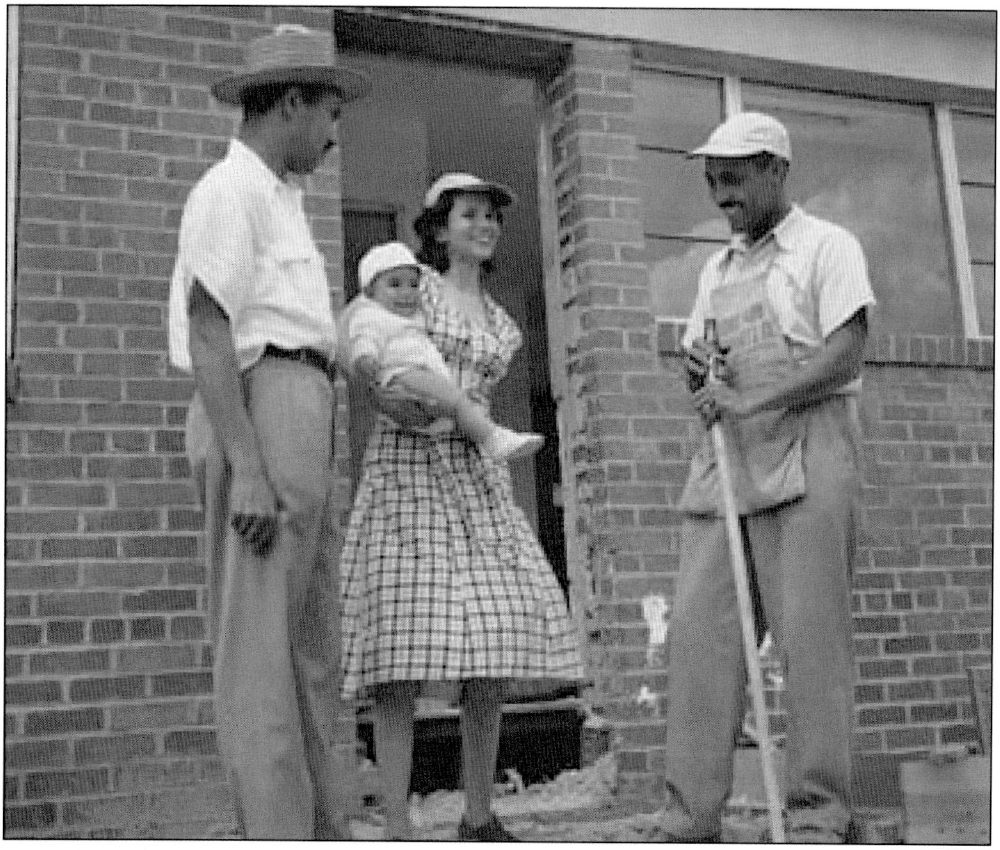

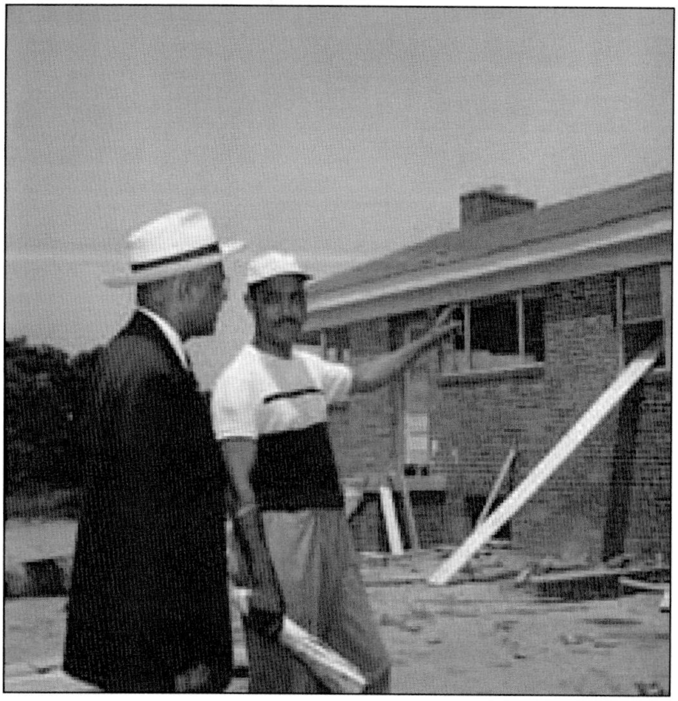

Documented by Scurlock. Civil engineer Wilber Ellis, his wife, Helen Ellis, and their baby, Dale, visit their 4021 Lane Place home under construction. Ellis designed and partially constructed the house. This moment was captured on film in 1950 by Robert Scurlock, a member of Washington's family of preeminent African American photographers. These are two of several photographs of the developing Eastland Gardens that Scurlock took in the 1950s, including the one where an architect and builder are in consultation at a construction site. (Both, NMAH.)

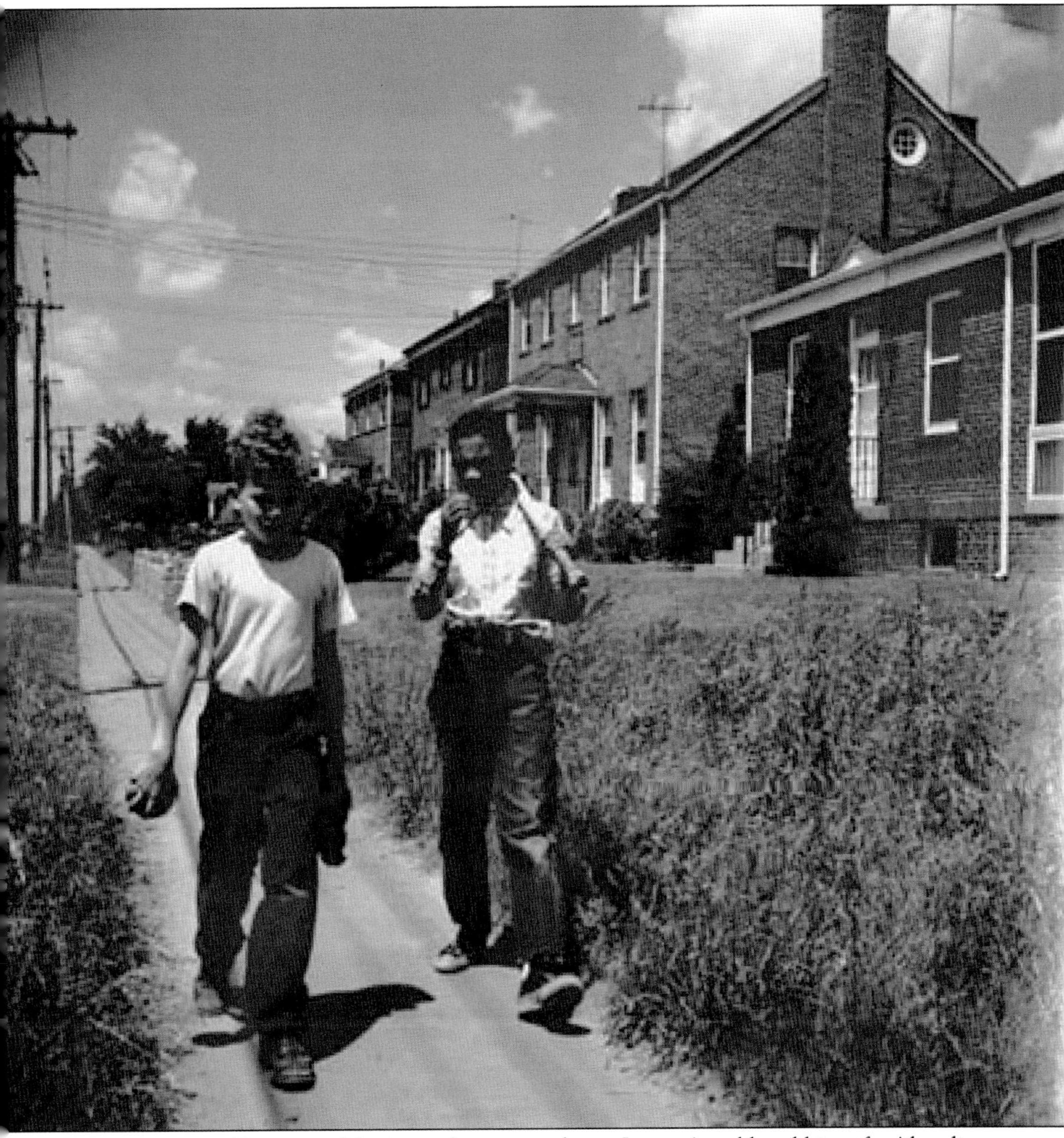

Infrastructure Progress. Hoping to keep costs down, James Arnold and his wife, Almedia Arnold, built their own Colonial Revival and were featured with some of their neighbors in *Ebony* magazine in 1951. Arnold, born in South Carolina, worked as a brick mason in his native state and was able to utilize his skills and experiences in this project. The Arnolds' son Larry (left) and friend Jerry Porter are seen some years later on the newly laid streets and paved sidewalks of Eastland Gardens. (NMAH.)

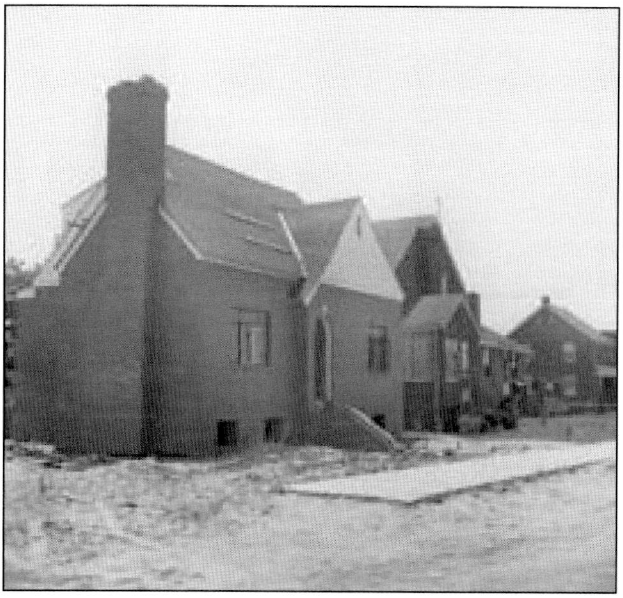

Building by Building. R.C. Archer Jr. (1890–1968) designed the 4425 Nash Street house for W.E. Alexander. While under construction in 1949, the streets and sidewalks were not yet paved. The delay in services was the subject of much debate between the active Eastland Gardens Civic Association, formed in 1931, and city government. Prospective property owners bought double lots rather than a single lot as was originally intended by the developer. On the double lots, they built detached homes and spacious gardens, which contributed to the suburban look of the community. (NMAH.)

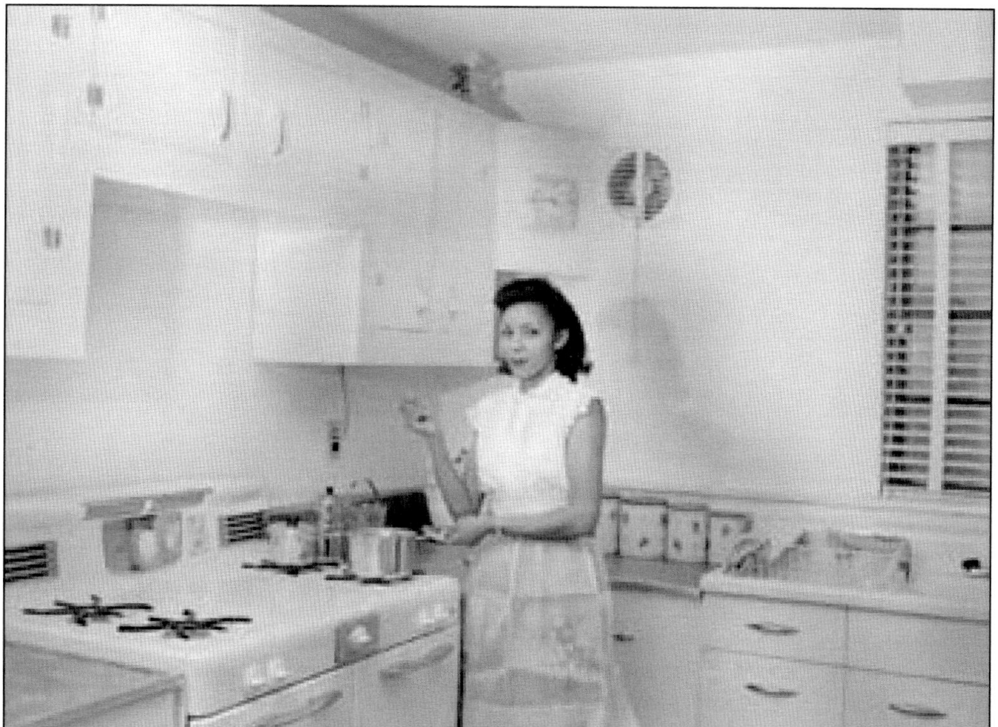

Suburban Kitchen. A stereotypical, 1950s middle-class existence was out of reach for many African Americans. However, this Eastland Gardens scene, captured by photographer Robert Scurlock, countered that notion. In this well-appointed kitchen, an unidentified person appears comfortable and ready to serve her family or guests. Undoubtedly, her home was designed by an African American architect and constructed by an African American builder. The ability to purchase a home with racial pride literally built into the foundation was a huge draw for Eastland Gardens. (NMAH.)

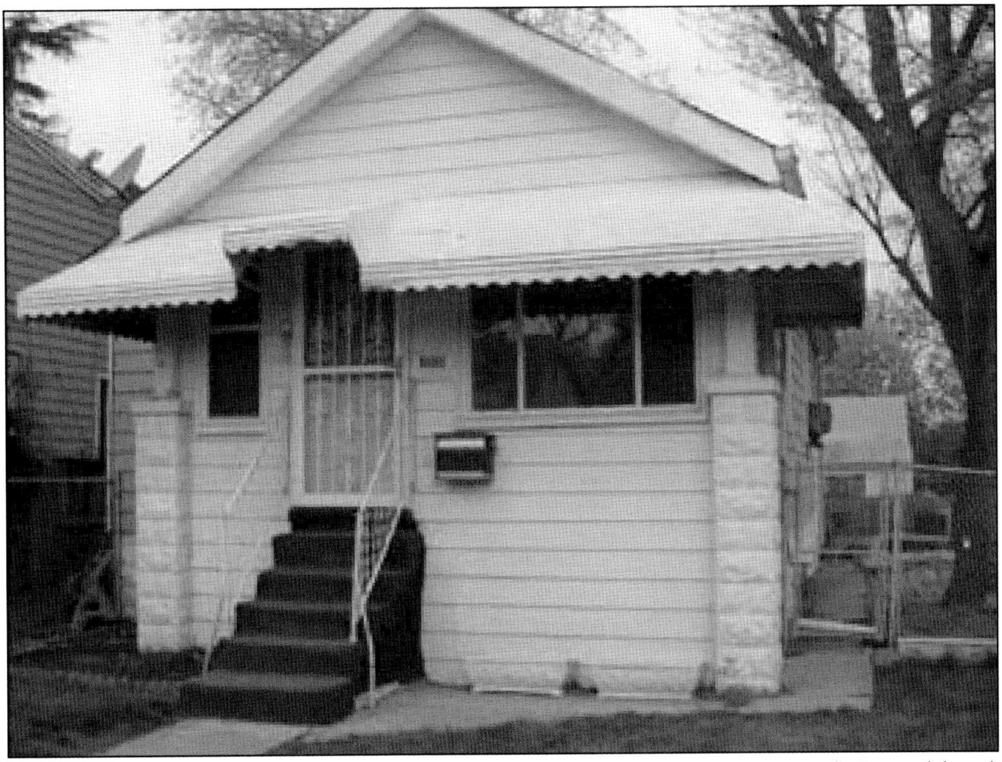

The Community Filling Up. Clifford and Estelle Glover moved into 4218 Meade Street (above) in 1930. When they first moved into the neighborhood, there were only two additional families on the block: Russell and Lorraine Chambers at 4210 and John Mundell at 4215. Like the original Glover house, the Chambers home was designed and built by EGI. The Mundell home was erected by builder Randolph Dodd. The 1930 city directory noted that Clifford Glover and John Mundell were laborers and Russell Chambers worked for an ice company. Chambers and Glover also helped found the Eastland Gardens Civic Association. As a contrast, the later and more contemporary house at 4001 Meade Street (below), pictured here in the 1970s, displays the suburban nature of Eastland Gardens. The owner is Margaret Harris, an Eastland Gardens Flower Club member. (Above, JB; below, DF.)

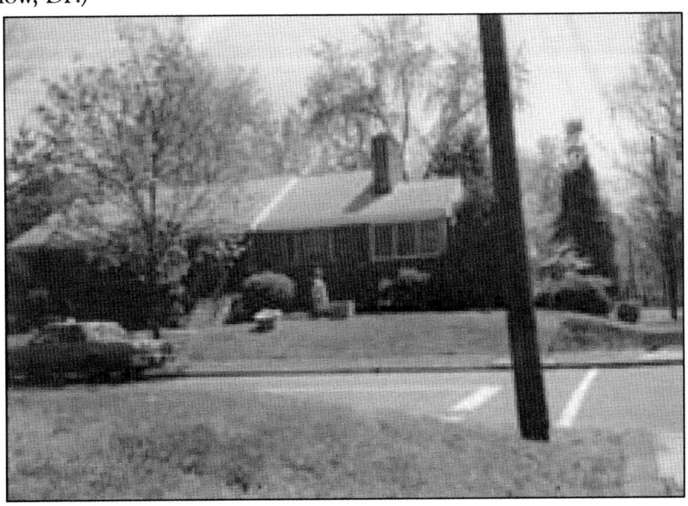

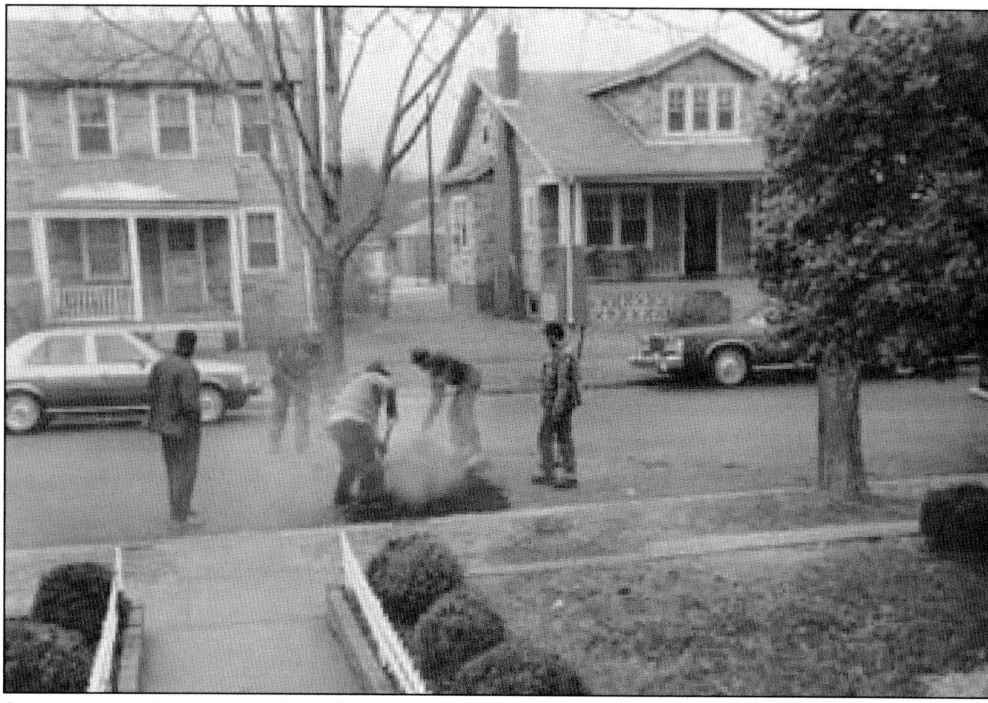

STREETS AND SIDEWALKS. Paved streets in Eastland Gardens made life easier for its residents, improved the look of the community, and added value to individual properties. Community activist Rhuedine Davis captured city workers filling potholes on Forty-second Street in front of her home. (Both, DF.)

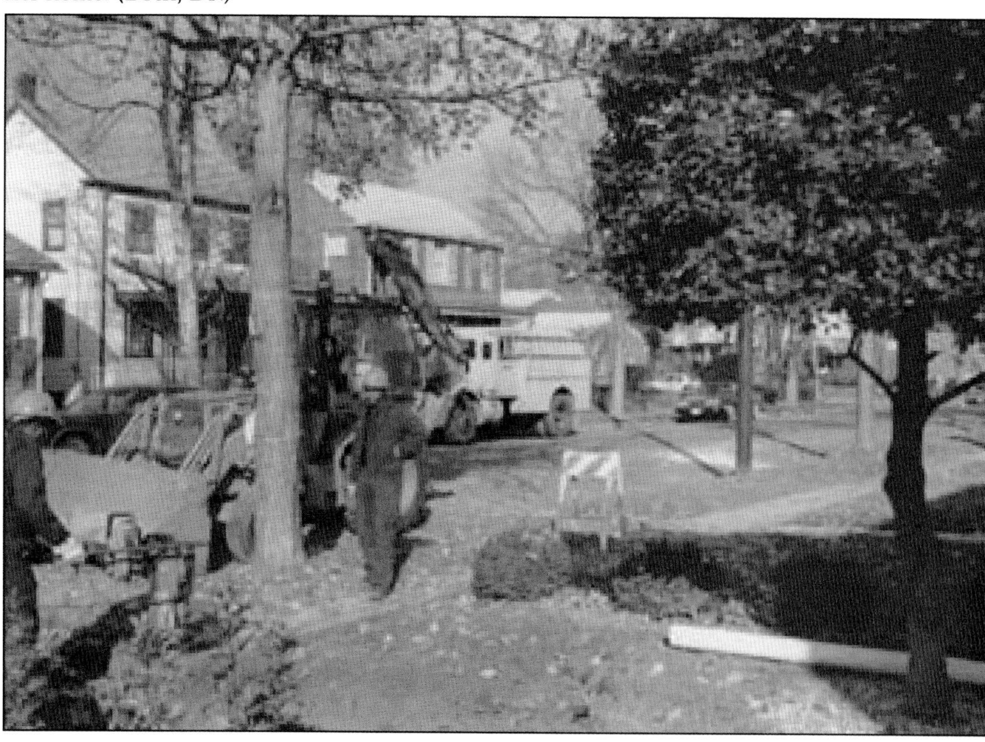

HOLLOWAY AND FROE. Across the street from the Harris's new house was this Federal Revival home built in 1948 at 4004 Meade Street. John B. Holloway Jr. (1913–1993) is the architect of record on this and at least four other Eastland Gardens houses. Froe Properties, a black-owned construction and real estate development company, built it. (JB.)

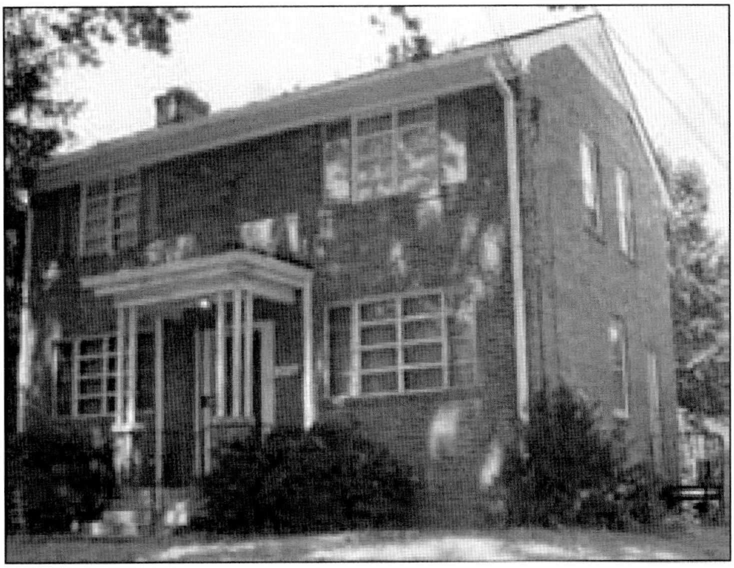

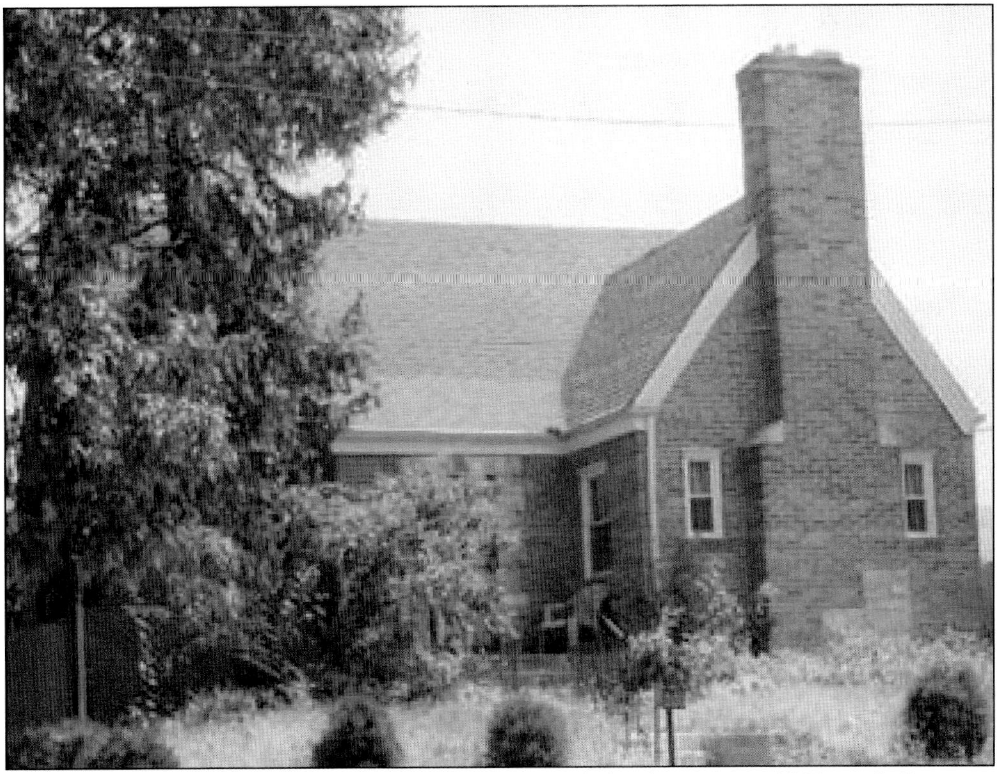

JOHN HOLLOWAY. John Bunyon Holloway Jr. designed this house at 1205 Fortieth Street in partnership with Froe Properties. The well-educated Holloway studied at Tuskegee Institute in the early 1930s under the renowned architect Robert Robinson Taylor (1868–1942), the first African American to earn a bachelor of science degree in architecture. Holloway relocated to Washington, DC, in 1937 and worked briefly with architects Albert Cassell and R.C. Archer. He later studied at the University of Illinois and the Catholic University of America. He opened an office in Deanwood and became a District of Columbia–registered architect in 1951. (JB.)

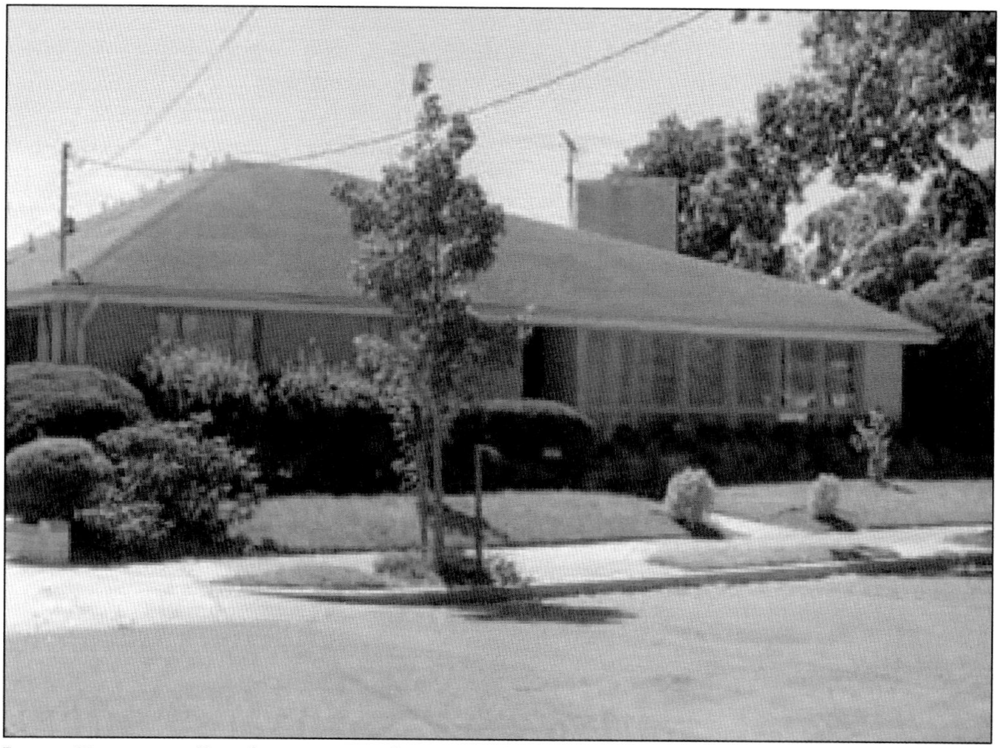

Lewis Downing. Development on the west side of Nash Street did not begin until the late 1940s. Most of the homes here were designed in mid-century modern styles. This attractive home, designed by Lewis K. Downing (1896–1967) and located at 4239 Nash, was constructed in 1951. The highly educated Downing, born in Virginia, earned degrees from Johnson C. Smith University, Howard University, the Massachusetts Institute of Technology, and the University of Michigan. In 1936, he began his tenure as dean of Howard University's School of Architecture. Downing's only other design in Eastland Gardens by 1955 is below. (Both, JB.)

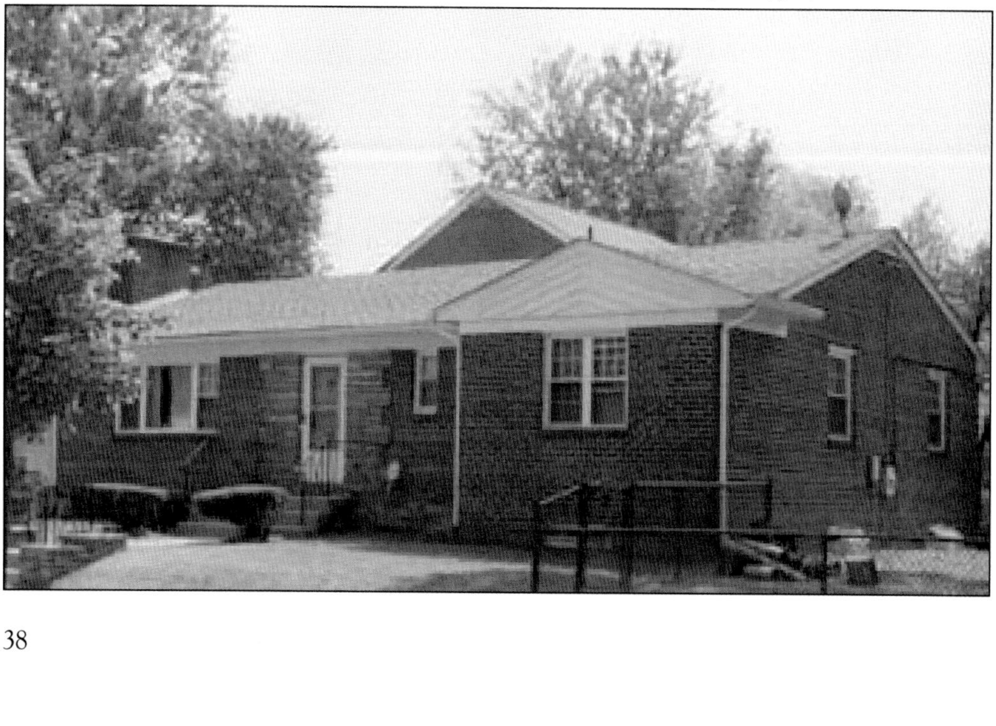

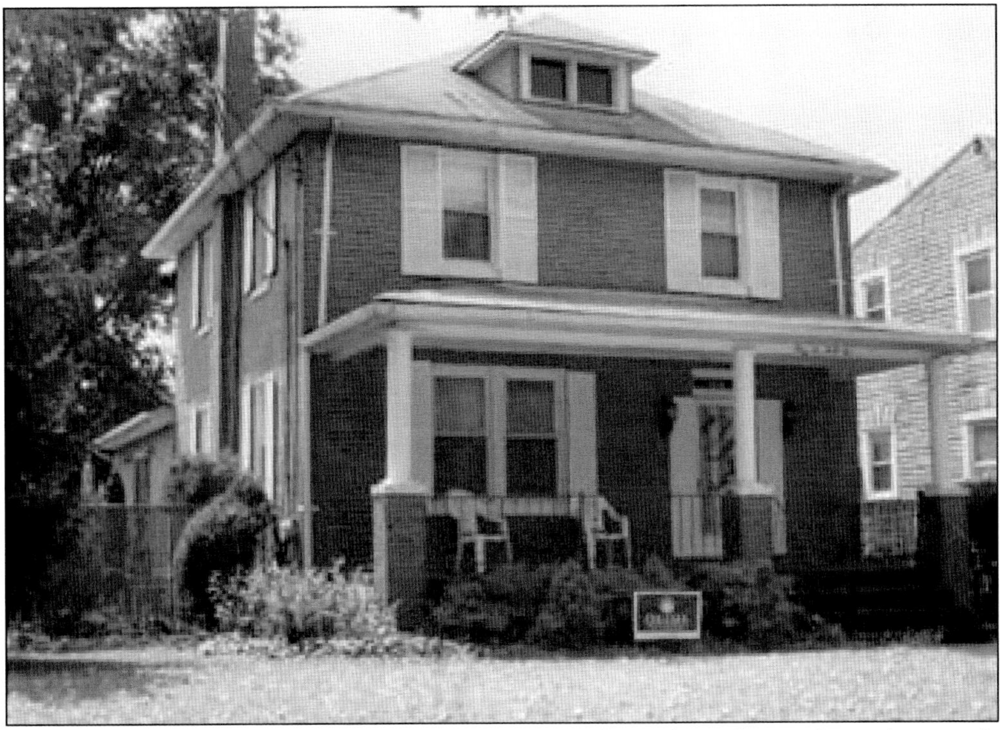

Giles and Dodd. Lewis Wentworth Giles Sr. (1894–1974) was the architect of record on a wide range of buildings throughout Washington, DC, including churches, stores, apartment buildings, and houses. He even designed, in 1921, the dance pavilion at Suburban Gardens, the black-owned amusement park in Deanwood. The Foursquare house (above) at 4245 Meade Street and the bungalow (below) at 4232 Lane Place are just two of Giles's more than 35 designs in Eastland Gardens. As a child, Giles relocated with his family from Virginia to Washington, DC. He graduated from Armstrong High School in 1913 and studied at the University of Illinois until drafted into the Army in 1917. Upon discharge, he returned to Washington, DC, and worked as chief architectural draftsman for Isaiah Truman Hatton (1883–1921), the African American designer of Industrial Bank and the Whitelaw Hotel, among other projects. Giles opened his own practice in 1921, relocating to Deanwood in 1929. He was frequently retained by Howard Gott and other white developers. He also worked with black builders Randolph Dodd, who constructed these homes, and Harry Entzminger. (Both, JB.)

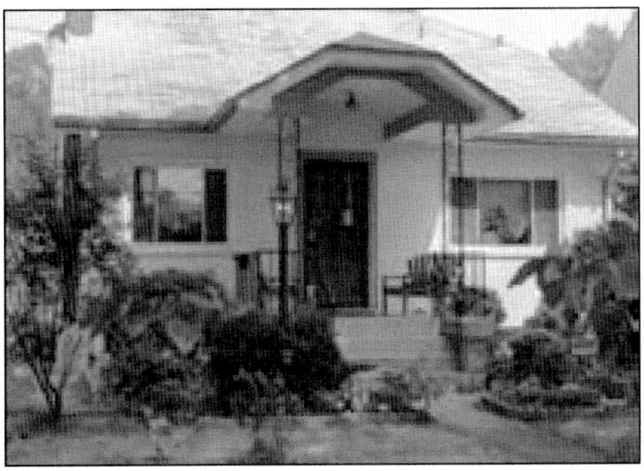

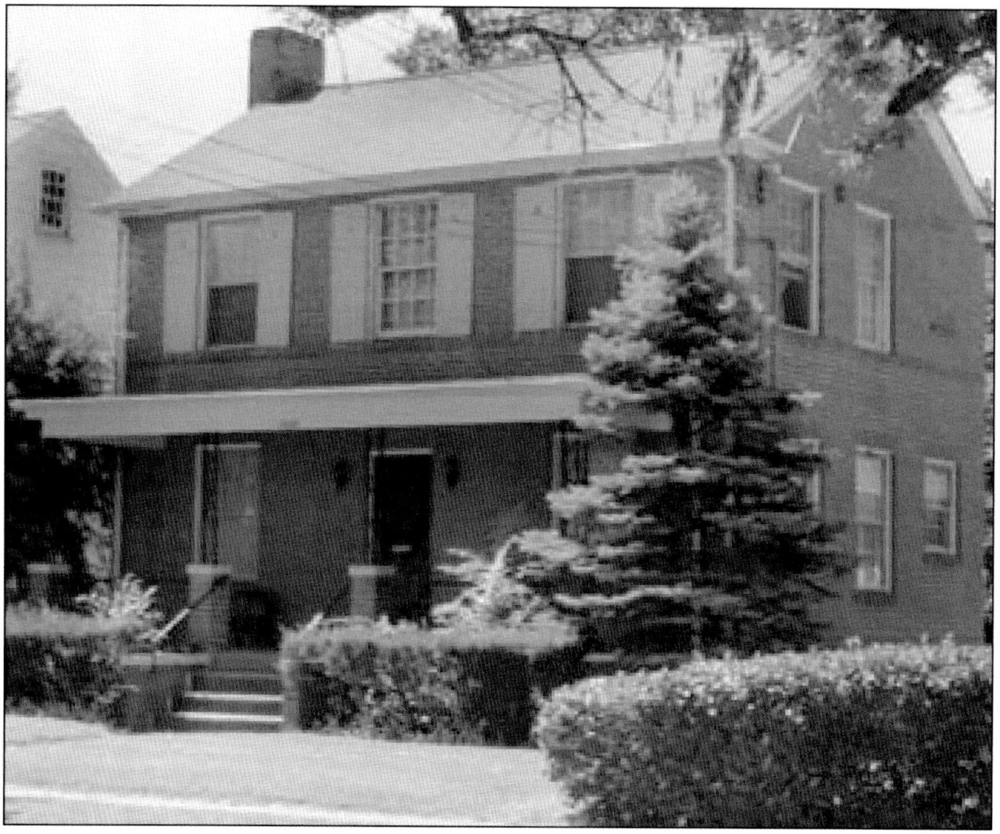

Archer and Dodd. By 1955, at least 13 of Eastland Gardens's homes had been designed by Romulus Cornelius Archer Jr., who was known by the initials "R.C." during his lengthy career. His father was a plasterer and building contractor in Norfolk, Virginia, where he was born. After studying architecture, he set up a practice in Norfolk. In 1921, he moved to Washington, DC, and established an architectural office. His first commissions were for churches and related buildings. On January 15, 1926, Archer received District of Columbia architect license No. 117, making him the city's second African American registered architect. These two houses stand at 1120 and 1125 Forty-second Street and were designed in 1939 and 1936, respectively. Randolph Dodd was the builder. (Both, JB.)

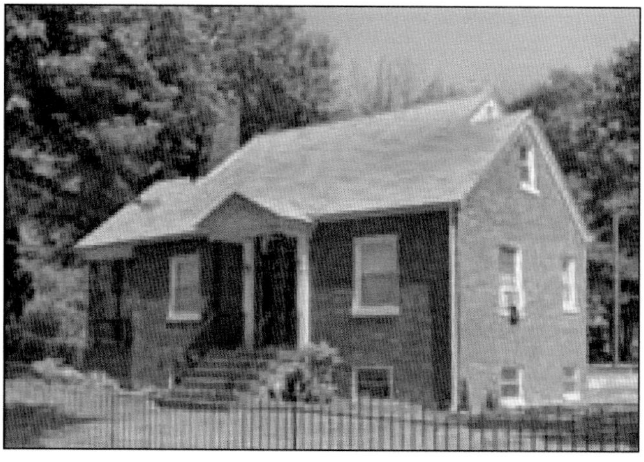

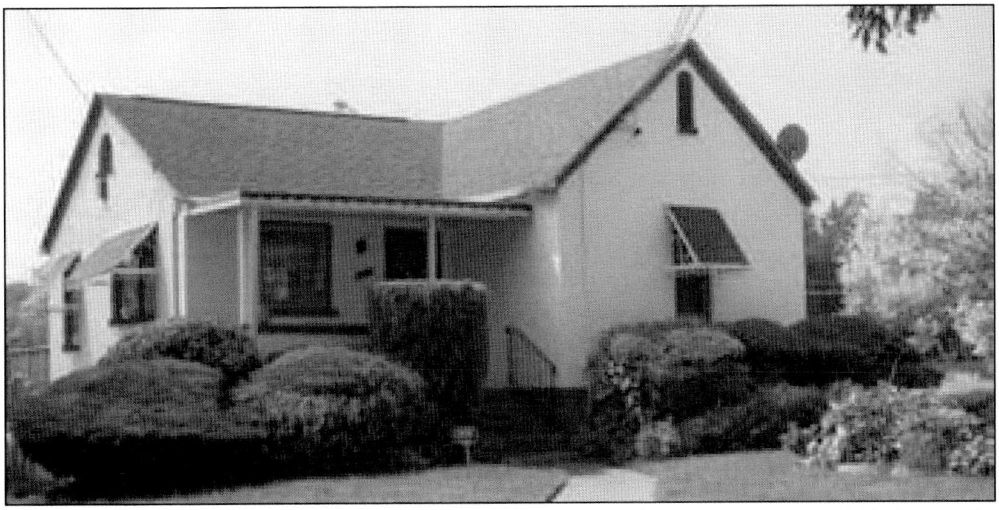

Plater and Dodd. The homes at 4115 Lee and 4021 Meade Streets are two 1940 designs by James Alonzo Plater (1908–1965), who was born and raised in Deanwood. Plater graduated from Armstrong High School and Howard University's School of Architecture in 1932. He worked under several prominent African American architects, including R.C. Archer Jr., Howard Mackey, and Hilyard Robert Robinson (1899–1986), the designer of Langston Terrace Dwellings. Although Plater set up his own practice in Philadelphia, he was registered in Washington, DC, and designed at least 20 homes in Eastland Gardens. Randolph Dodd built both homes. (Both, JB.)

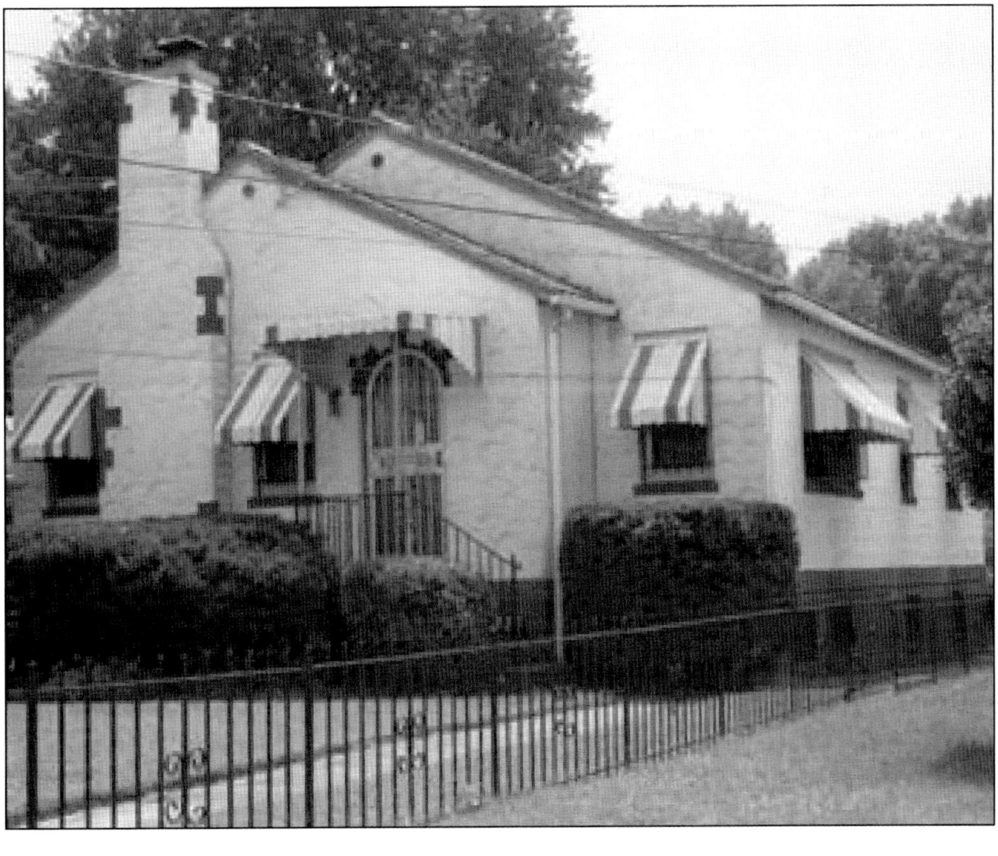

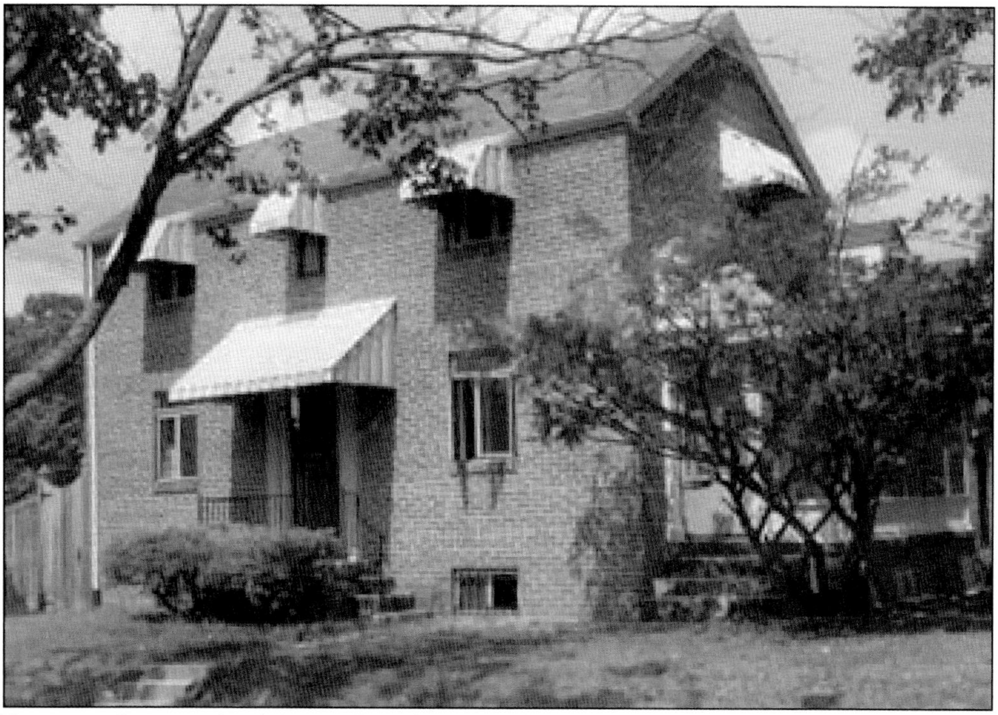

Bow and Cassell. Cyril Garner Bow (1899–1963), designer of this 1939 house at 4138 Meade Street, was a Buffalo, New York, native. He entered the School of Architecture at Cornell University in 1919, joining architect Albert Cassell. Although Bow did not graduate, he formed close ties with Cassell. Bow moved to Washington, DC, and worked in Howard University's Department of Building and Grounds, headed by Cassell. Bow also worked in Cassell's architecture firm from 1926 to 1951 as the chief draftsman. This was Bow's only Eastland Gardens design. Oliver Cassell, Albert Cassell's brother, built the house. (JB.)

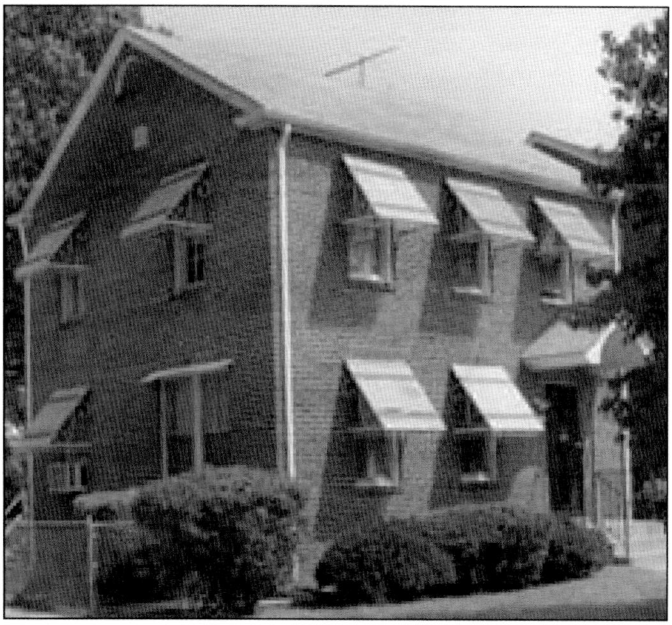

Bull and Dodd. Not much is known about architect Gustavus N. Bull, the designer of this stately dwelling at 4106 Lee Street in 1939. By 1936, he was listed in the city directory as an architect and was noted as the designer of several houses in Eastland Gardens and nearby Deanwood. Randolph Dodd was the builder of this house. As the photograph suggests, metal awnings were commonly applied over residential windows during the mid–20th century when most houses lacked air conditioning. (JB.)

BRANSON AND RUNSTEN. S. Leslie Branson is the designer of record for this home at 1133 Lee Street. Branson was a student at Howard University in 1937. As early as 1938, he was listed as the architect on several building permits for residences. Besides his three known projects in Eastland Gardens, his designs were also found in other Northeast Washington, DC, neighborhoods, including Lincoln Heights and Central Northeast. The builder on this property is J.B. Runsten. (JB.)

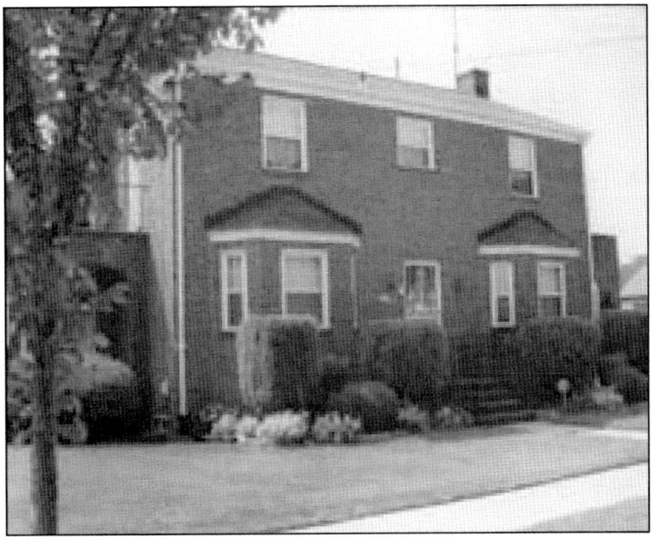

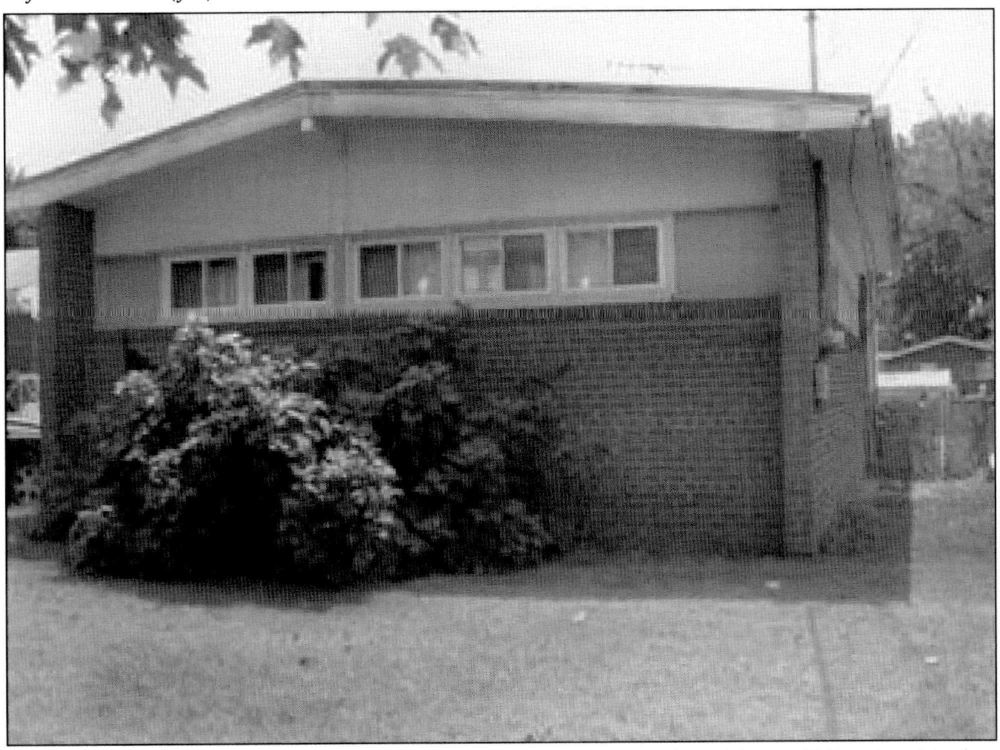

MACKEY. Philadelphian and 1924 University of Pennsylvania graduate Howard Hamilton Mackey Sr. (1901–1987) relocated to Washington in 1924 to teach at Howard University's new department of architecture. He became a licensed architect in Washington, DC, in 1935, earned a master's degree in architecture, and was appointed dean of Howard's architectural and engineering program in 1937. Mackey was called the "father of black architecture" because he taught so many architects. He also had the distinction of guiding Howard University's architecture program to accreditation in 1950, making it the first accredited architecture program at a historically black college or university. The International-style house at 4101 Meade Street is the sole surviving Mackey design in Eastland Gardens. Two others were razed for Interstate 295 construction. (JB.)

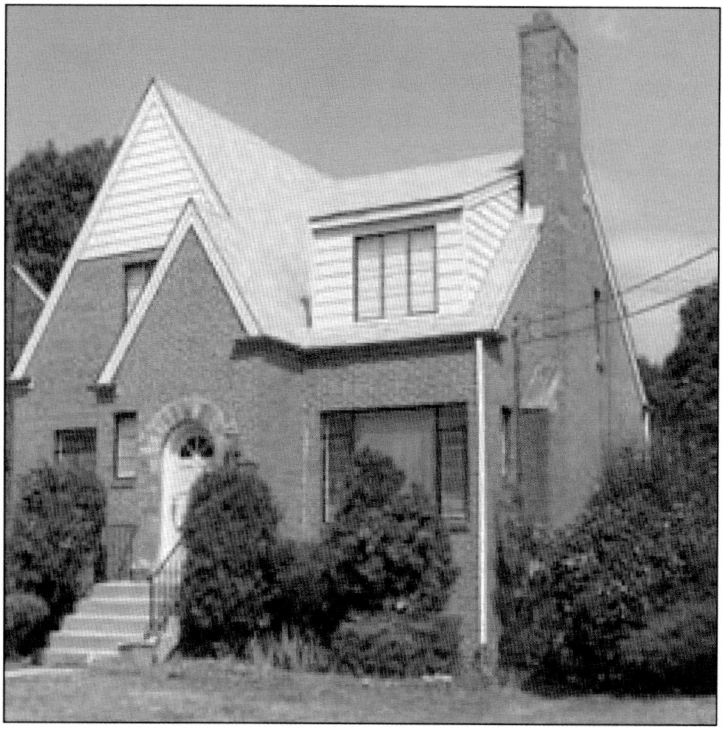

Homes for Jones and Boxley. This 1952 English cottage (left) at 4114 Lee Street is a standout in a neighborhood of classically derived designs. Owner Conway Jones was in the bond, insurance, and real estate business. The tastefully landscaped house below, at 4200 Nash Street, was designed in 1947 for the E.L. Boxley family. Both houses are the work of William Elbert Dickinson, a white architect. (Both, JB.)

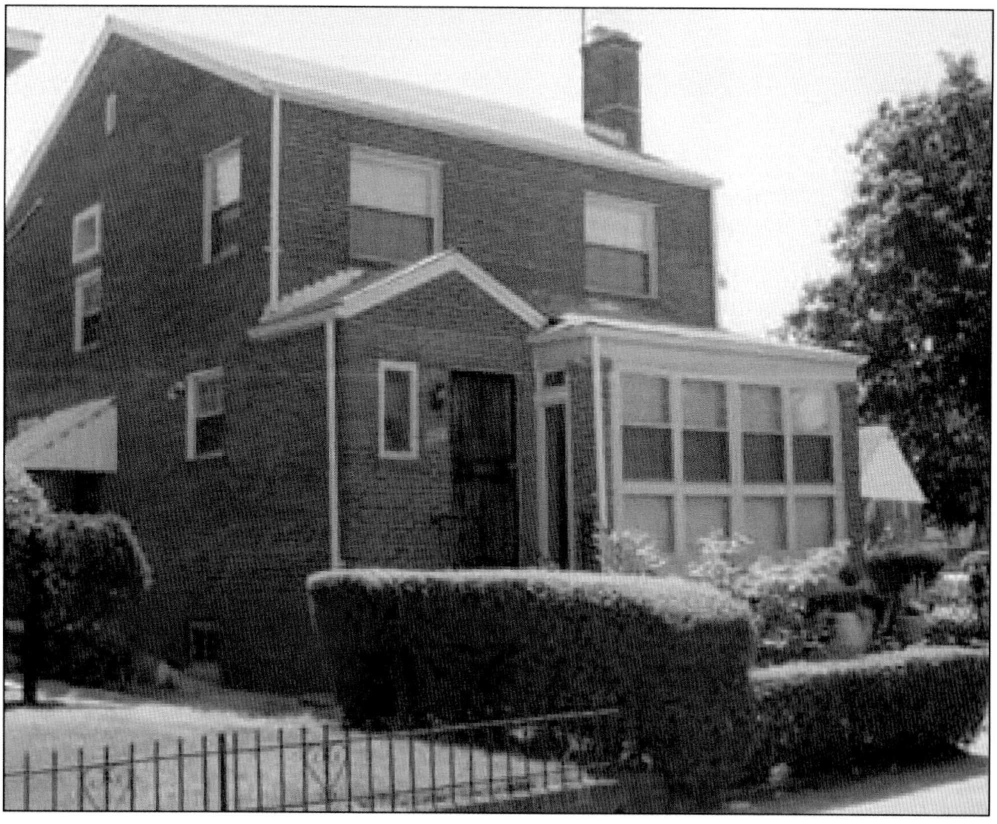

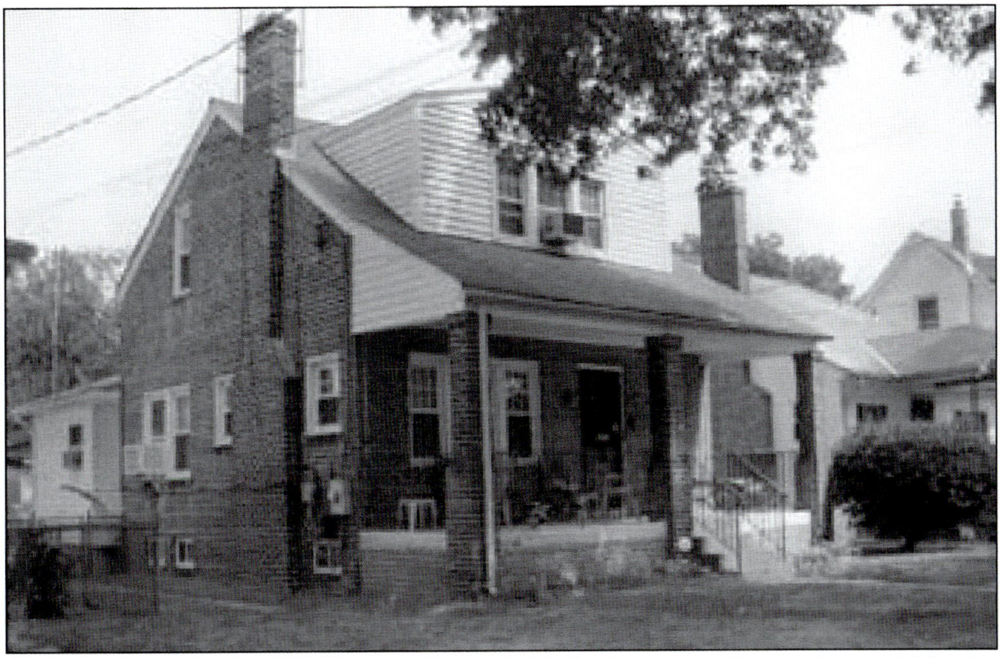

VAUGHN, MORRISON, AND MCKENZIE. District of Columbia–native Roscoe Ingersoll Vaughn (1884–1971) graduated from Armstrong High School in 1904 and studied architecture at the University of Pennsylvania, Columbia University, and the University of Wisconsin. He was also tutored in architectural design and structural engineering by black coworkers William Wilson Cooke (1871–1949) and Howard Dilworth Woodson (1876–1962) while the three were employed at the US Treasury. Vaughn became a teacher at Armstrong from 1919 to 1951 and served as head of its department of mechanical arts. He set up his own practice in 1918 and often partnered with Woodson and George Alonzo Ferguson (1895–1979). Vaughn is responsible for numerous designs in Washington, including the First Baptist Church of Deanwood, in collaboration with Ferguson. The homes at 4228 Lane Place and 4256 Meade Street (the latter for Howard University professor Frank Young) are two of several homes he designed in Eastland Gardens. The Morrison Brothers Company and Lawrence E. McKenzie served as builders. (Both, JB.)

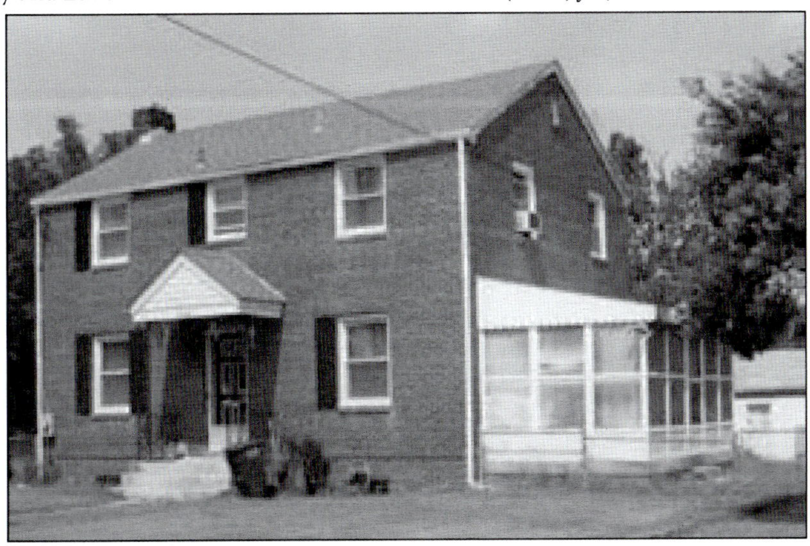

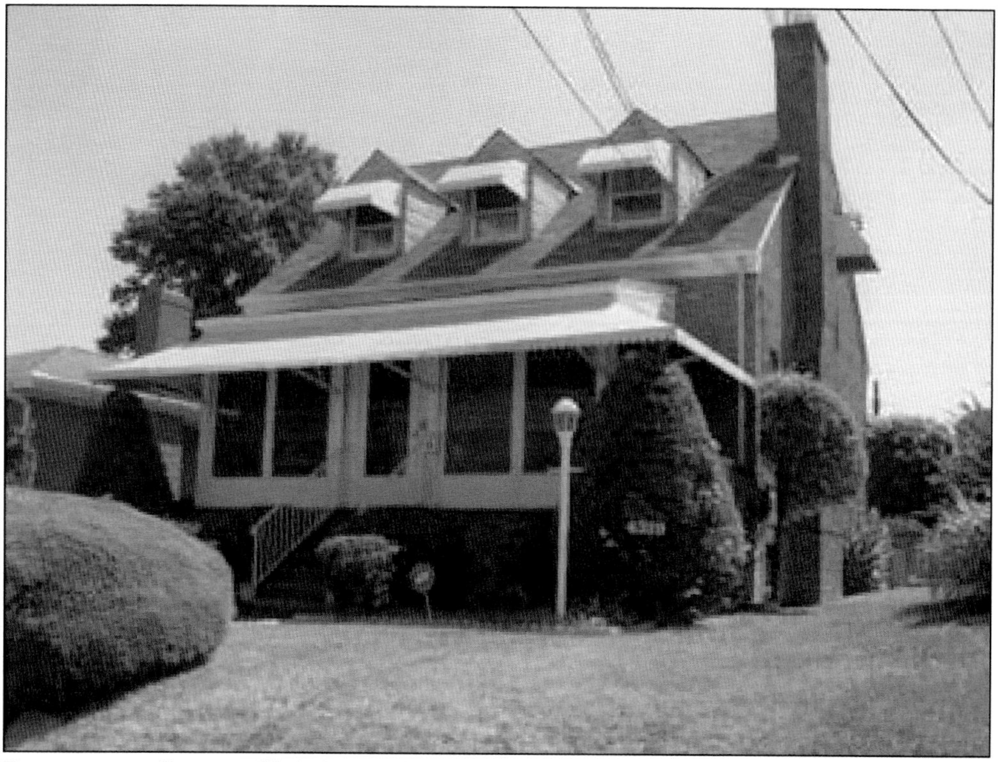

Drayton and Porter. Clyde Martin Drayton (1915–1983), a North Carolina native, attended Armstrong High School and Howard University's architecture and engineering program. He worked as a draftsman under Albert Cassell and Louis Fry Sr. (1903–2000), supervising numerous construction projects. He set up his own firm in 1942. Notable among his many commissions were his designs of Ed Murphy's Supper Club and Blackie's House of Beef, well-known Washington, DC, destinations. This house at 4319 Anacostia Avenue was one of two pre-1955 Drayton designs in Eastland Gardens. The builder is Lester N. Porter. (JB.)

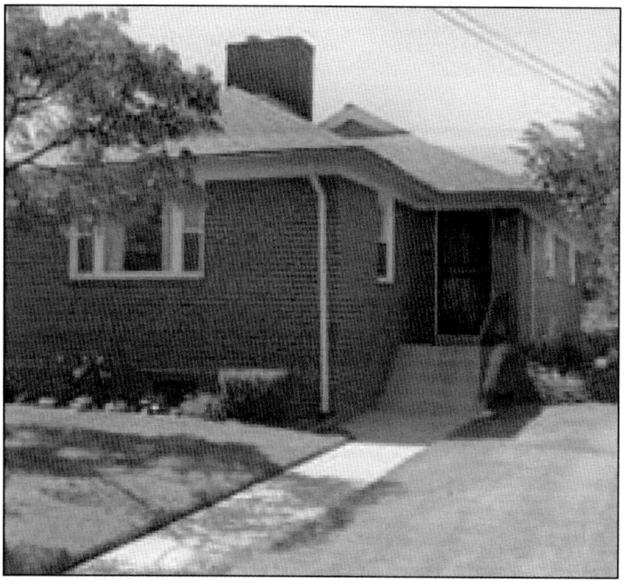

Giles and Entzminger. Designed in 1955 by Lewis Giles Sr., 1038 Forty-second Street was built by Harry Entzminger, who frequently worked with Giles on citywide projects. Entzminger, a member of Bricklayers Union No. 6, also partnered with G.W. Jones. Entzminger and his wife, Annie, were patrons of the 50th-anniversary celebration of the Eastland Gardens Civic Association held October 10, 1981. Five days later, Entzminger passed away. His legacy is the craftsmanship that Eastland Gardens residents and visitors continue to appreciate. (JB.)

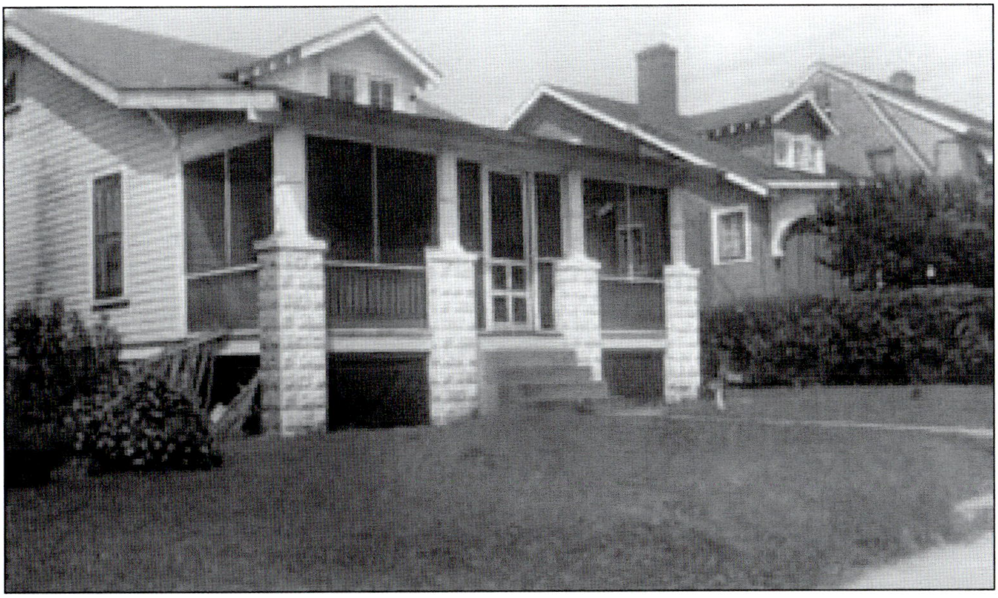

Dodd-Built House in 1948. Although oral history places the beginning of his career in 1900, Randolph Dodd's (1889–1945) earliest documented work was for a house in Deanwood in 1912, and his last was in 1944. He and his brother Jacob, both Deanwood residents, worked together until Jacob's death in 1930. One of their earliest collaborations was with Howard Gott of Kenilworth, who had joined the development game in 1910. As Dodd gained more experience, he developed his own properties in addition to contracting to build. This house on the 4200 block of Lane Place was designed by Kenneth Vieth and built by Dodd in 1929. John Irvin Slade purchased it in 1930. By 1948, the date of these photographs, Lane Place had seen significant development. (Both, WB.)

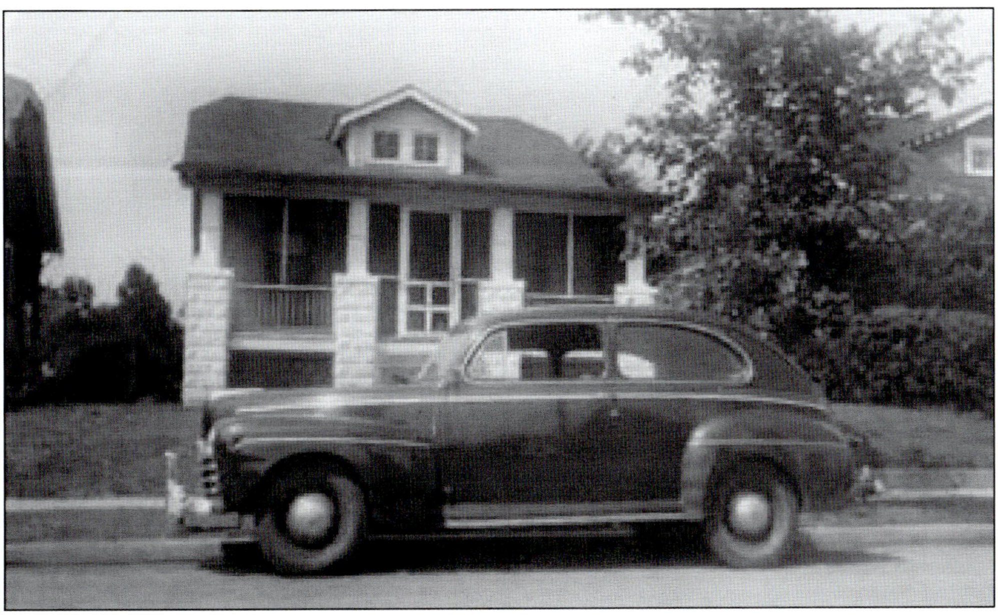

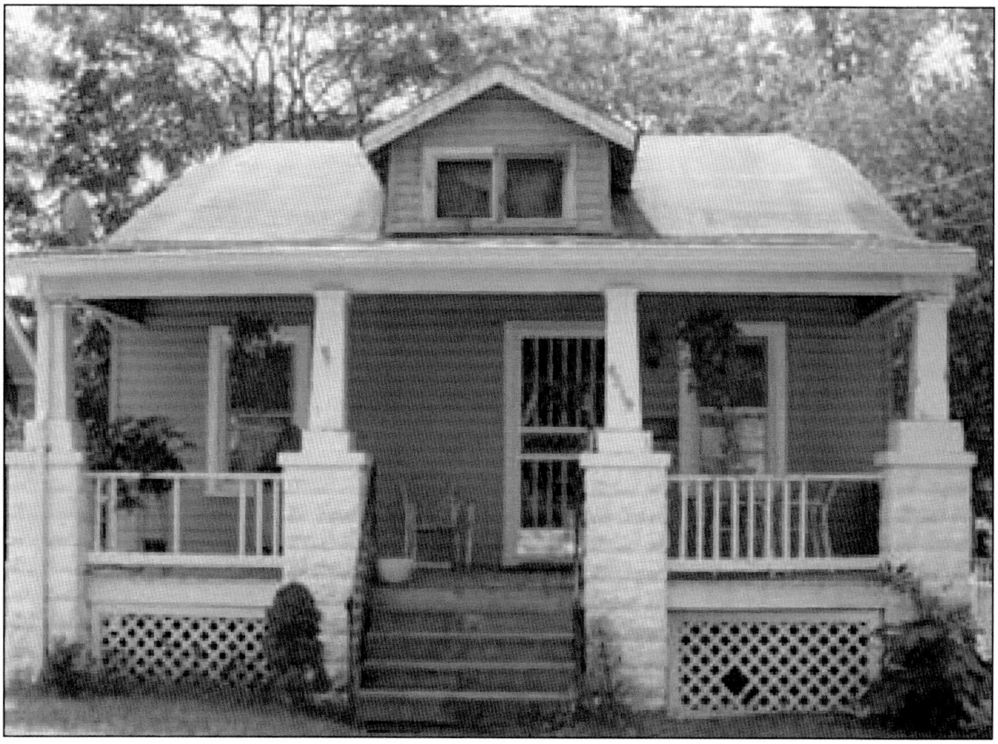

Randolph Dodd as Designer. One of the most prolific African American builders of his time, Randolph Dodd worked primarily in Far Northeast Washington communities, like Deanwood, Lincoln Heights, Capitol View, and, of course, Eastland Gardens. As a designer, he preferred the Craftsman style. This 1931 house at 4219 Meade Street is an example of his work. Ethel Jones, who took up residence here in 1932, had purchased two lots so she could have a "first-class" home. Although she owned investment property elsewhere, she was proud to be a homeowner. She frequently recounted how she worked two jobs many years to pay for this home. She did laundry and housekeeping and even moved to New York to earn money working in sweatshops. (JB.)

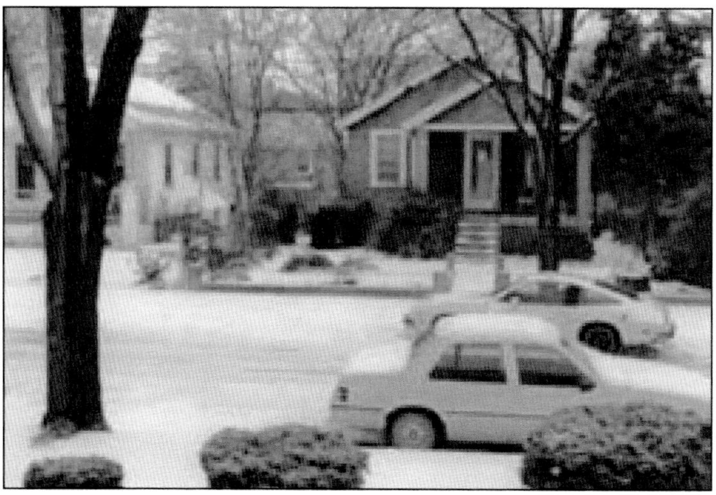

Winter Wonderland. A snowy scene enhances the streetscape of older Eastland Gardens homes. This Howard Gott house on the 1200 block of Forty-second Street had seen many snowstorms by the time this photograph was taken in the 1980s, which was when the home belonged to the Billingsley family. (CM.)

Three

Gardens of Eastland Gardens

At the end of a long winter, when the sun begins to warm the air and land, the green beginnings of last fall's forgotten bulbs push through the snow, and little nodes emerge on every tree's branch. There is an overwhelming sense of renewal and endless possibility for spring gardening in Eastland Gardens. In this haven, gardening conveys the message of stewardship and sustainability and a sense of control over the environment.

The Eastland Gardens Flower Club (EGFC) was a natural outcome of neighbors meeting over fences or gathering during evening walks to discuss their gardens, plants, and yards. As interest grew, resident and activist Rhuedine Davis invited a horticultural instructor from the city's adult education department to instruct and train neighbors in gardening. In 1957, EGFC formally organized. Founding members included Davis, who was elected president; Hattie C. Robinson; Charlotte Corbin; Virginia Brown; Gladys Brown; Genevieve Hardy; Isadore Hardy; George W. McKenney; Evelyn Billingsley; Theresa Jessup; Georgie Mae Carter; Margaret Harris; Almeda George; Grace Cabaniss; and James Cabaniss.

EGFC immediately put together an ambitious program that included a biweekly newsletter, participation in various flower shows, and community cleanups. EGFC became the first black flower club to join the National Capital Area Garden Clubs and to exhibit frequently at the National Arboretum across the river. An annual garden tour of the neighborhood regularly established and remains one of its most popular events, attracting citywide visitors. Members have won awards from flower show competitions and have worked to beautify local schools and senior homes through gardening. Member Diana Davis received a White House certificate for her work at Kenilworth Elementary School. Rhuedine Davis received a Beautification Award and a Women's Doer of the Year honor in 1965. EGFC lobbied for the erection of a pontoon bridge and provision of a shuttle so that residents and patrons could have easy access to both the aquatic gardens and the arboretum. EGFC successfully sought to beautify Eastland Gardens's entrance, a small park site belonging to the National Park Service. The group also received a $30,000 grant to create an attractive garden and flowering welcome to the neighborhood.

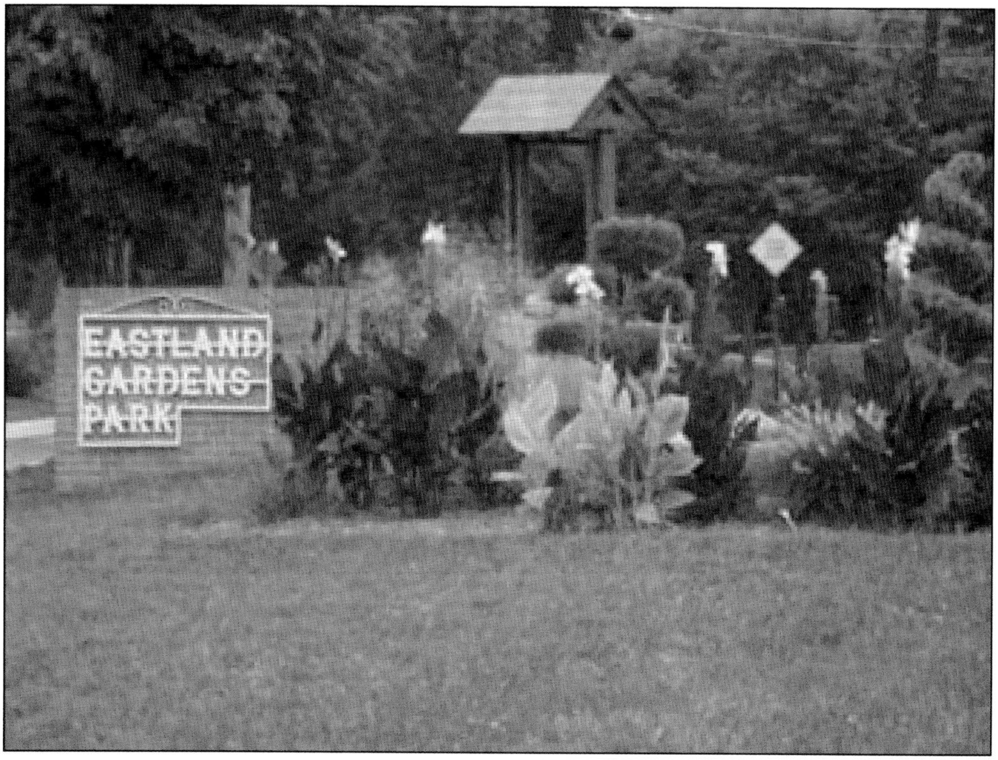

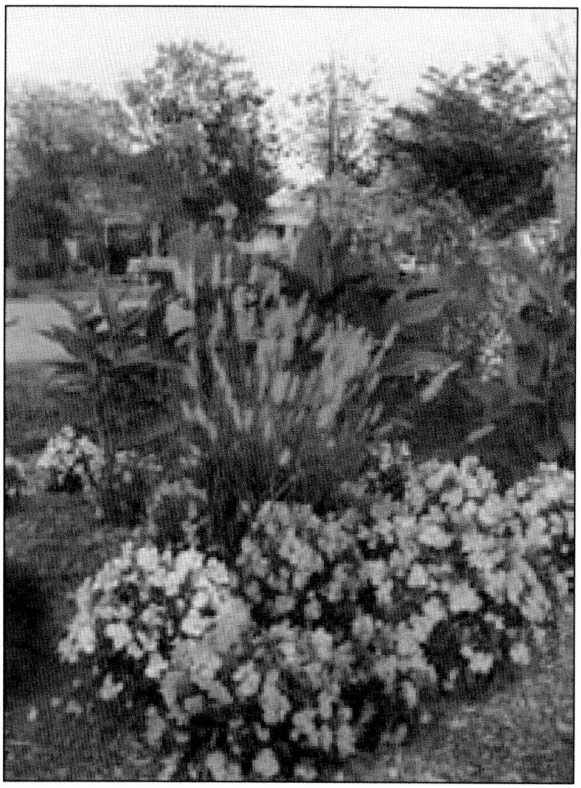

Welcome to Our World. Vibrantly colored flowers grace the entrance to Eastland Gardens. In the background, the Kenilworth Park, formerly a city dump, lends a majestic presence to the flowery garden. The setting represents a hard-won effort by EGFC to beautify the site and to herald a truly special neighborhood. EGFC members and other residents pitched in to plant the garden and continue to come together to maintain this showpiece. (Above, EC; left, JB.)

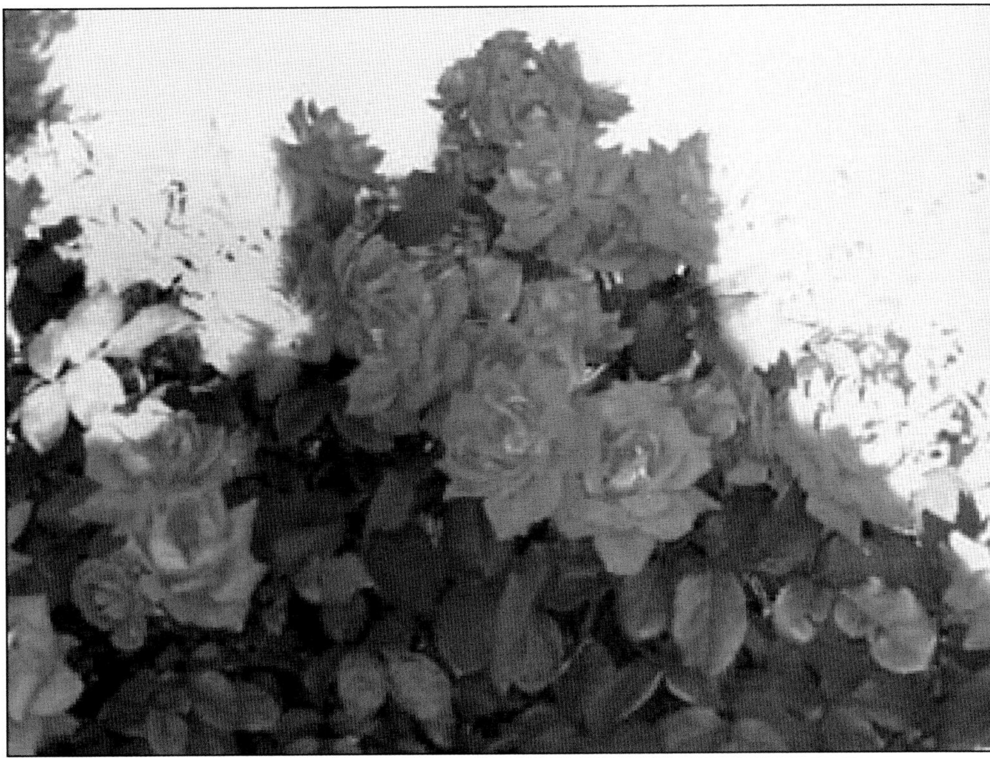

Roses. Aside from providing aesthetic appeal, inducing pleasure, and contributing to a sense of well-being, the rose gardens helped build stronger relationships between neighbors as they shared across-the-fence gardening tips. Illustrating this point, the photograph at right is of adjoining neighbors' yards, looking from the roses and shrubbery in the Billingsley's yard to the yard of neighbor Margaret Stevens, who is out on her porch. Roses became the pride of the community largely because a neighbor, a certified rosarian, generously provided first-hand knowledge and guidance. (Above, JB; right, CM.)

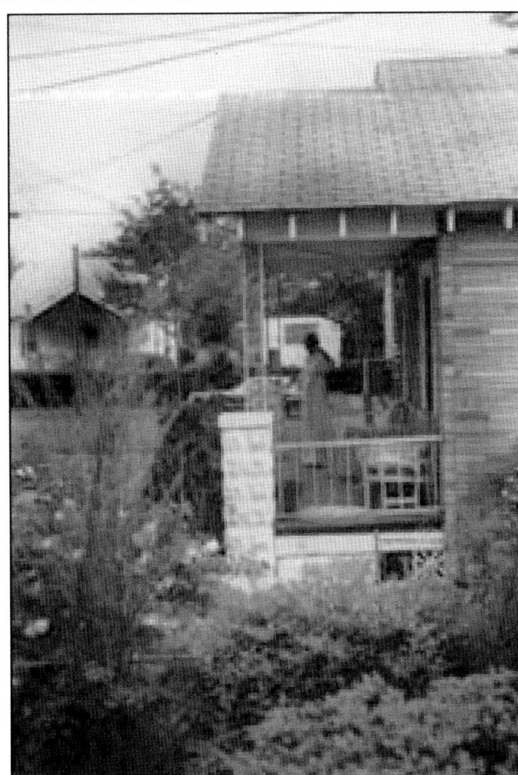

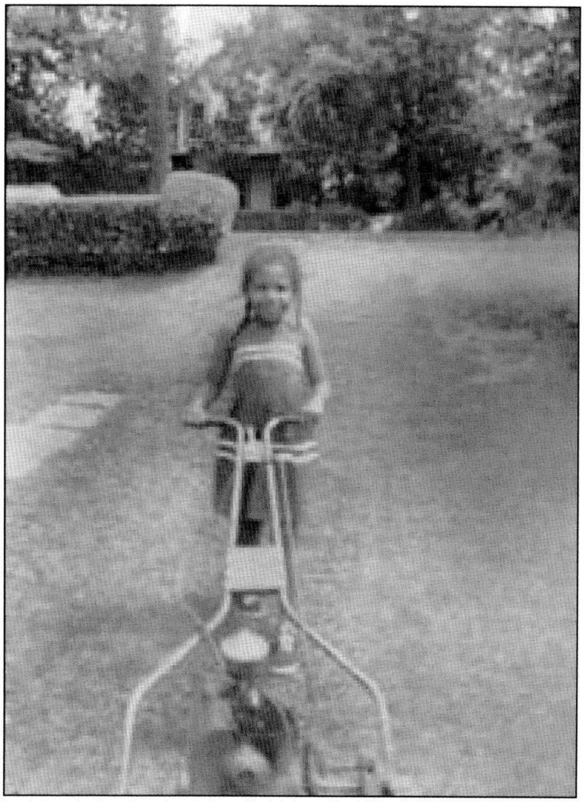

Lawn and Garden Upkeep by Youths. This 1960 photograph shows Bernetta (Matthews) Francis helping maintain the family's spacious yard. Eastland Gardens parents tried to ensure that their children learned the value of taking care of their property for the benefit of the family and for the community. The Matthews were proud property owners who had a long held tradition of stewardship in their neighborhood. (FM.)

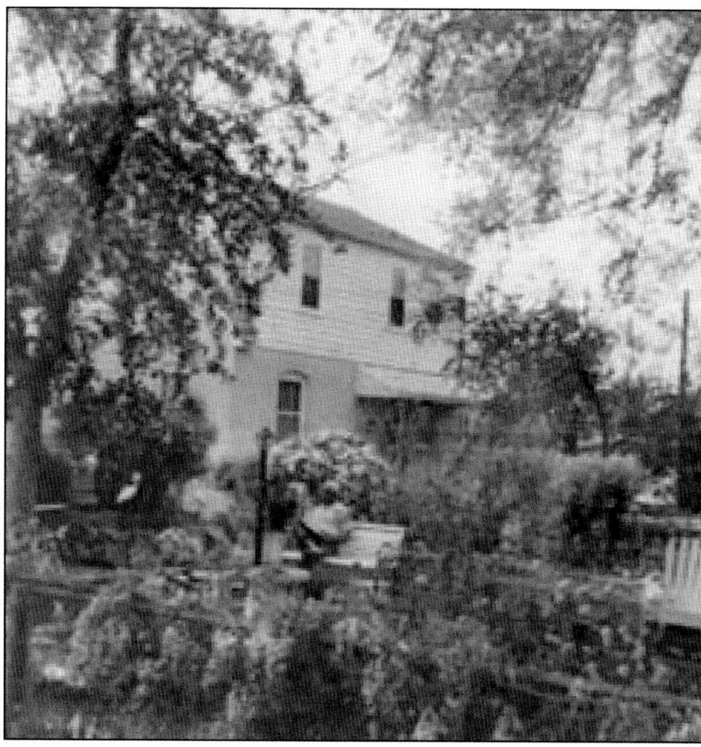

Flowering Gardens. Robert Roland enjoys some backyard solace in 1958. His backyard, located on Forty-second Place, is flush with flowering shrubs, lilacs, and other colorful and fragrant foliage. In the foreground is a fence over which he and his neighbor exchanged gardening tips and concerns about the neighborhood's needed city services. (CM.)

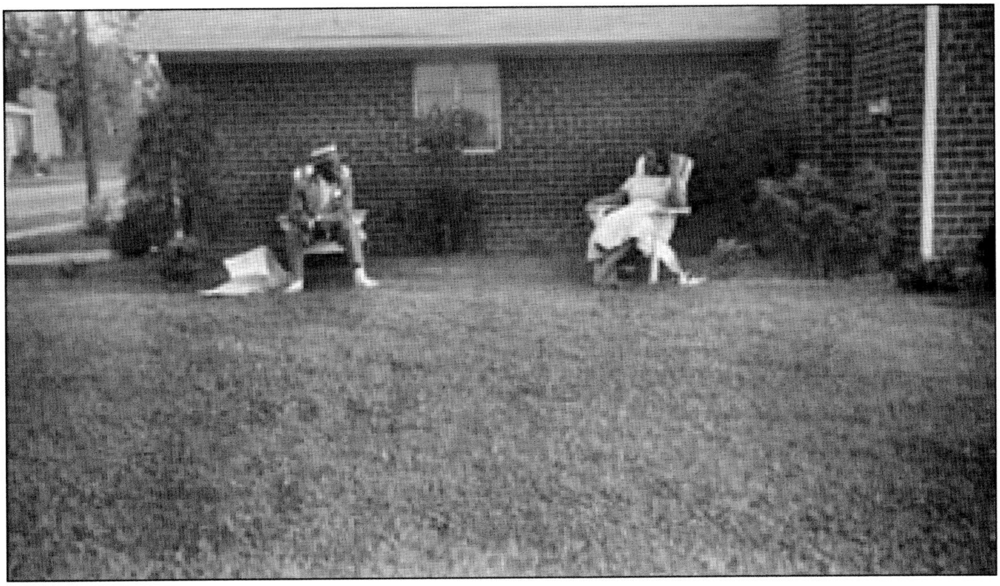

Cromer Gardens. John Cromer and Lunetta Nelson Cromer moved to Eastland Gardens in 1953. They were drawn to the neighborhood because of the spacious city lots. They immediately set out to transform their front and rear yards into floral courtyards. They would later spend many evenings on their screened porch admiring their bountiful perennials and colorful annuals. Their well-manicured lawn and impressive flower gardens made their home a popular stop on the annual community garden tour. Below is Lunetta Cromer in 1958 beside a bed of calla lilies. (Both, LC.)

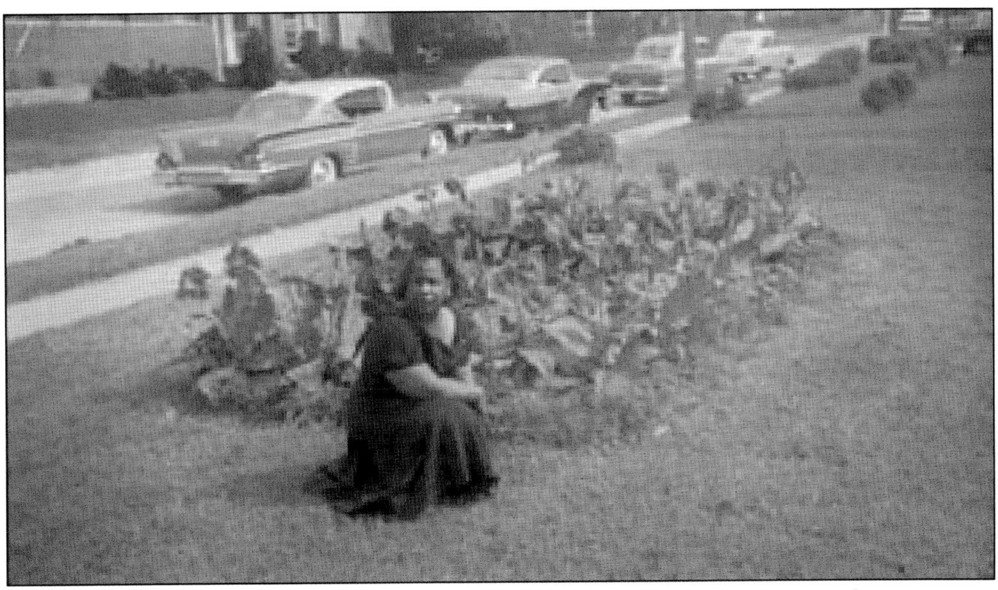

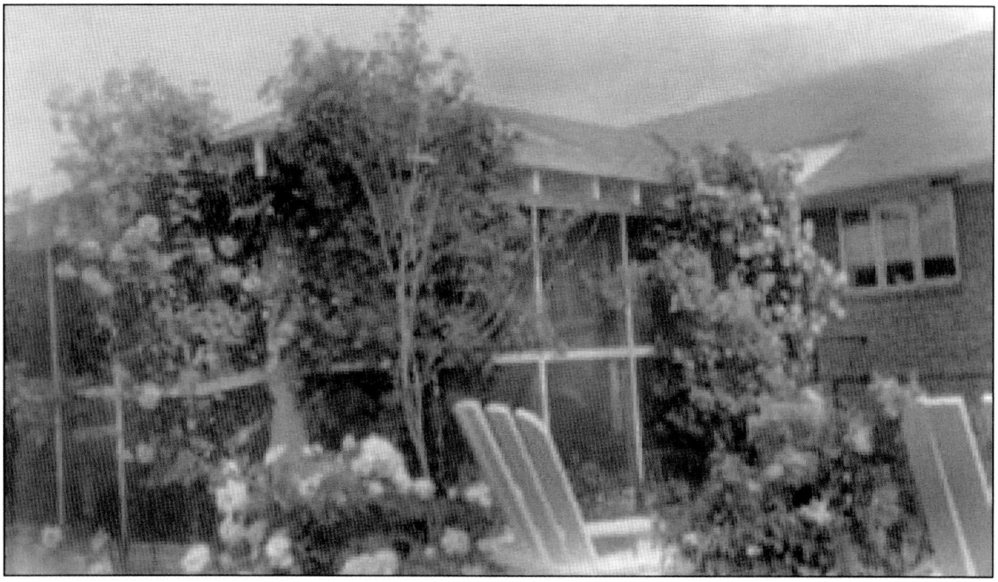

Floral Backyard. Like many of their neighbors who built and designed their homes, the Cromers' creativity did not stop with bricks and mortar. They designed their backyard to have an English-garden feel with ornate lawn furnishings and lush bushes surrounding the property. The screened porch John Cromer added to the rear of the family home was enjoyed as much as the Adirondack chairs in the less formal section of their outdoor garden. (Both, LC.)

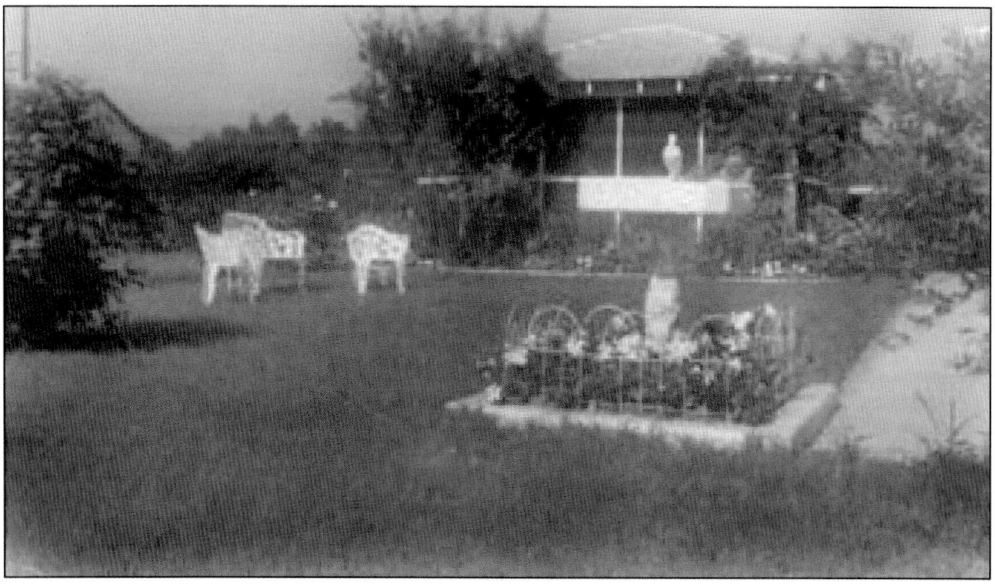

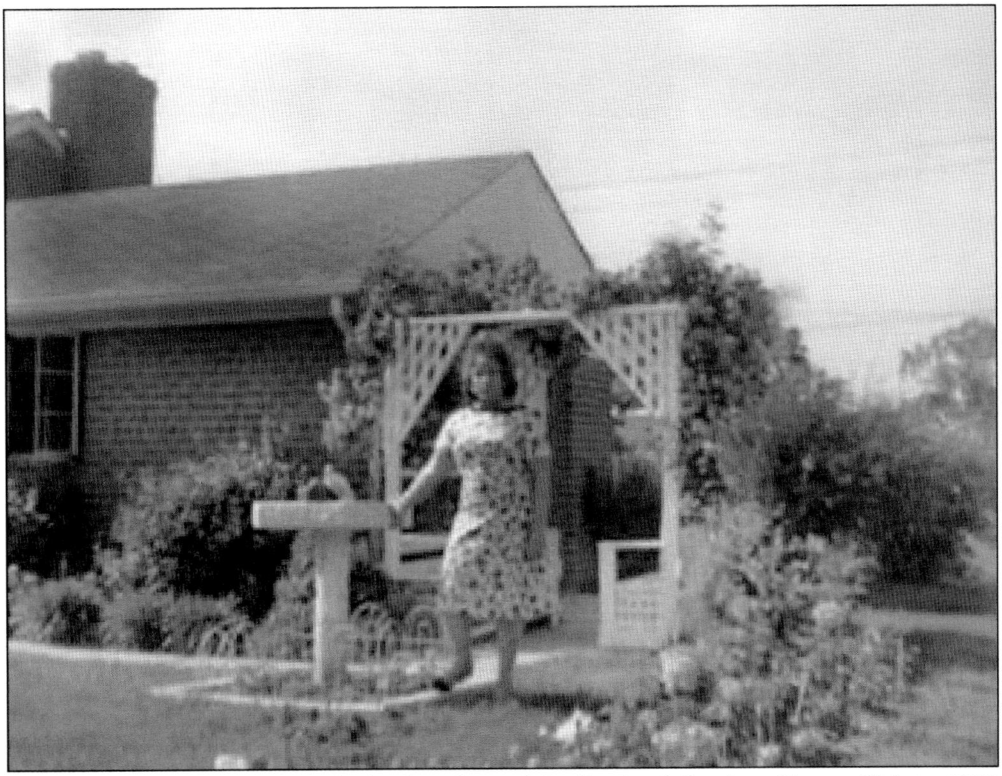

ANNUAL GARDEN TOURS. With the founding of the Eastland Gardens Flower Club in 1957, annual garden tours of the neighborhood became a tradition. The Cromers and their neighbors competed to present their best green thumb skills for their own pleasure and that of the community. Residents also competed in citywide flower shows, including ones held at the National Armory and the National Arboretum. Above, Lunetta Cromer is standing at the entrance of her backyard garden, awaiting flower garden tourists. (Above, LC; below, DF.)

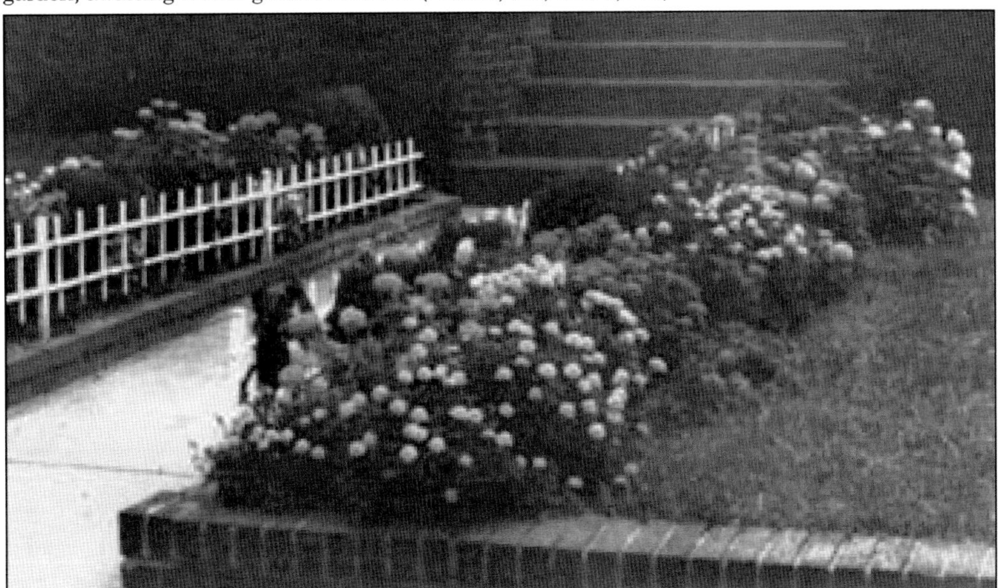

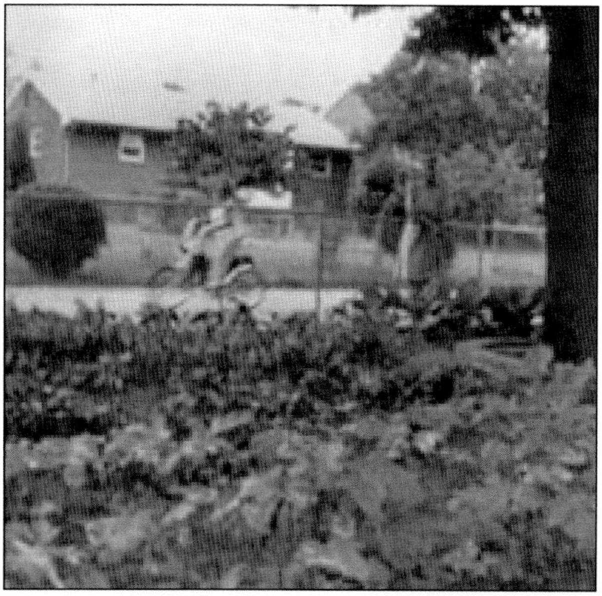

Backyard Vegetable Gardens. The alleys of Eastland Gardens were wide and kept clean. Backyards were manicured and bursting with color from annuals, perennials, and vegetables. Residents, like Louis and Ruth Logan, believed that landscaping framed a house just like a good painting, bringing out its good features. Louis, an independent brick mason, built and landscaped his home located on Anacostia Avenue. He also designed the masonry around his oak tree. The Logans backyard fruit and vegetable garden included kale, tomatoes, and onions, which they shared with neighbors. (EC.)

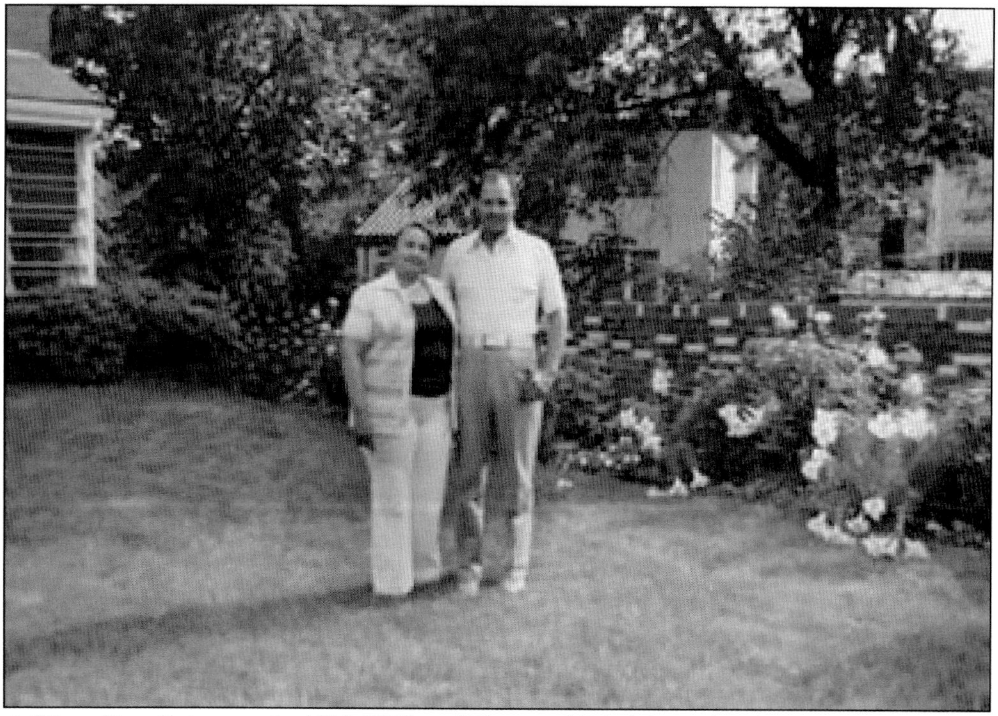

A "Best Yard" Award. In 1954, William White and Ethel (Lucas) White moved into a new home at 4010 Lane Place, built by Froe Properties. Ethel, a National Security Administration employee, made headlines in 1969 when she used the family car to block a truck convoy hauling raw sewage through the neighborhood. William retired as a truck driver from Safeway Stores, after 46 years of exemplary service. In 1958, he started and coached the Eastland Gardens Tigers football team, which was sponsored by the Metropolitan Police Boys Club. The team won several championships. He also contributed to his community by designing the logo for the Eastland Gardens Civic Association. In 1982, his yard received the EGFC "Best Yard" award. (DF.)

Four

"Our Spirits Glow in the Beauty"

Taken from the conclusion of a condensed history of the Eastland Gardens Civic Association (EGCA), the chapter title describes the families that settled in the community. The pioneers of Eastland Gardens were a diverse and motivated group of professional and working-class families. Residents included college professors, doctors, attorneys, ministers, officers, local and federal government workers, teachers, truck drivers, and masons. From the creation of lots in 1927 and the sale to "Coloreds" for $500 per lot, a new community arose seeking a high quality of life for middle-class African Americans.

The majority of the families demonstrated their love of the community through activism, seeking to protect and preserve the safety and aesthetics they enjoyed. Befitting of the community's name, gardening was a family pastime that both men and women enjoyed. They believed that "life is revolved around gardens and nature where people and plants age gracefully together."

Among the earliest families were Walter and Betty Robertson; Helen and Viola Cross; Margaret and James Stevens; Mason and Beatrice White; Josephine and Gaston Briggs; Clifford and Estelle Glover; Henry, Leonora, Henry Jr., and Mabel Spencer; Alvin and Teresa Sewell; Samuel and Ella Gibson; Russell and Lorraine Chambers; John Mundell; James and Mary Catlett; William Norman; James and Nora Butler; Harriett and William Williams; and Jacob and Olive Handy.

Colie Davis was working as a pastry cook at St. Elizabeth's Hospital in 1931 when he paid $10 down and $45 a month for two lots on Forty-second Street. At the time, there were only three houses on the street. In 1952, he retired and opened a store at Kenilworth and Dean (Nannie Helen Burroughs) Avenues, which he operated until it was taken to construct Interstate 295. His wife, Nannie, worked as a nurse at Providence Hospital. Together, they raised their children, Diana Michelle, Colie Jr., and Christopher.

Another family, headed by Reuben Richard Nichols Sr. and Maude Nichols, moved to Forty-second and Meade Streets with their children, Edna and Reuben Jr. Edna recalled seeing builder Randolph Dodd working on a house in the community. She remained in the community when she married Joseph Douglas, who later served as president of the EGCA.

In 1929, Marion Louise Rose moved to Meade Street and lived there with her sister and brother-in-law, Josephine Rose Briggs and Gaston Briggs. In 1932, she met and married William A. Stewart. They bought a house in the community, at Forty-second Street and Anacostia Avenue, where their sons William, Joseph, Reginald, and Aloysius were born.

Elsie Coleman Johnson, with her children Kenneth and Beatrice (Fuller), and her mother, Florence Irene Denund, moved to Forty-second Place in 1931. They later moved to Meade Street. Elsie worked as a public school teacher. Kenneth, a commissioned officer, gave his life heroically in World War II and was awarded the Silver Star and Purple Heart. Beatrice, who rose to become a head nurse at the National Institutes of Health, recalls the razing of the racetrack and the loss of the small commercial area to Interstate 295.

Though some of the community's pioneers have passed on and some have relocated, many have chosen to enjoy their golden ages in Eastland Gardens. They reared generations in the community, many of whom have remained where their spirits have grown in beauty.

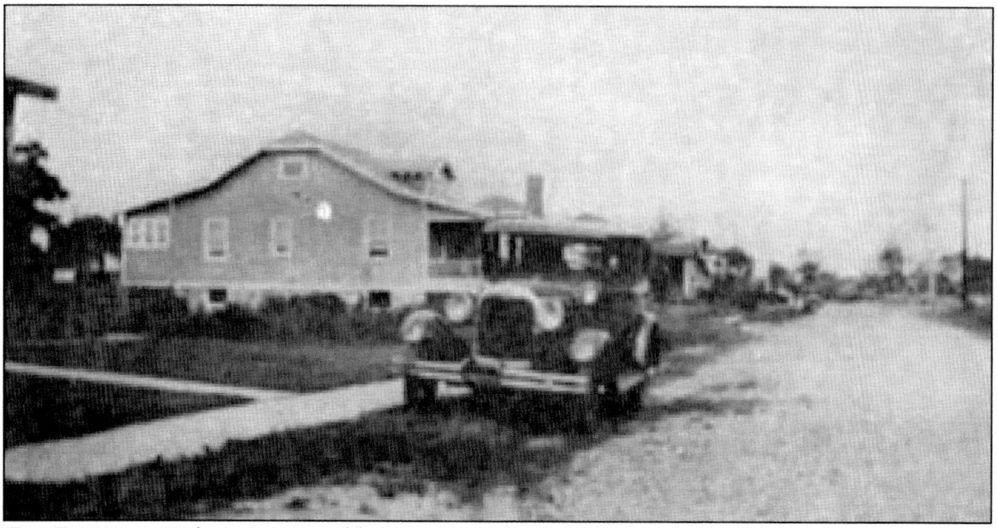

The Bowsers. Hobson Sr., Matilda Bowser, and son Hobson Jr. came to Eastland Gardens in August 1931 and lived with neighbors Walter and Betty Robertson while awaiting completion of their home at 4220 Lane Place, pictured above in the 1930s. Bowser Sr., who passed away in 1935, was a real estate agent for Howard Gott Properties. Matilda, who died in 1963, served as the first recording secretary of the Eastland Gardens Civic Association (EGCA). Hobson Jr. grew up to love the community. After attending college, he returned home with his wife, Doris, and served as EGCA president and vice president. He retired as a superintendent from the US Postal Service and, subsequently, became ordained as a permanent deacon for the Catholic Archdiocese of Washington. (PA.)

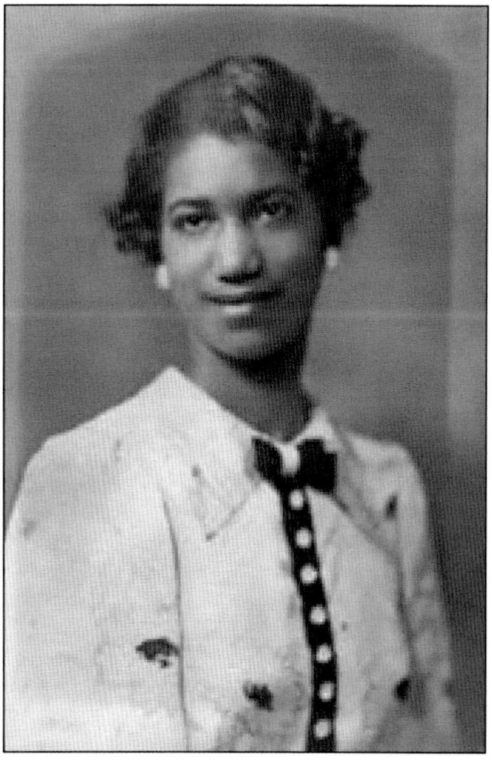

Burdette Household. Wilhelmina Burdette has been a resident of Lane Place since 1971. In her work as a child-care provider, she continued in the avocation she learned as a teenage helper to her grandmother. When she moved to Eastland Gardens, she continued caring for a first and second generation of nieces and nephews. Today, many are outstanding professionals. She has enjoyed the tranquility of the community, which has enabled her to indulge in one of her favorite pastimes, reading. (WB.)

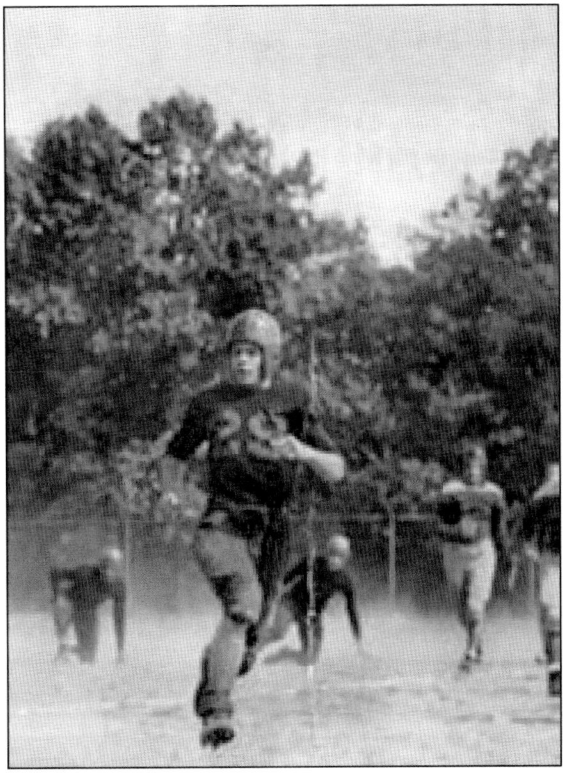

The Chinn Family. Louise (Nash) Chinn, Harold Bruce Chinn Sr., "Billy" (Harold Jr.), and Ann Louise moved from Foggy Bottom to Eastland Gardens in 1940. Their home, located in the 4100 block of Meade Street, was designed by Roscoe I. Vaughn and built by Randolph Dodd. Harold, a military veteran who served in Italy, was well known for his civic activism. He taught at Howard University and later at Street Academy in Washington, DC, where the newly renovated library has been named in his honor. Louise also taught at a Washington school. In addition to being ardent community activists, the Chinns were also active leaders in the Boy Scouts and Girl Scouts. In the 1950s, Billy, wearing No. 29, played guard on Howard University's football team. Pictured below are Billy Chinn (left), a friend, Chinn's son Michael, and granddaughters Dominic (front) and Mysha (right). (Both, MC.)

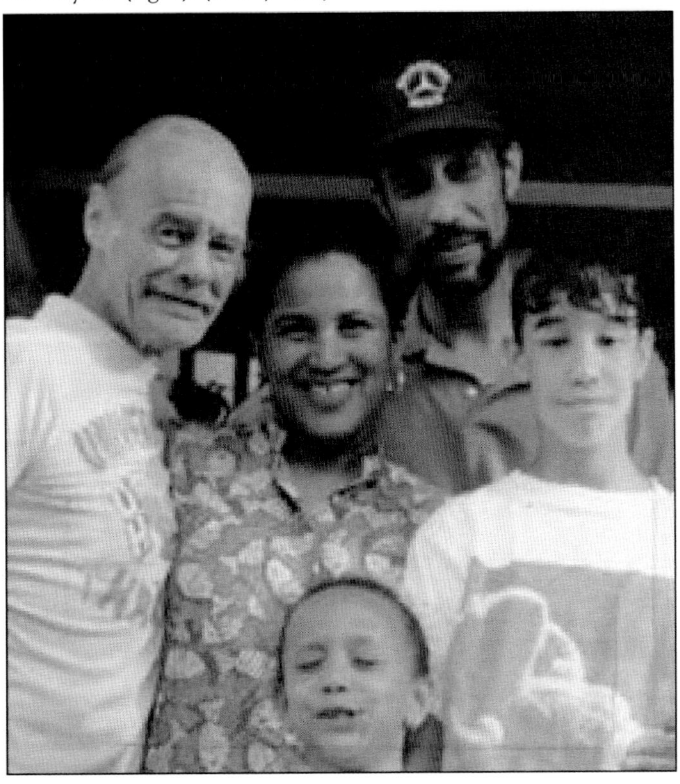

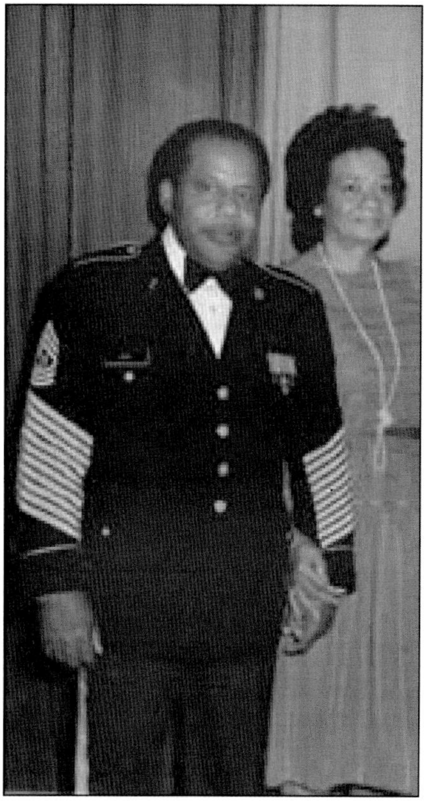

The Clay Family. Erman T. Clay Sr. and Vanetta Clay raised their two children, Paul and Erman Tommy Jr., in Eastland Gardens. A much-decorated World War II veteran, Erman was drafted into the all-black 544th Quartermaster Battalion and participated in the invasion of Normandy. In 1973, he was one of two African Americans to attain the rank of command sergeant major in the US Army. He met Vanetta Murray, a Johnson C. Smith University graduate, at the US Veterans Administration, where they both worked. Once married, they both served their community—he served as president of the Eastland Gardens Civic Association, and she served as president of the Eastland Gardens Flower Club. A widower, Erman is still an active gardener, cultivating vegetables, strawberries, and herbs. (EC.)

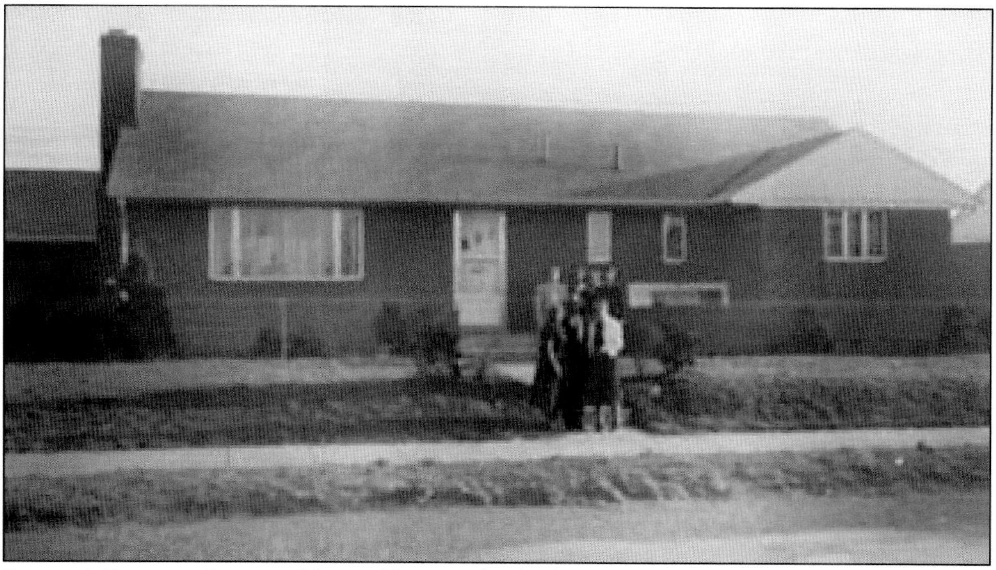

John and Lunetta Cromer. John and Lunetta (Nelson) Cromer moved into this Harry Enztminger house on the 4200 block of Nash Street in 1953 with their family of four. John Cromer worked as a cement finisher and made additions to their home, including their beloved front and back porches, which quickly became places of family relaxation. Lunetta was a professional dressmaker and worked for numerous families in the city's Georgetown neighborhood. Together, the Cromers made a comfortable and inviting home for their family and friends. (LC.)

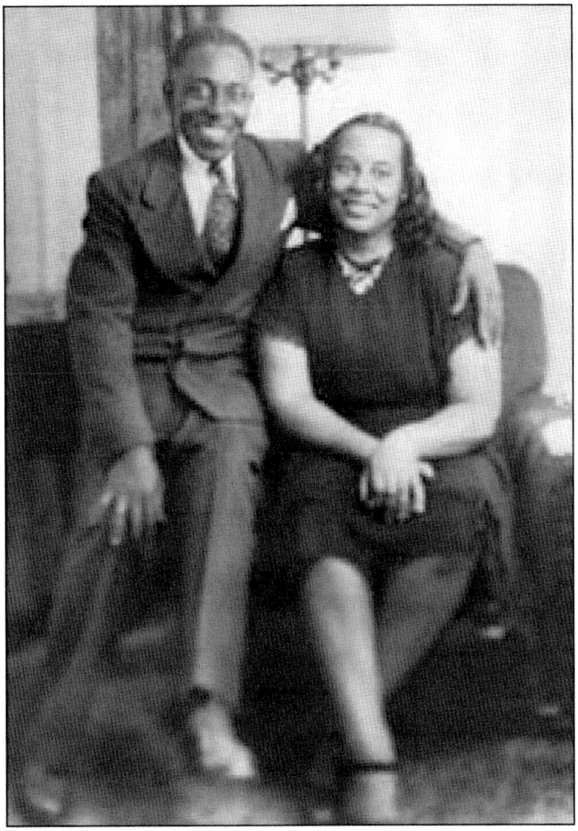

The Cromer Family. John Cromer enjoyed growing rose bushes in his backyard and was a frequent participant in the Eastland Gardens Flower Club garden tours. He earned several commendations over the years. Lunetta Cromer, with her sewing skills and sense of fashion, loved to decorate and was noted for making all the home's window treatments. In 2011, at 91 years old, she still enjoys the Eastland Gardens community. She is pictured below, in the center, with a friend and second, third, and fourth generations of her family. (Both, LC.)

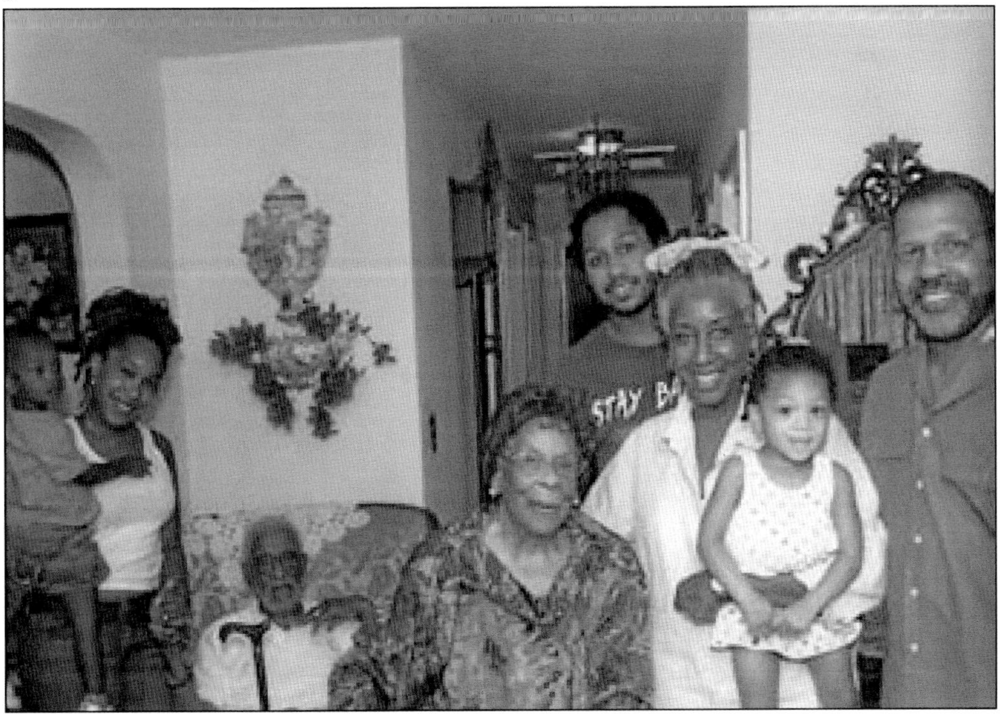

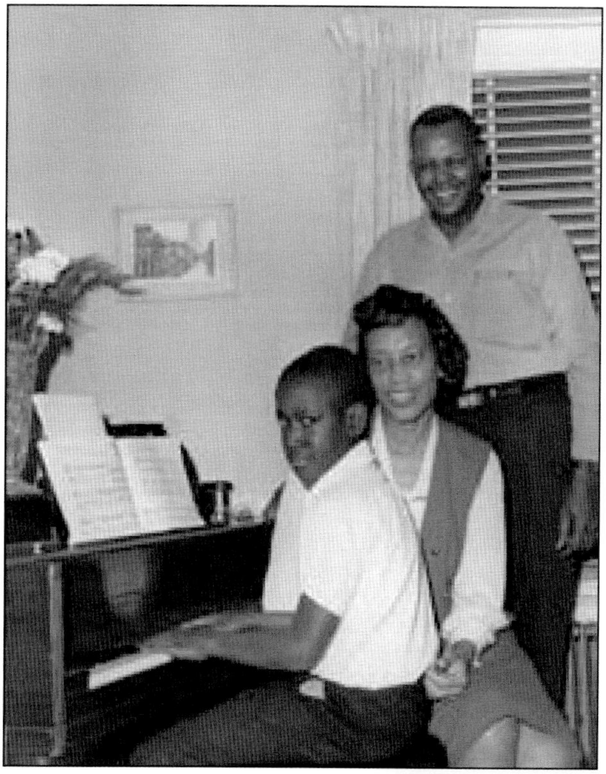

THE DAVIS FAMILY, 1965. Deputy police chief Owen Davis and Rhuedine Davis moved to Eastland Gardens as newlyweds in 1939. This photograph shows the couple in their Plater-Dodd home with son Alan upon receiving news that Owen had been named the first black captain on the police force in Washington, DC. He joined the department in 1939, and his first beat was Seventh Street NW. In spite of their demanding jobs (Rhuedine was a realtor), the Davises were probably the most civically active of Eastland Gardens residents. Owen served as president of the Kenilworth Parents and Teachers Association and was a member of the neighborhood safety patrol team. Rhuedine was founder and president of the Eastland Gardens Flower Club (EGFC) and the KEMP Senior Citizens Club. (DF.)

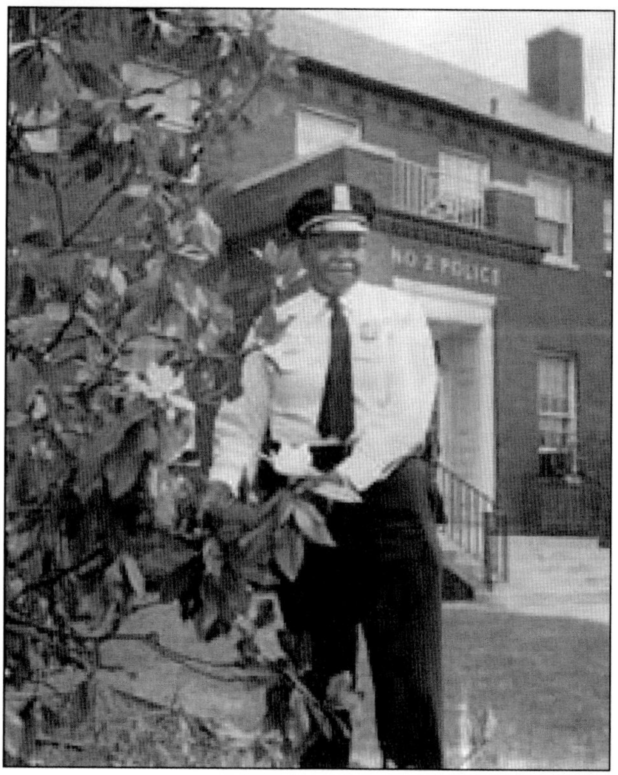

"FIRST DC NEGRO CAPTAIN TO HEAD 2ND PRECINCT." Owen Davis made the front page of the *Sunday Star* in 1965 when he was named the first "Negro" to command a precinct. Modest and humble, Davis was quoted by the *Star* as saying, "It's more important to me to be a police captain than to be the department's first Negro police captain." He was transferred to head the 11th Precinct in Anacostia during the civil unrest of the late 1960s and was credited for preventing serious disturbances (MLK-W.)

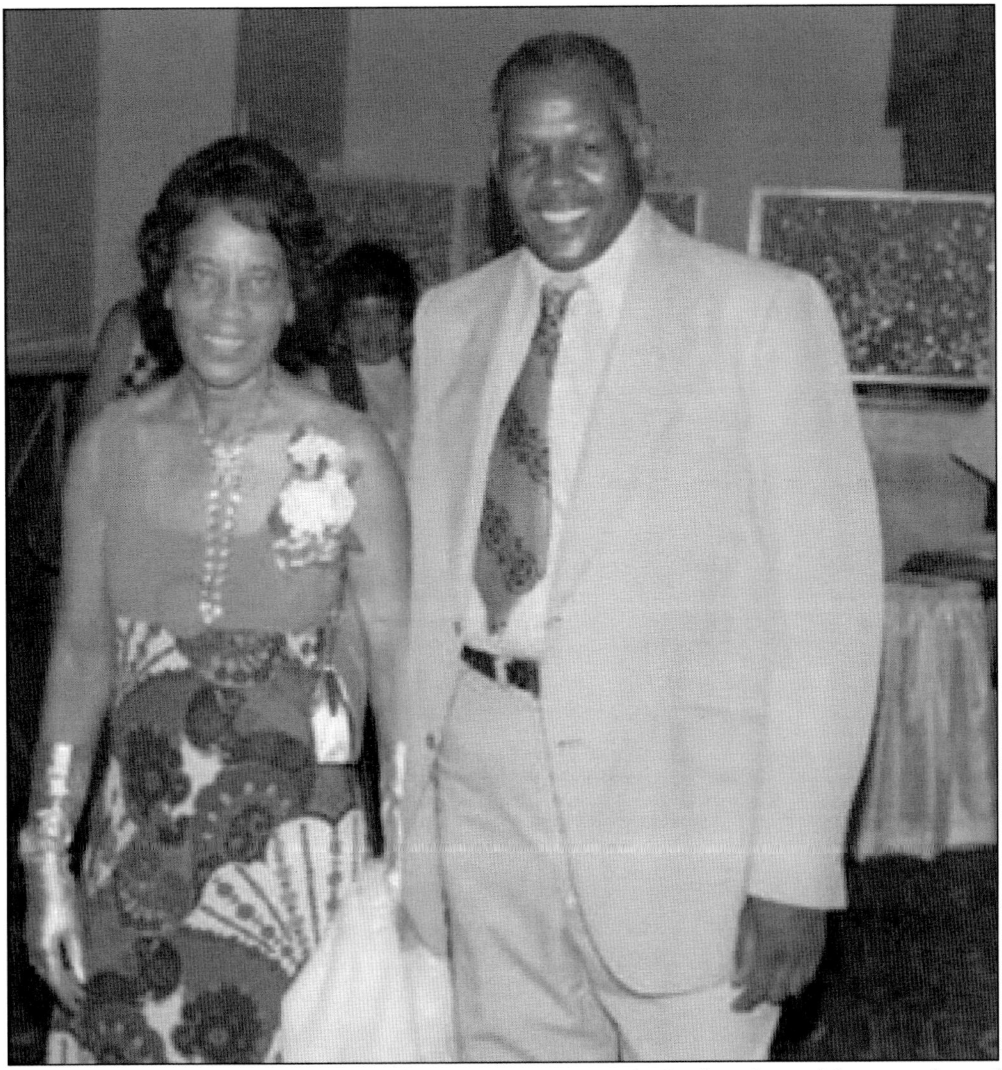

Peerless Community Leader. Rhuedine Davis was not only the founder and first president of the EGFC, she also assumed the leadership helm in other aspects of the community. She became involved with Lady Bird Johnson's beautification program, eventually winning national recognition as a Women's Doer. She spearheaded the cleanup of the community and included neighborhood children in cultural activities and community outreach, such as trips to parks, galleries, sporting events, and local social activities. (DF.)

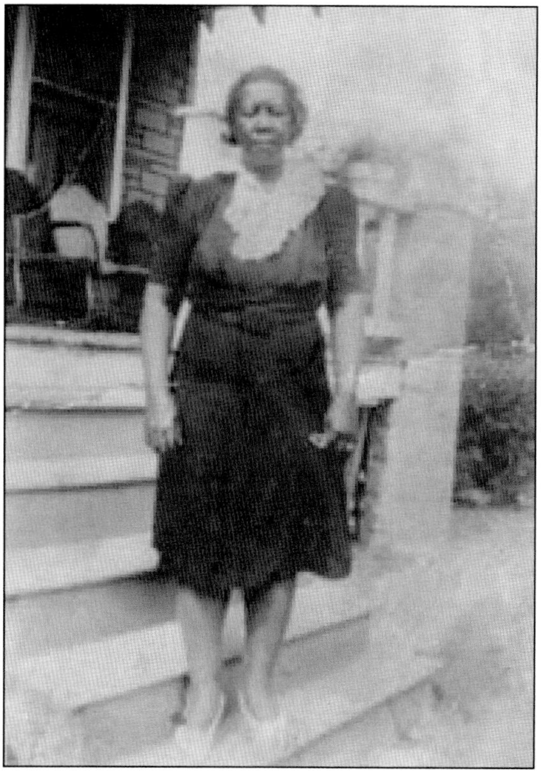

The Glovers. The first family to reside in Eastland Gardens was that of Clifford "Henry" and Estelle Glover. True pioneers, they moved in 1929 to 4218 Meade Street, where today their grandchildren and great-grandchildren continue to live. Clifford was one of the seven founders of the EGCA for which he served as sergeant-at-arms. Known as a hardworking family man, he and Estelle raised several children. The Glover home soon became the "hangout," as Estelle always cooked enough to feed neighborhood children who played with her grandchildren. (Both, GF.)

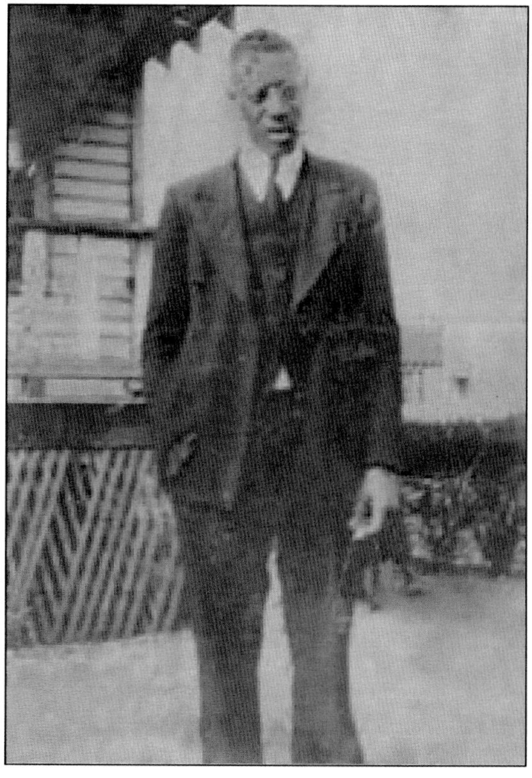

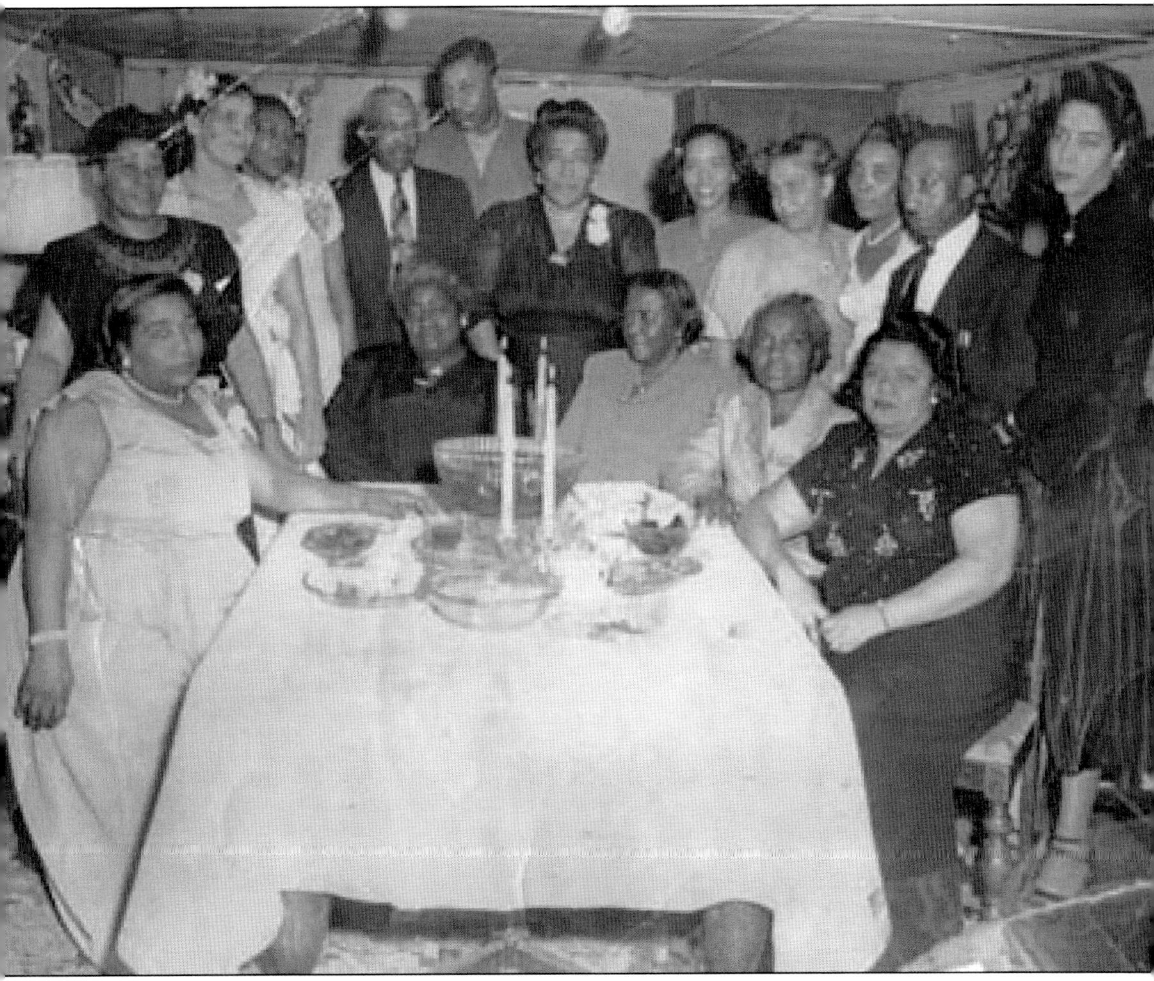

The Glovers Entertain. Known for their generosity and penchant for entertaining, the Glover family held many parties in the basement of their home, as was typical in the age of segregation when there were few decent restaurants and clubs in Northeast Washington that catered to African Americans. This lavish affair brought together extended family members and friends in the early 1940s. (GF.)

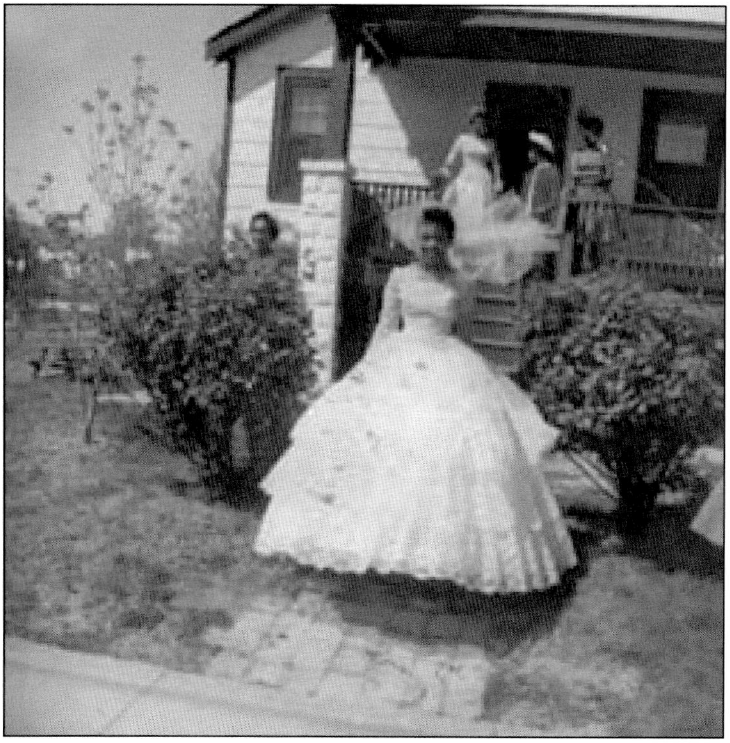

A Wedding in the Glover Family. On her wedding day in 1962, Brenda (Glover) Cooper is pictured across the street from her family home at her aunt's house at 4220 Marne Place. Resplendent in her wedding dress, she is ready for marriage. Brenda is the daughter of Jesse "Jake" Glover and Ruth Glover. On the porch are other members of the Glover family, including Doris, Louise, and Ruth. The next generation of Glovers, includes Gregory "Koolgalou" Williams, the neighborhood griot or historian. (CM.)

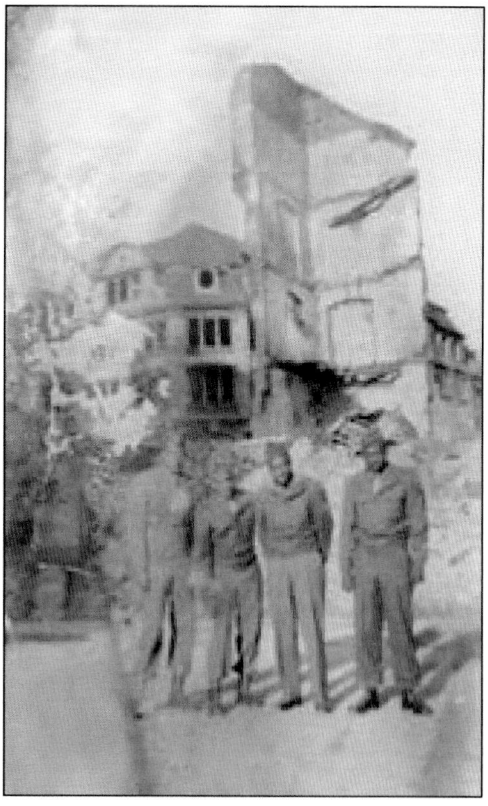

Serving Their Country in World War II. Although the identities of these Eastland Gardens men are unverified, two may well have been the Handy brothers who grew up at 4245 Meade Street with their parents, Jacob and Olive, who bought their home in 1932. Sgt. George Handy, a Howard University graduate, and Pfc. Emmett Handy, a Bowie Normal School student, reconnected on a road in Normandy, France, in 1944. This was the first time they had seen one another in two years. Another brother, Jacob Jr., was stationed in Texas, and the final brother, Francis, was a new pre-medicine graduate. There were at least three daughters in the Handy family. (DF.)

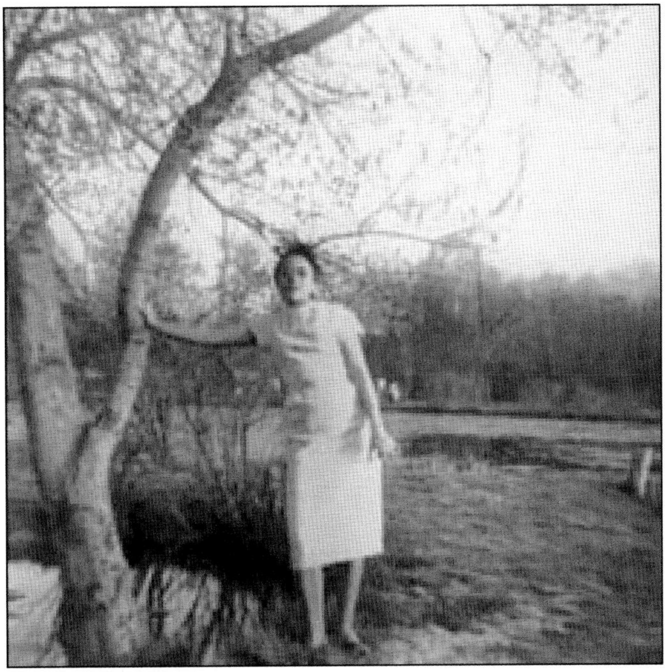

Helen Haynes. Helen Haynes has been an EGFC member for more than 30 years. In the spring of 1960, she was photographed during one of her many visits to Kenilworth Aquatic Gardens to enjoy the best of nature. She continues to be very active in the club and volunteers in many outreach activities of the community. (HH.)

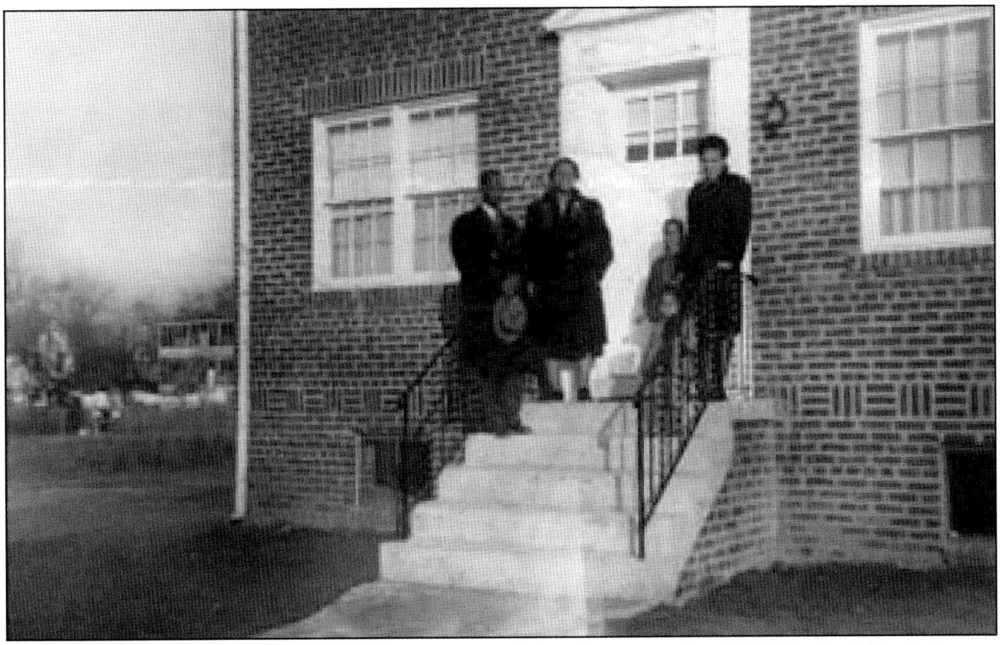

The Herndon Family. After the construction of their home in the 4400 block of Nash Street, Laurence Herndon and Helen Herndon moved in. Their home, designed by James L. Turner in 1948, was featured in a 1951 issue of *Ebony* magazine in an article titled, "Amateur Home Builders." The article captured the determination of black families to attain a piece of the American dream in the midst of segregation and racism. Pictured in front of their home are Laurence's parents, William and Nina Herndon (left), Helen, and two of the four Herndon children, Sandra and Diane. Through 1989, Laurence was a great gardener and participated in the EGFC annual garden tour, where he once won first prize for "Best Yard." (HF.)

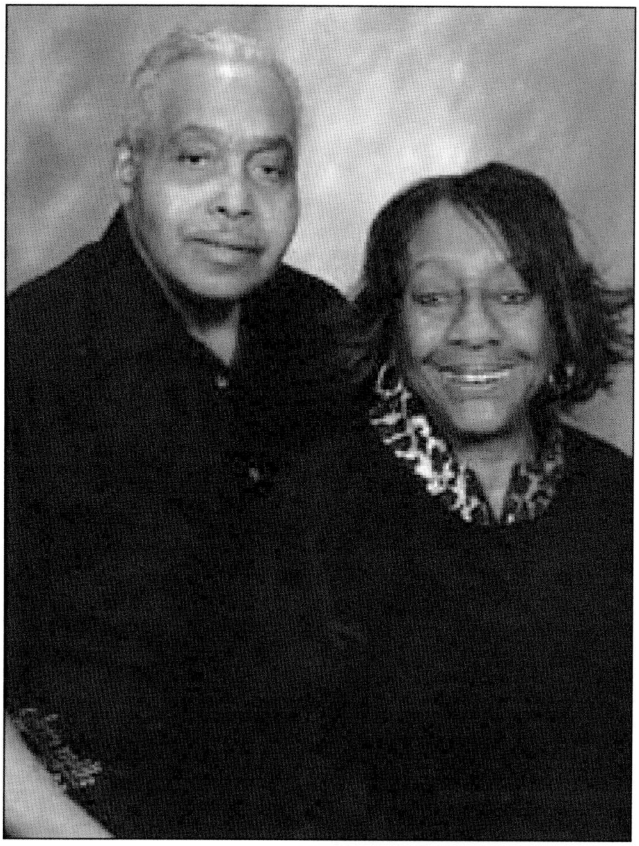

The Jacksons. Geraldyne (Tasby) Jackson and Cedric Jackson, both native Washingtonians, moved to the 4100 block of Anacostia Avenue in 1967 with their son Stanley. Cedric and Geraldyne worked at the US Postal Service and the Department of Housing and Urban Development, respectively, until retirement. They started and actively participated in the Christmas tree decorations at the entrance park. Geraldyne also served on the board of the EGCA and was the Eastland Gardens reporter to the *Capitol Spotlight*. They were recognized for their contributions with a 1993 Certificate of Appreciation and a 2000 Award of Merit from the EGCA. (GJ.)

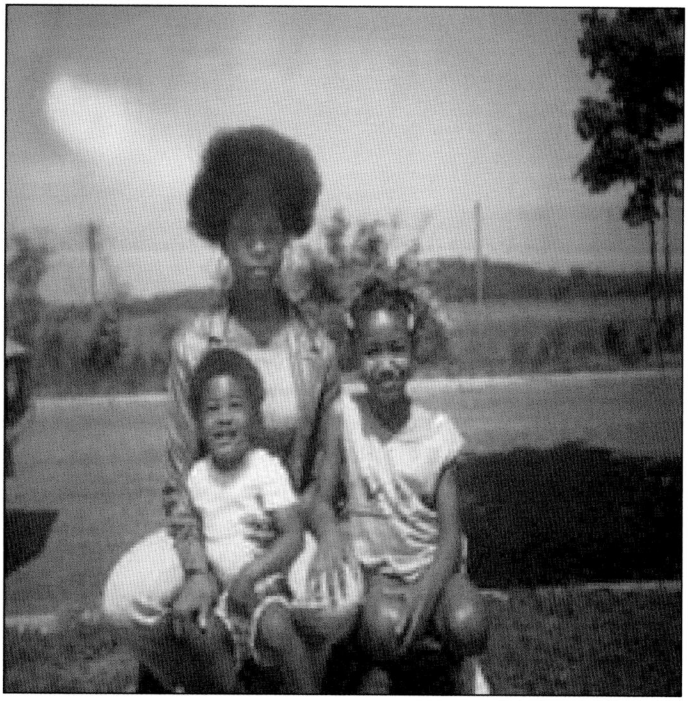

The Lincoln Children. James Lincoln and Mary (Swift) Lincoln moved to Eastland Gardens in 1968 with daughter Teresa. Mary worked as a registered nurse for 27 years before retiring in 2008. She often said that she loved the neighborhood because it was a good place to rear children. In addition, Eastland Gardens was the perfect place to indulge another of her passions, gardening. Mary readily has participated over the years in the annual garden tour of the neighborhood. Her children, James and Teresa, are pictured to the right with their babysitter. (ML.)

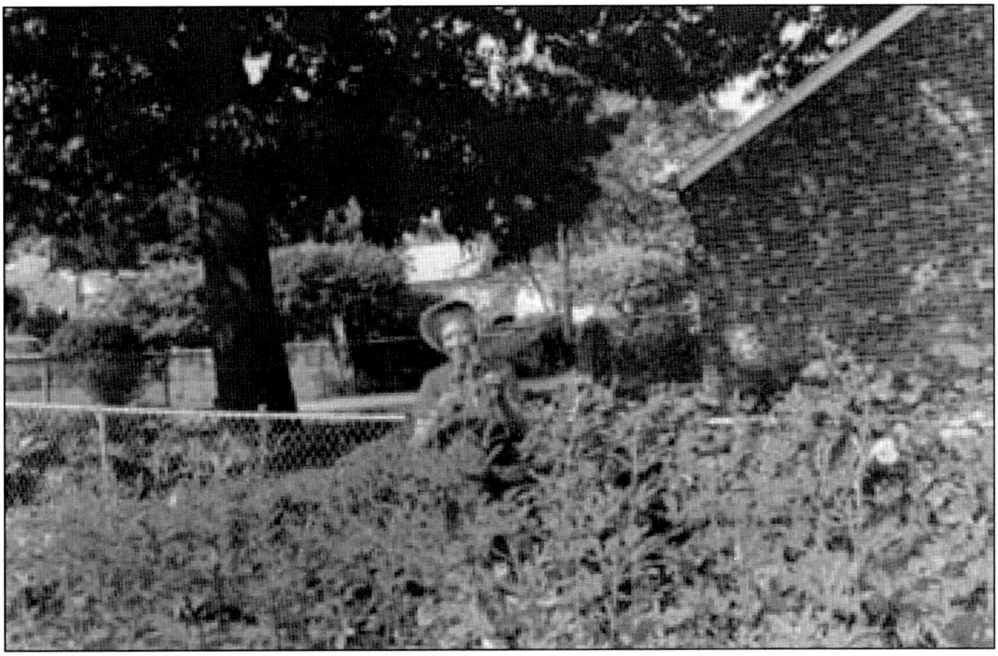

The Logan Family. Louis Logan and Ruth Logan built their home on Anacostia Avenue in 1971. A professional bricklayer, his craftsmanship can be seen on several apartment buildings in Deanwood, as well as the First Baptist Church of Deanwood on Forty-fifth Street. He also erected the brick wall that graces the Eastland Gardens entrance. (KL.)

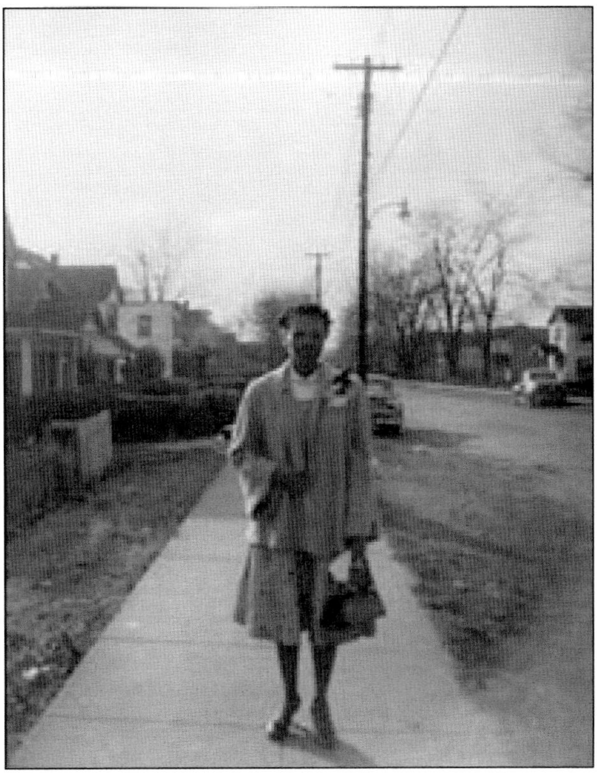

Matthews Family. Several generations of the Matthews family have lived on Douglas Street when it was a small enclave of African Americans in the predominantly white suburb of Kenilworth. Frank Matthews and Sadie Matthews were the first generation, moving into their house in the first decade of 1900. Over the years, the white population decreased as the black population increased with the development of Eastland Gardens. Second-generation Thomas L. Matthews and his wife, Beatrice (Williams) Matthews (pictured), lived in the family house and raised Florence, Frank, Bernetta, and Tommy. (FM.)

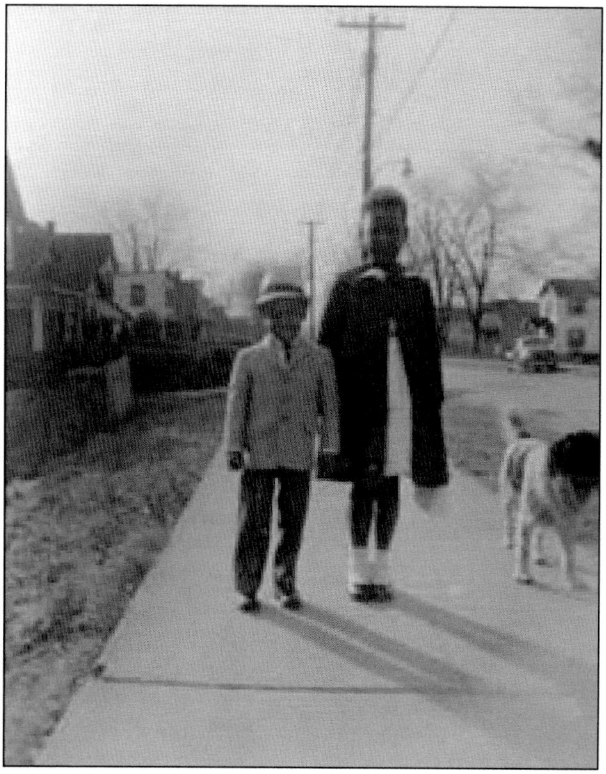

THIRD-GENERATION MATTHEWS. The grandchildren of Frank and Sadie Matthews grew up in the family house. Frank Matthews and sister Bernetta (Matthews) Francis are pictured left in the 1950s with their dog Skippy. The two children are also pictured in their yard, with Frank wearing his favorite cowboy hat. Frank now lives in his childhood home, where he in turn raised his daughter Franyana. (Both, FM.)

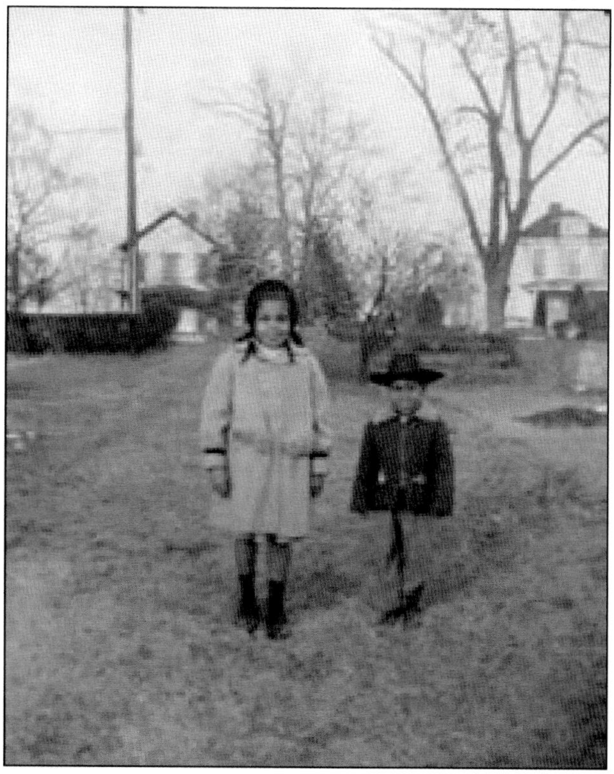

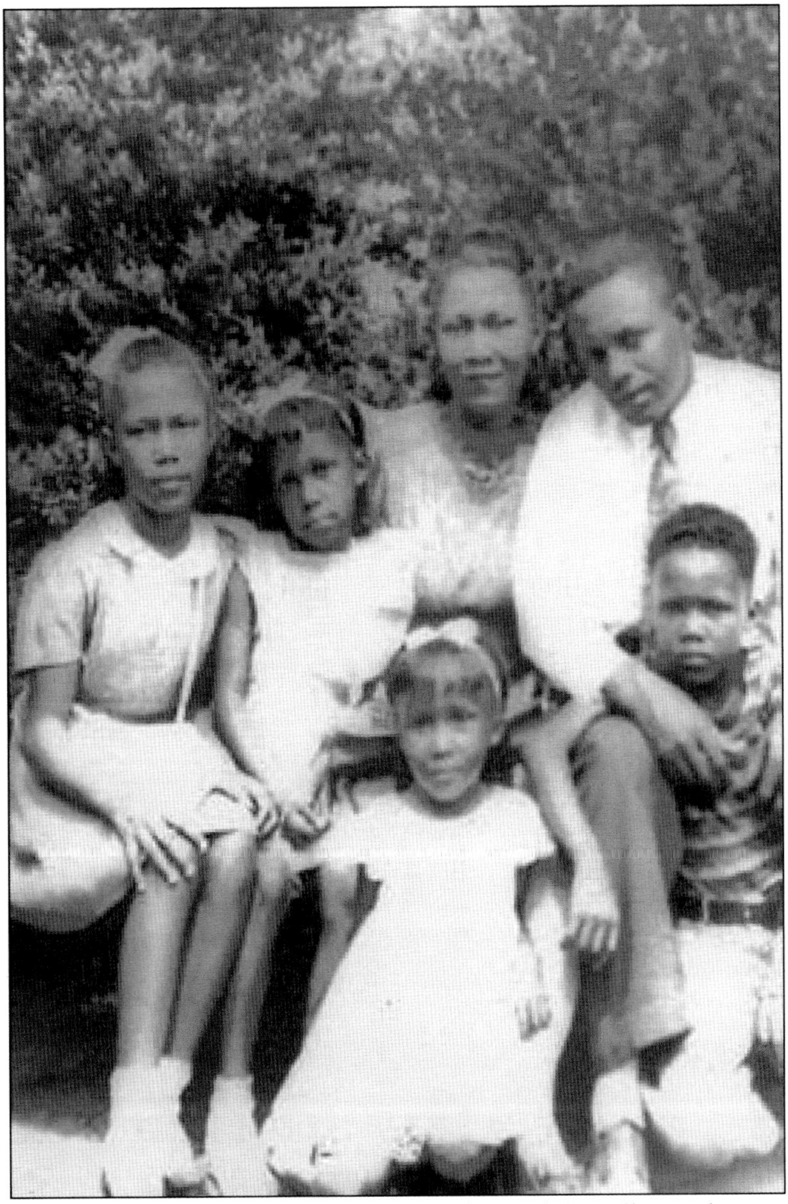

The Overall Family. In November 1941, Walter and Norvel Overall moved into an Eastland Gardens house at 1220 Forty-second Street, built by Randolph Dodd and designed by Lewis W. Giles. The Overalls immediately became active, occupying over the years various positions in the EGCA. In 1975, Walter and Norvel received the first Eastland Gardens Walter L. Robertson Award for outstanding community service. In 1981, Norvel chaired the association's coordination committee in planning the 50th anniversary. Over the years, Walter served as financial secretary of the association. Two descendants of the Overall family continue to live today in the neighborhood, Elaine O. Hymes, one of the first African American teachers to teach at Kenilworth Elementary School, and educator Lerleen O. Ennis. The two live across the street from one another, having reared their families there and carried out their parents' legacy of community activism. Pictured are, from left to right, (kneeling) Lerleen and Walter Jr.; (sitting) Elaine, LaFloma, Norvel, and Walter Sr. (EOH.)

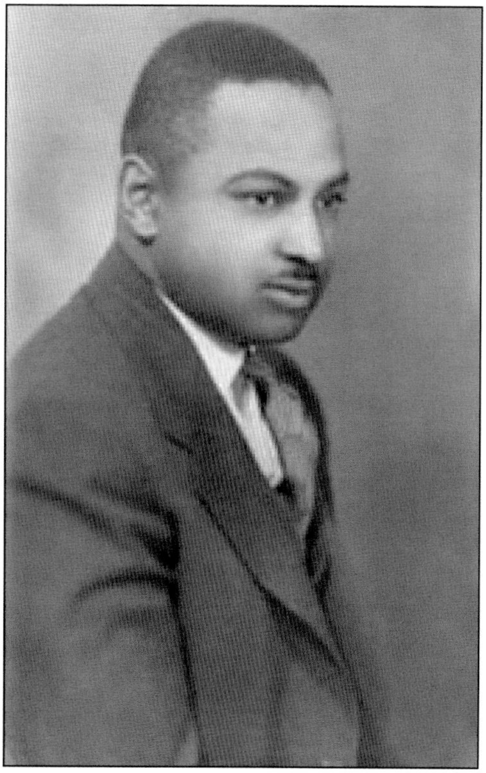

The Slade Household. John Irvin Slade moved to the 4200 block of Lane Place in 1930. His home was built by Randolph Dodd. Until his retirement, Slade was a master mason and worked on projects in the Washington and Philadelphia areas. He also worked part-time as a chauffeur for well-known musicians. A 32nd-degree Freemason, he amassed an extensive Bible collection before passing away in 1971. (Both, WB.)

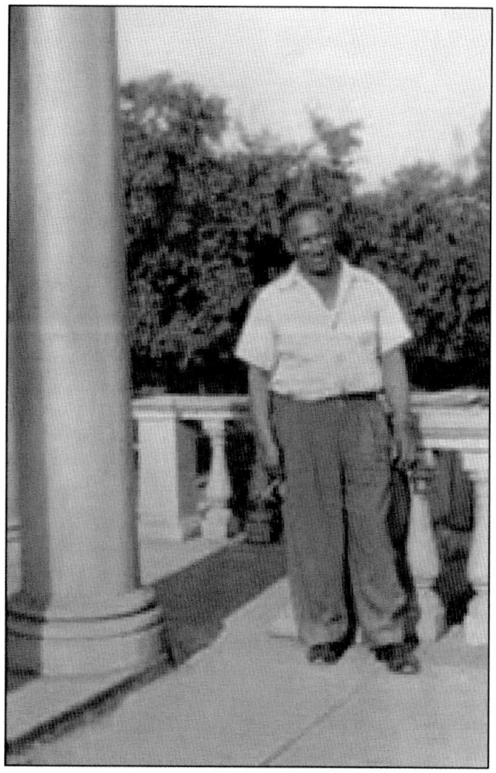

The Stewart Family. In 1974, Anita (Mayers) Stewart, Willie Stewart, and their one-year-old son Troy moved to a home on the 4300 block of Douglas Street NE. Both were teachers in the District of Columbia Public School System and saw the area as a peaceful place to rear their new family. The family grew, and today, Anita and Willie are enjoying their home and community with their grandchildren. Pictured are, from left to right, Anita, Troy, Tyron, Todd, and Willie Stewart. (WS.)

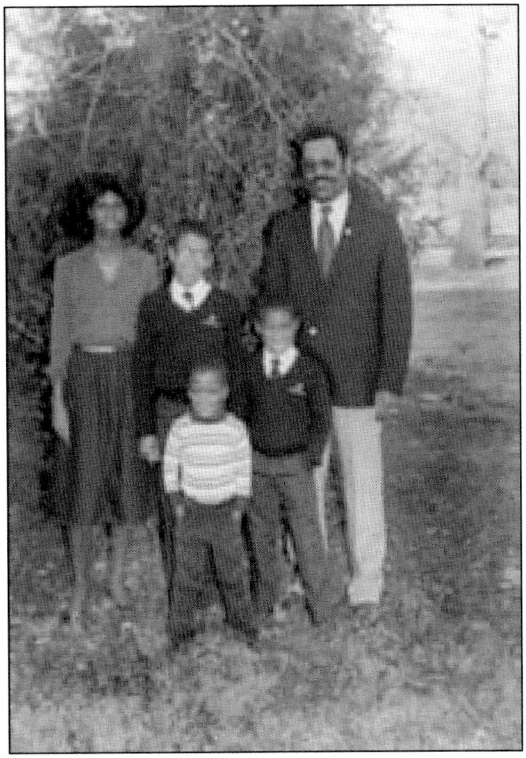

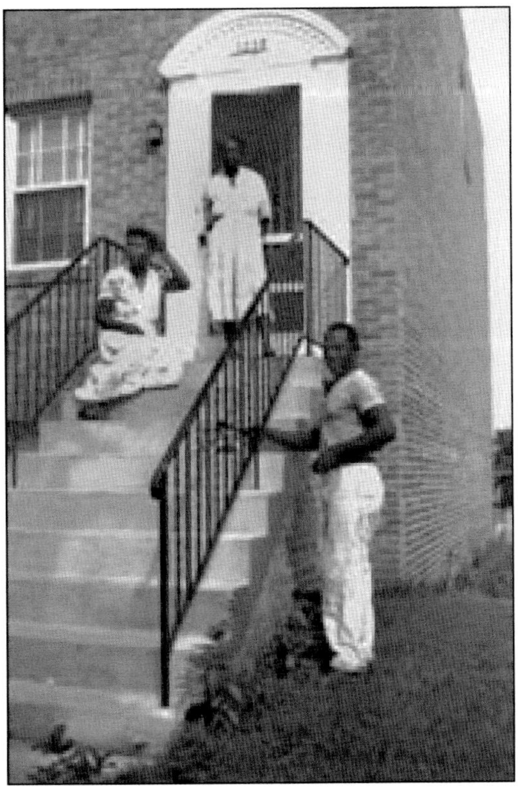

The Washington Family. Edwin B. Washington Sr. (standing), his wife, Lola Bates Washington (seated), and mother-in-law Bettie Ann Davis Bates (standing) relax on the front porch of their home in the 1200 block of Kenilworth Avenue. Edwin Washington Sr. retired from the US Postal Service and continued to work part-time as a taxi driver. Their home design was a joint venture of Roscoe I. Vaughn and George Ferguson and was built by Lester Porter in 1948. Unfortunately, in 1954, their home was razed for the construction of Interstate 295. (EBW.)

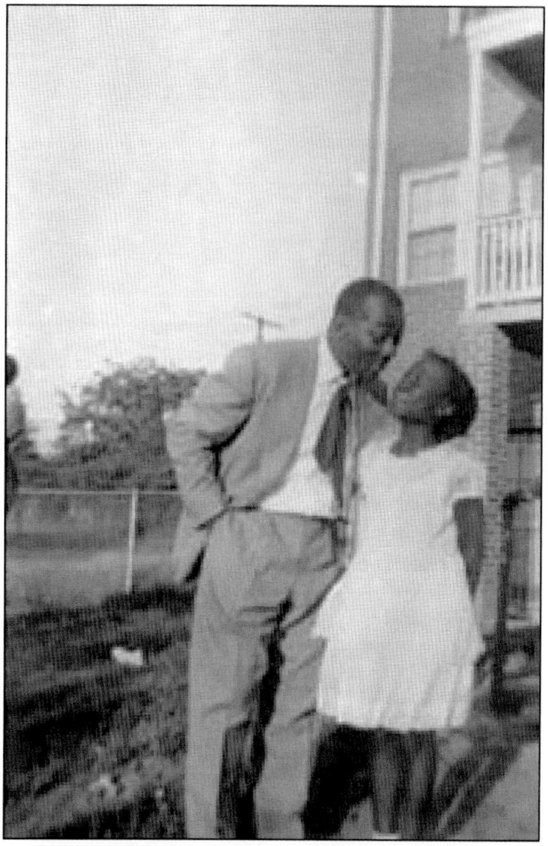

THE WASHINGTONS REMAIN. The family subsequently moved two blocks away to the 4200 block of Marne Place. Betty Washington is shown with her father, Edwin Sr., in the backyard of the family's first Eastland Gardens home. Below, Edwin Washington Jr. (left) is shown with cousins Martin Bates and Kenneth Bates. Not shown are the Washingtons' two other children, twins Melvin and Deborah. In 2011, Lola Bates Washington, at 99 years old, continues to live in the family home with daughter Betty. (Both, EBW.)

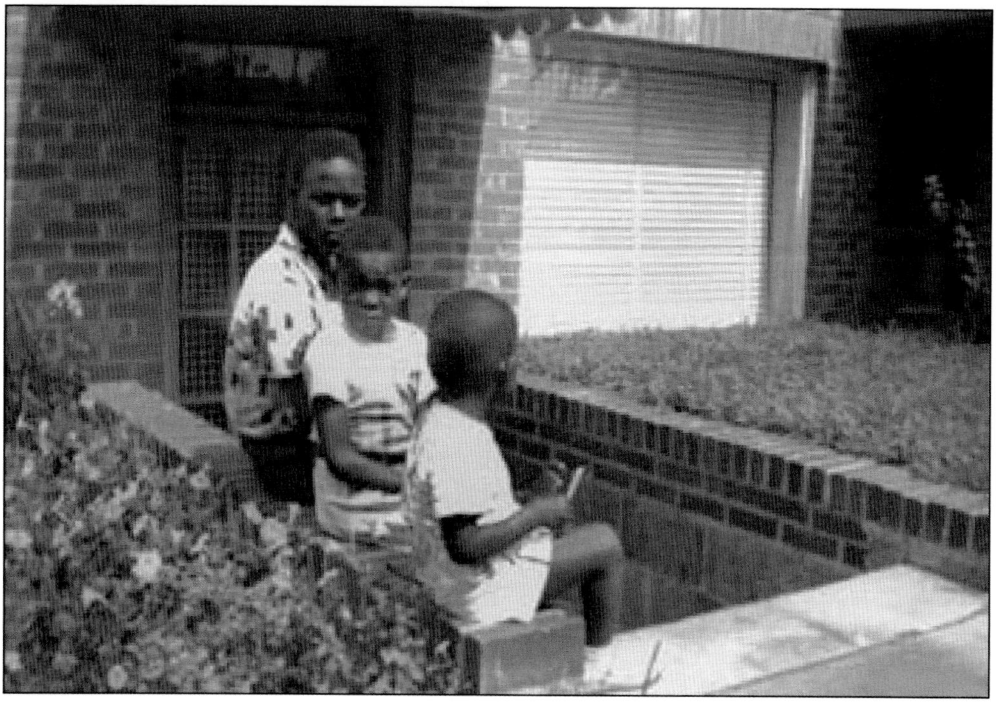

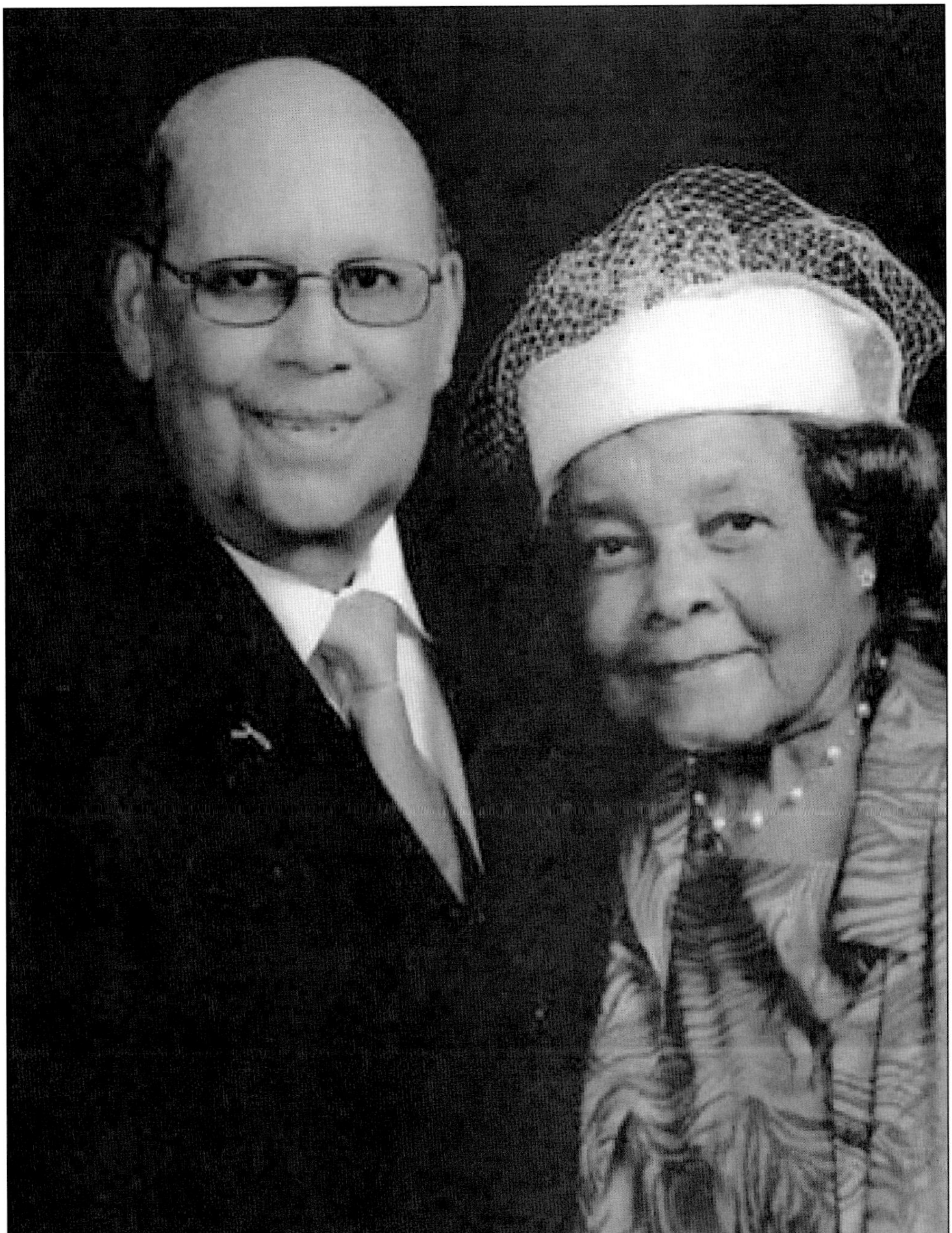

THE WHITE FAMILY. There were no sidewalks and only three houses on Anacostia Avenue in 1962 when Herbert Hoover White Sr. and his wife, Lucille Dill White, took residence on the block. The Whites were familiar with the area—Herbert's brother and wife, William and Ethel White, had been residents since 1951—and it was convenient to their places of work, the Pentagon and Fort Meade. Herbert and neighbor Charlotte Corbin, though, had to lobby for sidewalks to be installed and cherry blossom trees to be planted on their street. Herbert helped his brother coach the youth football team and taught swimming once the local pool was built. Both of the Whites' two children, Deborah and Herbert Jr., were born and raised in Eastland Gardens. (LW.)

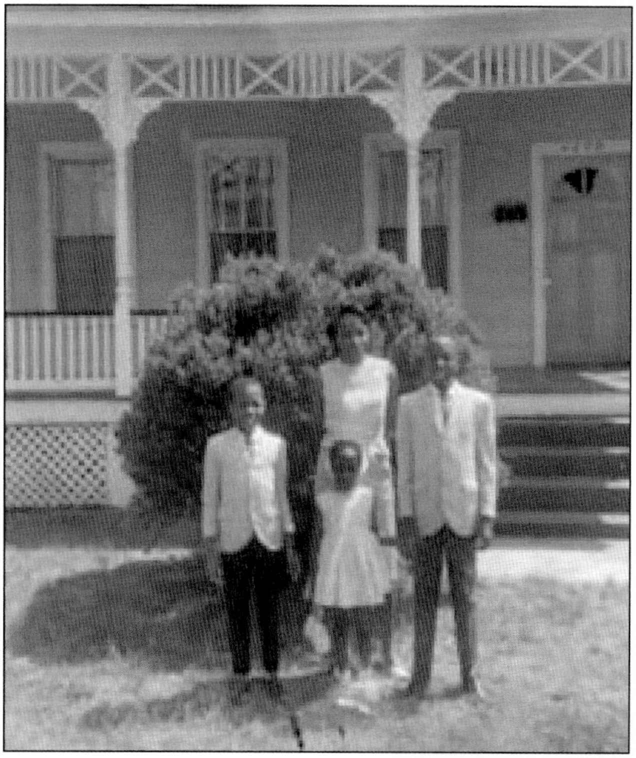

The Wood Family. William Wood and Frances Wood moved to Eastland Gardens with their three children, Timothy, Francine, and Larry, in February 1960. Their 1910 home was on the 4400 block of Ord Street. They referred to Eastland Gardens as a "little oasis of the city." Shown at left are Frances Wood and her children in their Sunday attire. She worked as a library technician for 38 years. William Wood was employed as mail personnel at the US Department of Navy for 48 years. Pictured below are the Woods some years later with son Larry and daughter-in-law Carmen on their wedding day in the backyard of the family home. Frances continues to enjoy the tranquility of the community. (Both, FW.)

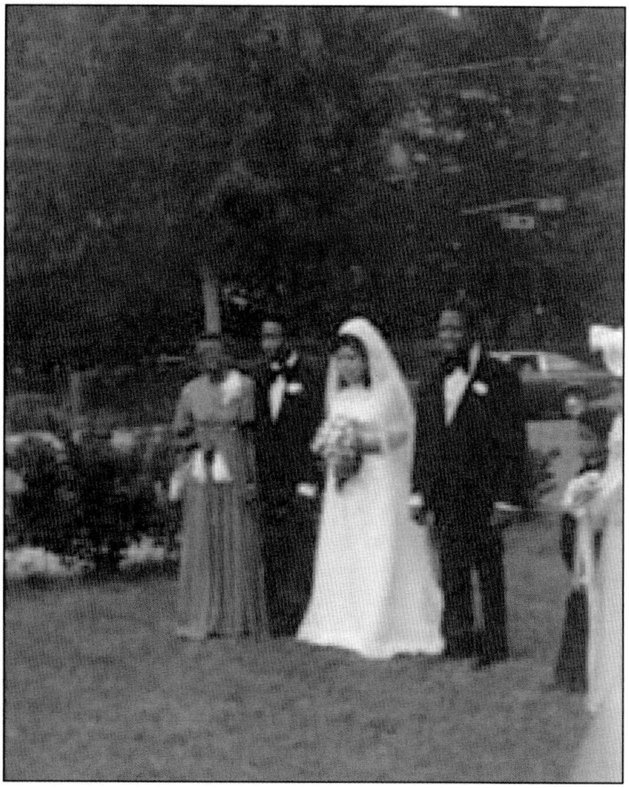

Five

Worshipping in Our Neighborhood

The Eastland Gardens community has had two places of worship within its boundaries. Although some residents attended the numerous churches in surrounding communities and throughout the city, many Eastland Gardens residents attended church "at home."

The oldest church, Kenilworth Presbyterian Church, actually predated Eastland Gardens. The developer of the neighboring Kenilworth subdivision, Allen W. Mallery, offered a portion of the property he had purchased from the Fowler family to erect a church. The church was built in 1901 at 1322 Kenilworth Avenue. Mallery hired one of Washington's most prestigious white architects, Appleton P. Clark, to design the edifice. The original building was later replaced by a charming brick building. When city officials decided in 1954 to extend Interstate 295 through the Kenilworth and Eastland Gardens neighborhoods, Kenilworth Presbyterian was razed. The church congregation subsequently merged with Eastern Presbyterian Church in Bladensburg, Maryland.

Zion Baptist Church was originally founded in Deanwood on Sheriff Road. The quaint frame church designed in 1908 by African American architect W. Sidney Pittman (1875–1958) served Zion Baptist for many years until the congregation outgrew the building. Under the leadership of Rev. Leon C. Collins, the church secured land and erected a new building at 1234 Kenilworth Avenue. The congregation moved in 1966 to the new building, where it remains today.

In 1967, pastors James Peeples and Betty Peeples moved Jericho Baptist Church to Kenilworth just beyond the Eastland Gardens neighborhood boundary. In 1997, they relocated the popular church to Prince Georges County, Maryland. Renamed Jericho City of Praise, the congregation increased to more than 19,000 members and became one of the largest and most influential churches in the area. Jericho City of Praise retains ownership of the Kenilworth property, which is now occupied by New Smyrna Missionary Church.

A fourth church building is in the area, Fellowship Haven Church. It was founded in 1975 by Mennonite missionaries.

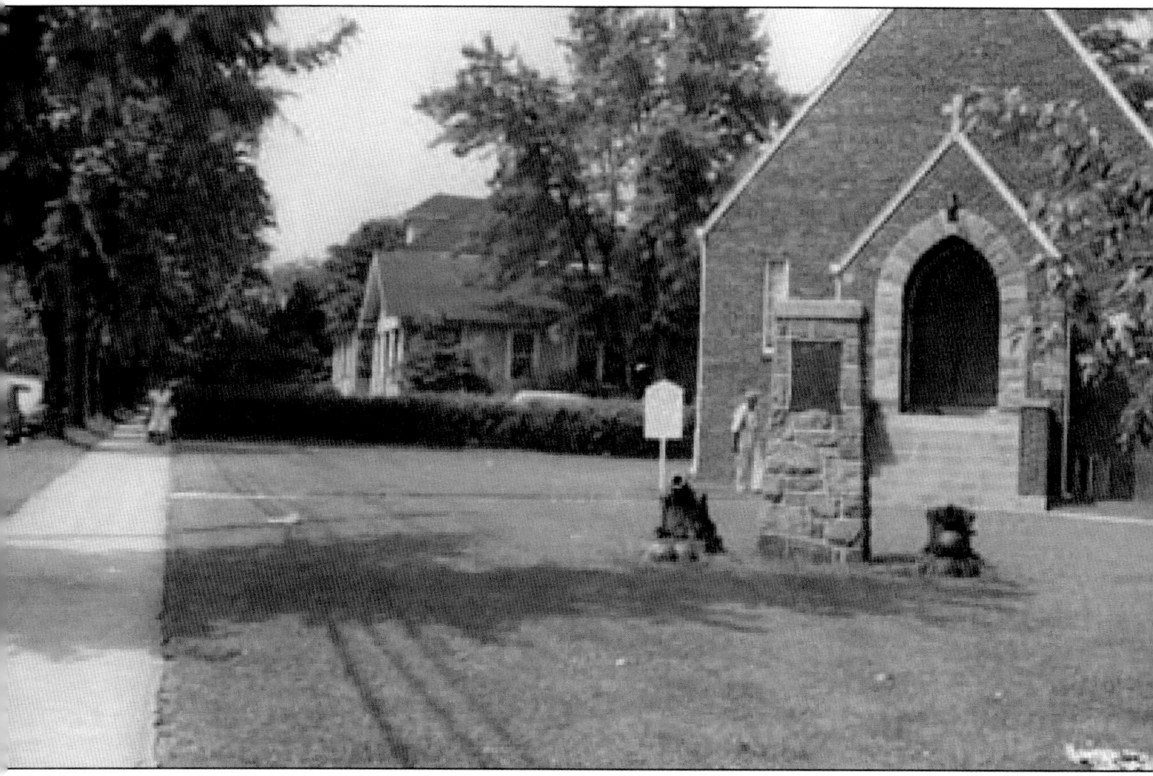

CHURCH OF BYGONE DAYS. Kenilworth Presbyterian Church's first edifice was erected in 1901, designed by Appleton P. Clark for the white congregation. It was replaced in 1942 by the building shown here, designed and constructed by E. Mortenson. The church was an active part of the community, hosting Boy Scouts and Girls Scouts, taking a stand against a pool hall in neighboring Kenilworth, Maryland, and participating in temperance activities. (HSW.)

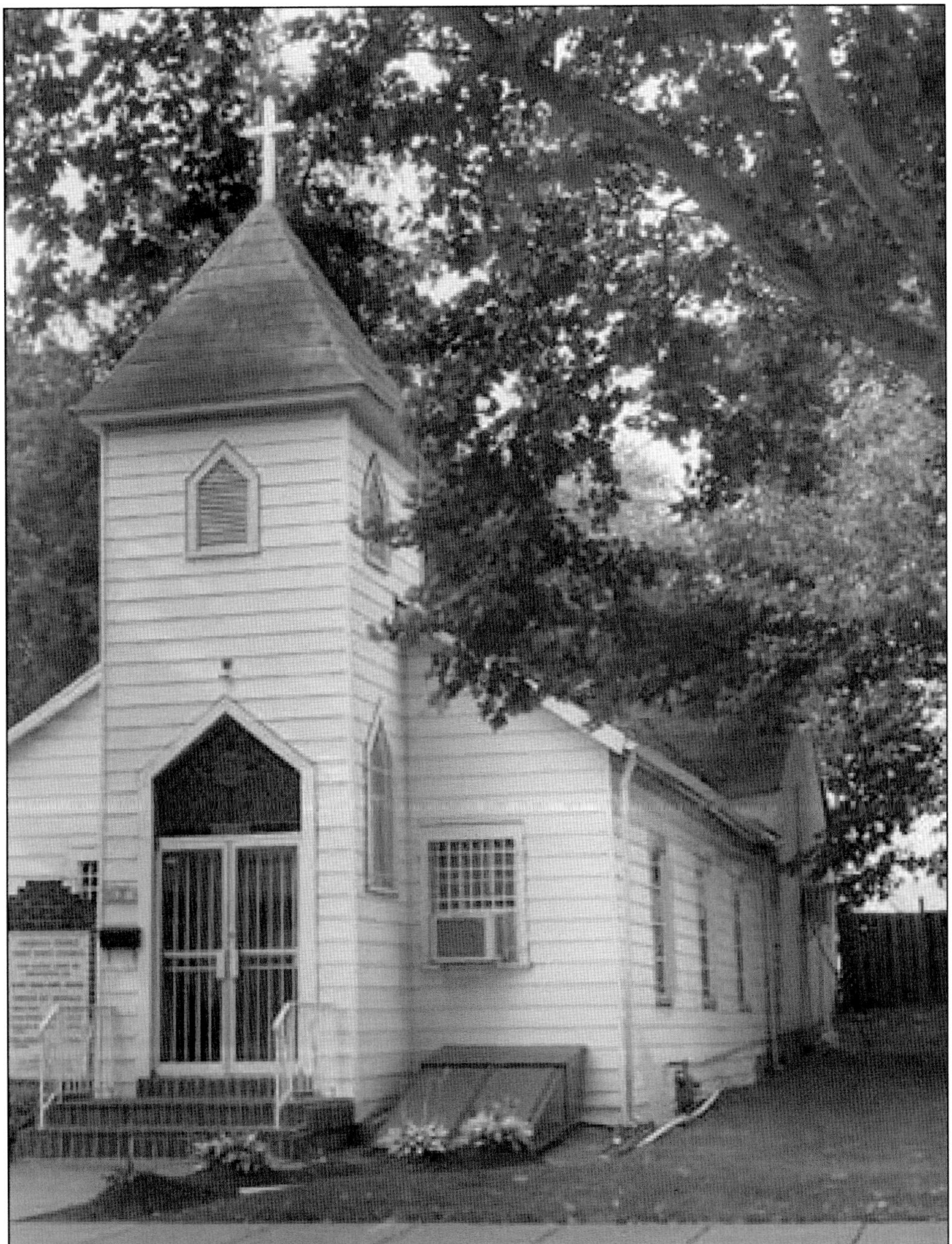

The First Zion Baptist Church. Originally located at Forty-fourth Street and Sheriff Road in Deanwood, Zion Baptist Church was completed in 1908 under the leadership of Rev. Charles Henry Strothers. One of the nation's earliest African American architects, W. Sidney Pittman, designed the edifice along with the building next door that most likely served as the parsonage. A subsequent minister, Rev. Leon C. Collins (from 1948 to 1986) worked with the congregation to raise the necessary funds to relocate to Eastland Gardens as a larger building became necessary. (DCHPO.)

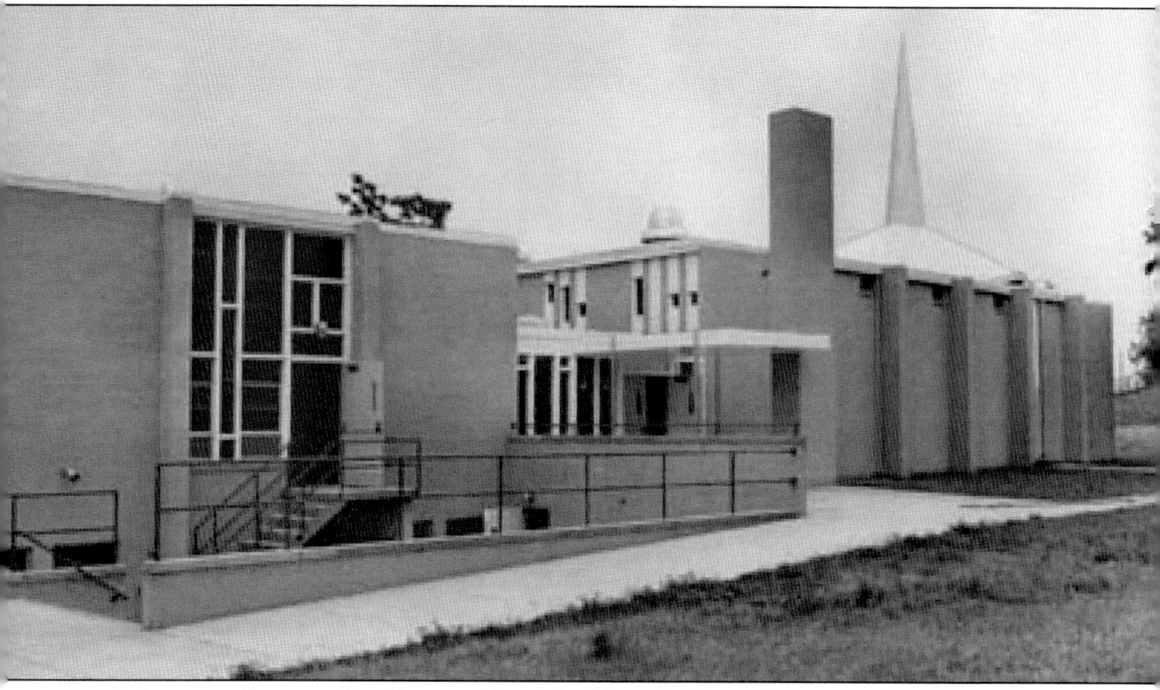

A Spiritual Leader. Zion Baptist Church had been led by Rev. Leon C. Collins for more than 30 years when ground was broken for the new building at 1234 Kenilworth Avenue. Built to seat 500 in the sanctuary and 250 in the fellowship hall, the church was designed by the prominent African American firm Madison, Madison & Madison. The church is now known as Zion Baptist Church of Eastland Gardens to distinguish it from the much older church of the same name in Northwest Washington. Subsequent pastors included Rev. Fentress Hickman (1987–1999) and Rev. Harold Brooks (2002–2004). (MLK-W.)

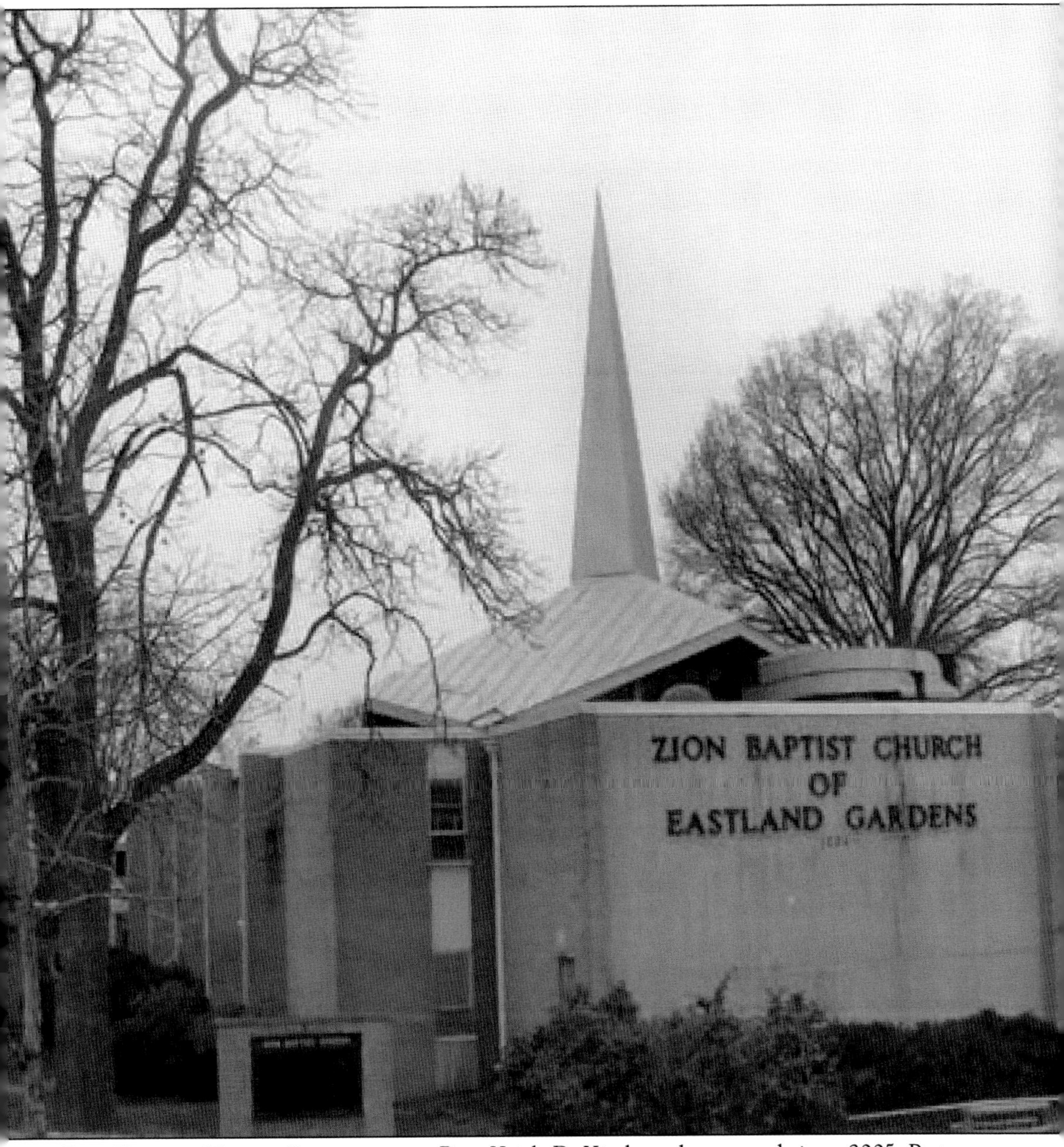

Zion Baptist Today. Current pastor Rev. Keith D. Kitchens has served since 2005. Pastor Kitchens is interested in developing a ministry that caters to spiritual, cultural, and physical needs of attending worshippers and those living in the contiguous neighborhood and community. Zion also operates an active childcare center, a before- and after-school tutorial program, and a summer youth all-day program. (ZBC.)

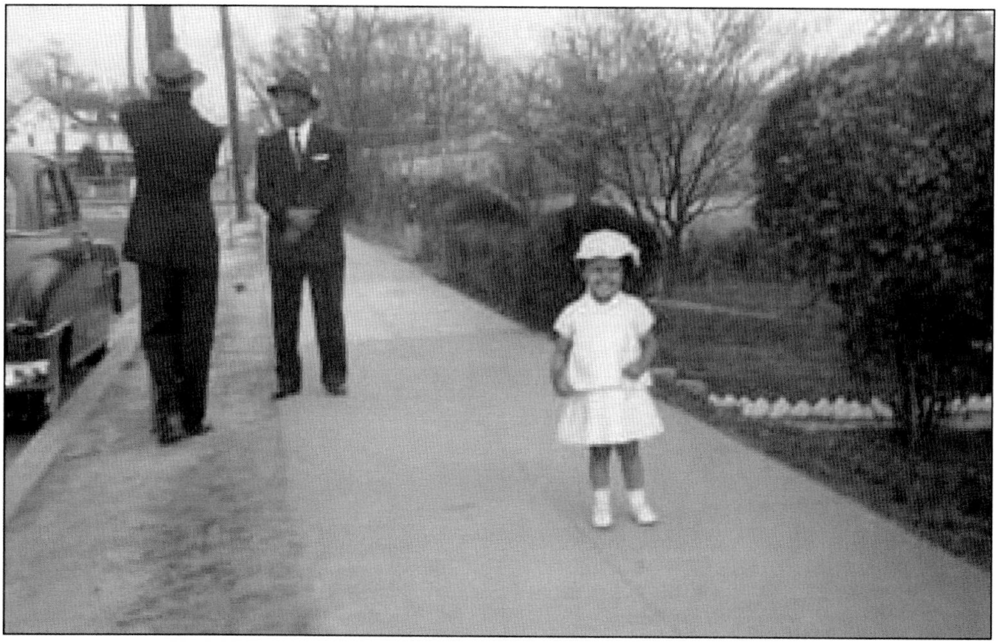

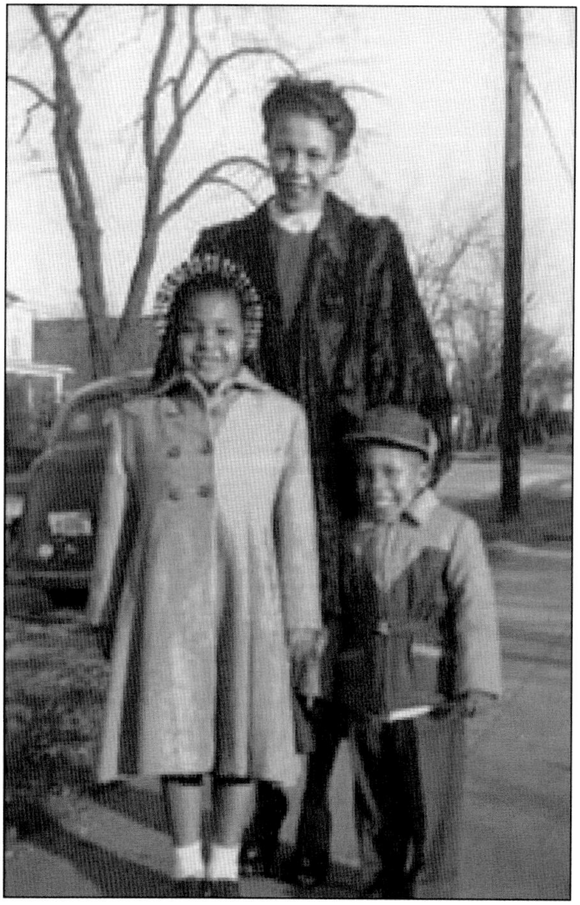

MATTHEWS FAMILY OFF TO CHURCH. Prior to the location of the first African American church in the community, which was Zion in 1939, black families in Eastland Gardens and Kenilworth attended services elsewhere. The Thomas L. Matthews and Beatrice (Williams) Matthews family, pictured here on Douglas Street in the 1940s, continued the tradition started by Thomas's parents, Sadie and Frank, and attended a church in nearby Cedar Heights, Maryland. Above, Thomas faces the camera, with neighbor Robert McCabey and Alvena Winestock, Beatrice's granddaughter. To the left are Beatrice Matthews with children Bernetta and Frank. (Both, FM.)

JERICHO BAPTIST CHURCH. The building at 4417 Douglas Street now houses the New Smyrna Missionary Baptist Church. It was once the home of Jericho Baptist Church, founded by Pastors James Peeples and Betty Peeples in 1964. Over the years, Jericho offered a training center, a convalescent home ministry, a radio ministry, and a youth ministry, among other services. The congregation quickly outgrew its first modest building on Douglas Street; it acquired additional property on Douglas and constructed this 800-seat structure in 1977. Jericho expanded again in 1987 to include a 2,000-seat sanctuary, 17 classrooms, and a professional kitchen where the congregation remained until it moved to Maryland. (JB.)

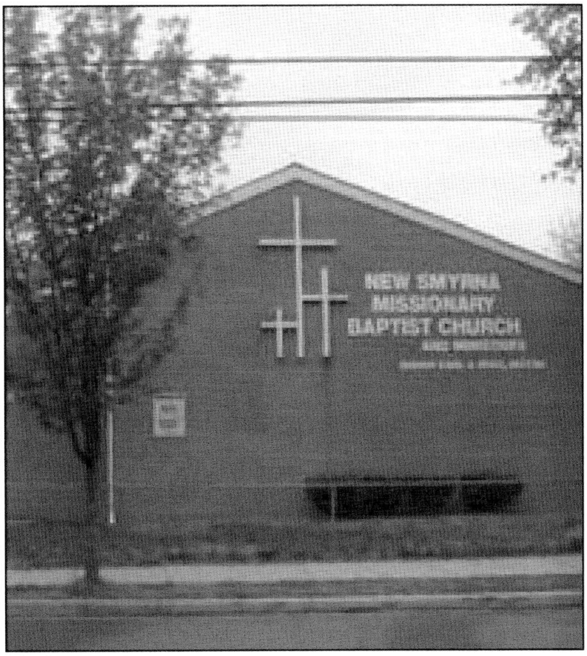

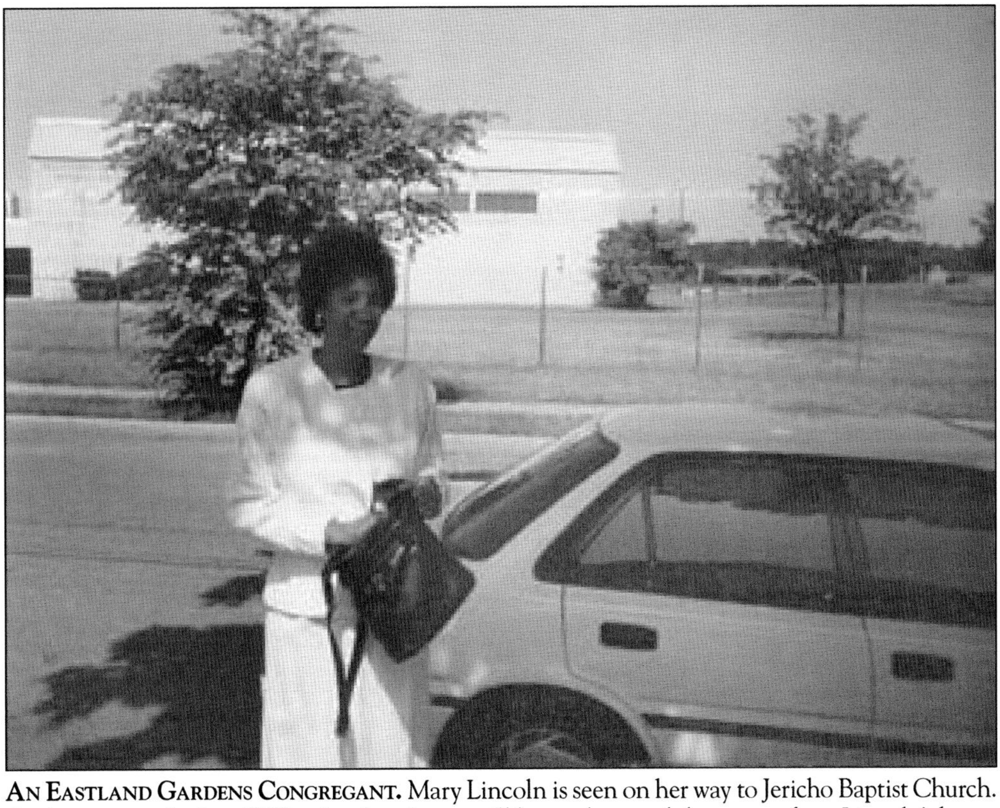

AN EASTLAND GARDENS CONGREGANT. Mary Lincoln is seen on her way to Jericho Baptist Church. At the time in the late 1980s, the church was still located around the corner from Lincoln's home in Eastland Gardens. She and her children were among the local residents who found spiritual and social sustenance at Jericho. (ML.)

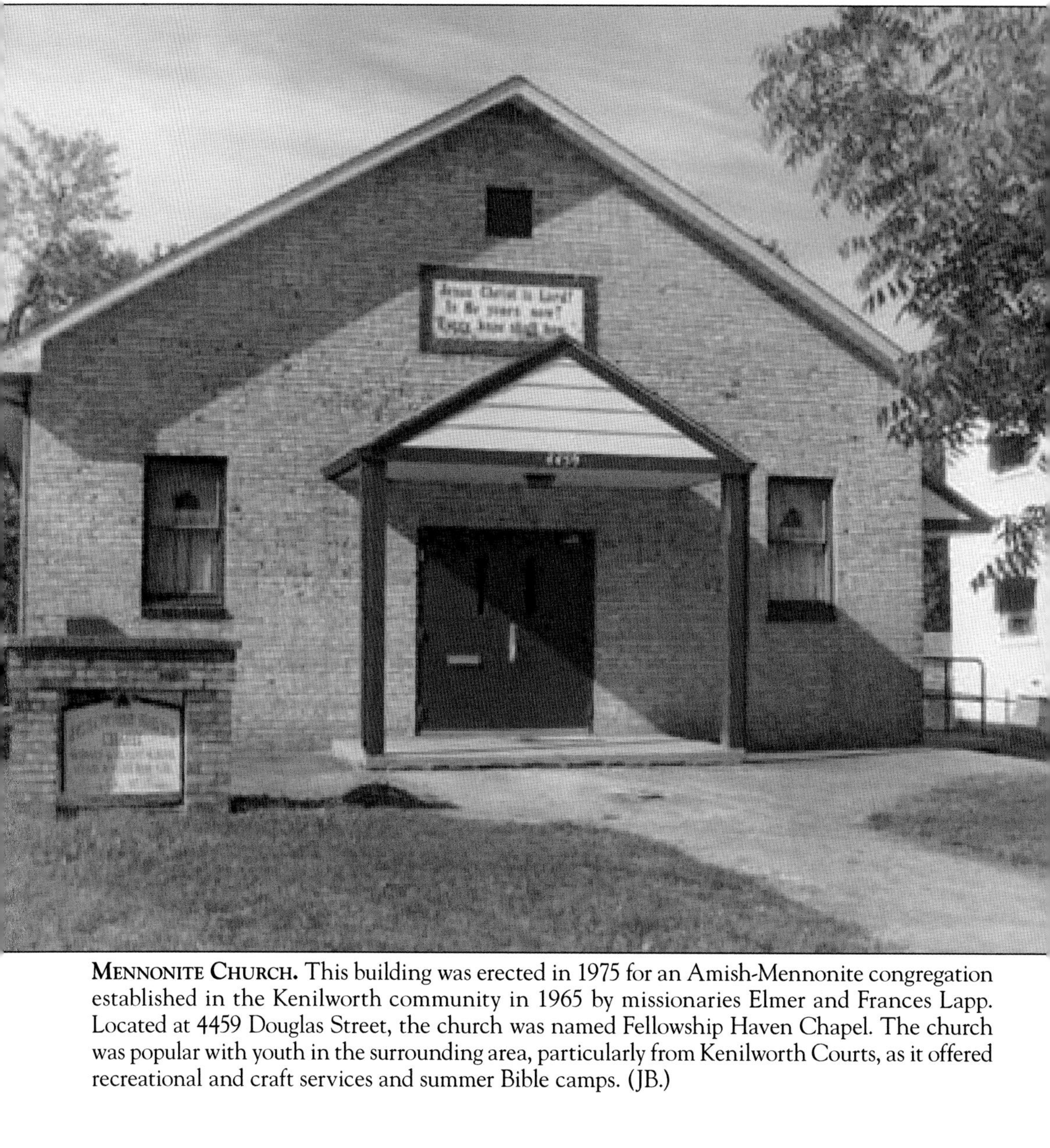

Mennonite Church. This building was erected in 1975 for an Amish-Mennonite congregation established in the Kenilworth community in 1965 by missionaries Elmer and Frances Lapp. Located at 4459 Douglas Street, the church was named Fellowship Haven Chapel. The church was popular with youth in the surrounding area, particularly from Kenilworth Courts, as it offered recreational and craft services and summer Bible camps. (JB.)

Six

"From These Seeds, We Shall Continue to Grow"

This chapter title is a quote from Hilda Banks, a resident and community activist, that aptly coins the sentiment of adults in Eastland Gardens. Until 1954, when schools in Washington, DC, were legally desegregated, many schools in the "colored division" were overcrowded and in disrepair. Fortunately, many of the schools had top-notch, well-educated teachers enabling students to flourish.

The neighborhood school, Kenilworth Elementary School, was erected in 1901 for white students. Although it would be another 25 years before Eastland Gardens would be developed, bringing in a large number of black students, there was a small settlement of African Americans on Douglas Street in Kenilworth. Douglas Street children were legally prohibited from attending their closest school. Instead, they attended Carver Elementary School in nearby Deanwood. They had to cross busy streets and railroad tracks to get to and from the school. Eastland Gardens students joined their Douglas Street friends at Carver Elementary.

Schools for black students usually increased through the transfer of a building from "white" use to "Negro" use. These "new" buildings were the result of a newly constructed building for white students or because of decreased enrollment. The latter was the case for Kenilworth Elementary School. During the 1953–1954 school year, only 34 students attended Kenilworth Elementary. White school superintendent Hobart Corning recommended the transfer of Kenilworth Elementary to the "colored division" to alleviate severe overcrowding at Carver and Thomas Elementary, a move vigorously supported by Eastland Gardens parents and civic association leaders. White parents, on the other hand, objected to transferring their children to the nearest white school, Benning Elementary, located a mile away, because their children would encounter hazardous traffic conditions. Eastland Gardens parents prevailed. The transfer took place in February 1954, two months before the landmark US Supreme Court decisions, *Bolling v. Sharpe* and *Brown v. Board of Education*, which declared that the "separate but equal" doctrine for public schools was unconstitutional.

Beyond elementary school, nearby public school options for Eastland Garden children were limited. There was no junior high school nearby until 1949, when Kelly Miller Junior High School, in Lincoln Heights, opened. Prior to Kelly Miller, the closest junior high school was Browne (1931), located across the Anacostia River. Dunbar High School and Armstrong High School in Northwest served black students until the opening of Cardozo High School and Spingarn High School.

Kenilworth Elementary School continues to bring the community together. It hosts the Eastland Gardens Civic Association meetings, Police Service Area meetings, Eastland Garden Flower Club special events, fundraisers, and Election Day polling.

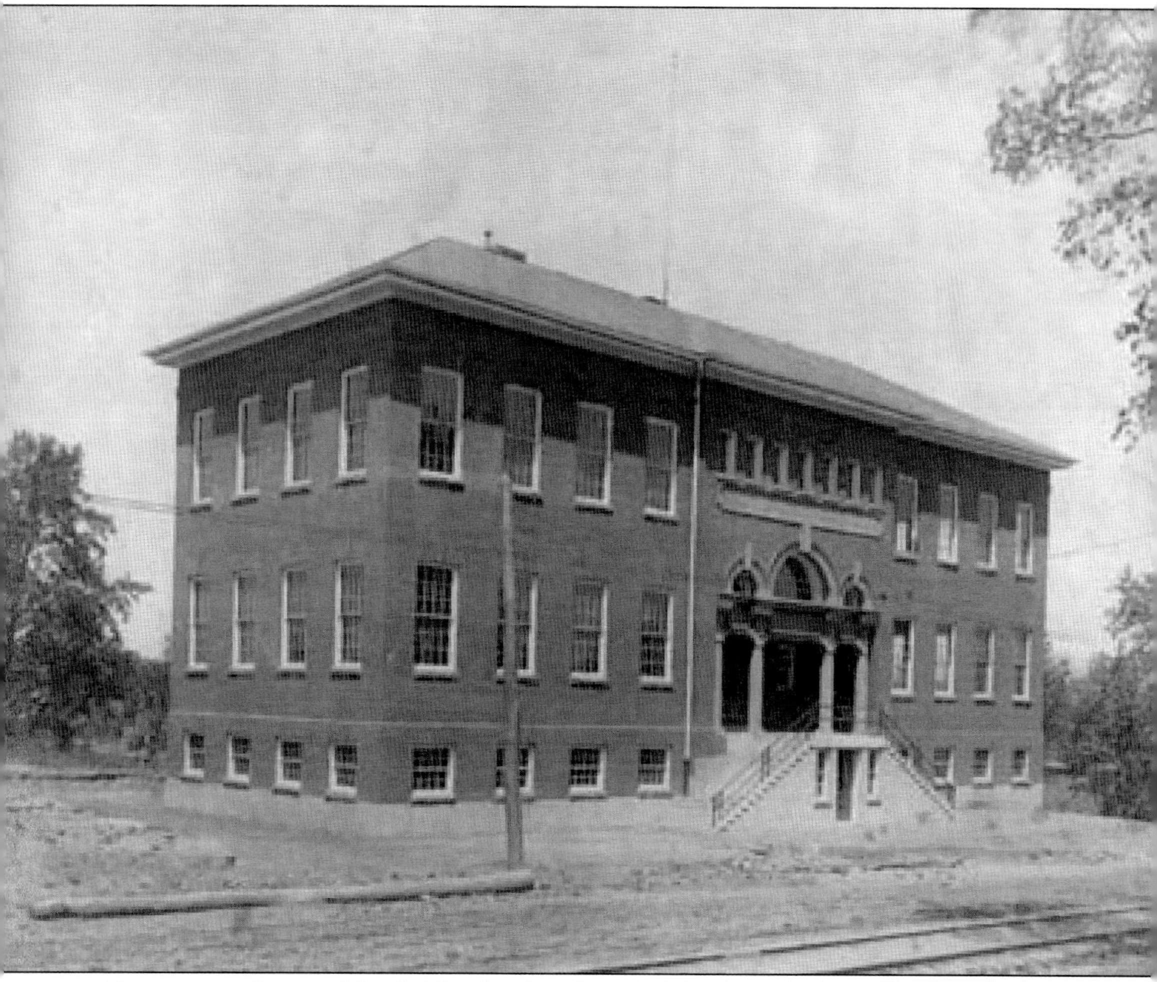

Kenilworth School No. 1. The first Kenilworth School was built on Kenilworth Avenue between Ord and Polk Streets. Designed by the municipal architect for a capacity of 160, the school served white students who lived in the area. When it was dedicated in November 1902, the city commissioner stated, "Kenilworth, with all its suburban attractions . . . cannot have all the things that the city of Washington had, but it is the purpose of the government . . . to give to the outlying towns and villages of the District, now so numerous, all that they need, and as rapidly as possible." (CSSMA.)

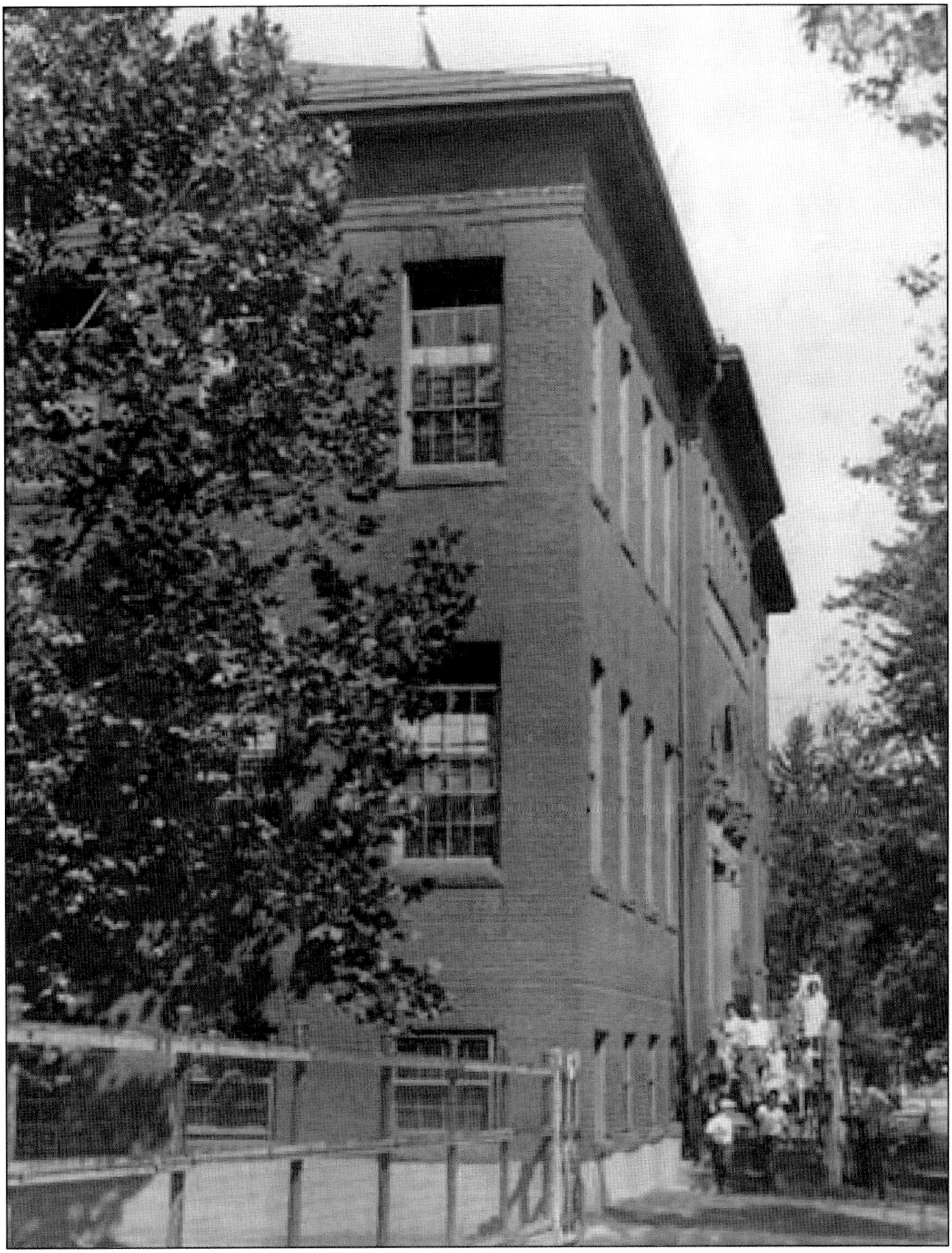

Early Integration. Kenilworth School enjoyed a bit of controversy in 1904 when the local white citizens' association alleged that three students might be black. White parents threatened to boycott the school. However, when John Colvin threatened to sue the city insisting that he and his children were white, city officials accepted his word and his children remained. Fifty years later, the school was legally desegregated and black students from the surrounding neighborhood began to attend the school. (MLK-W.)

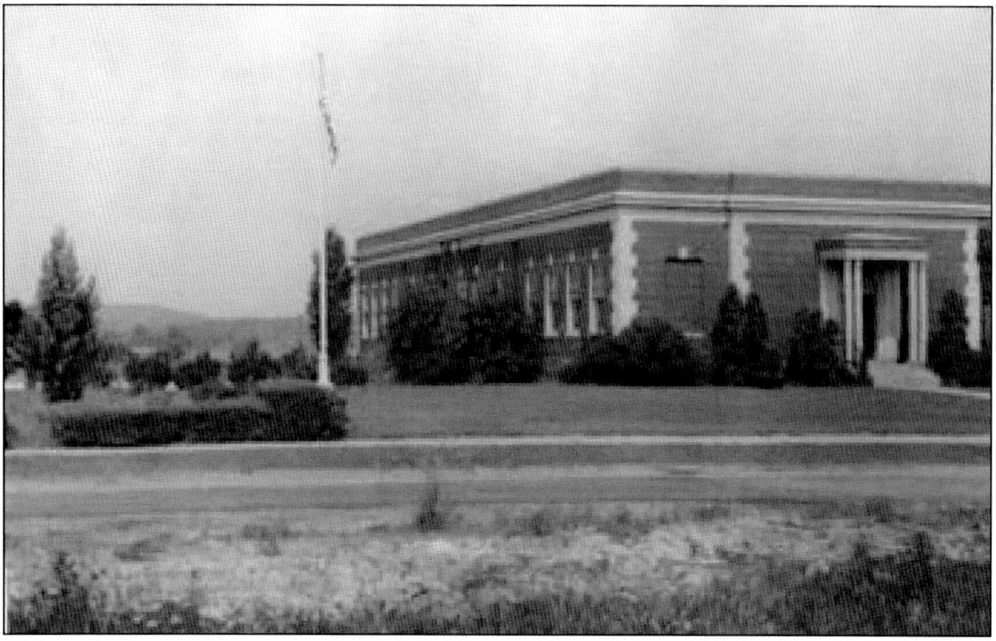

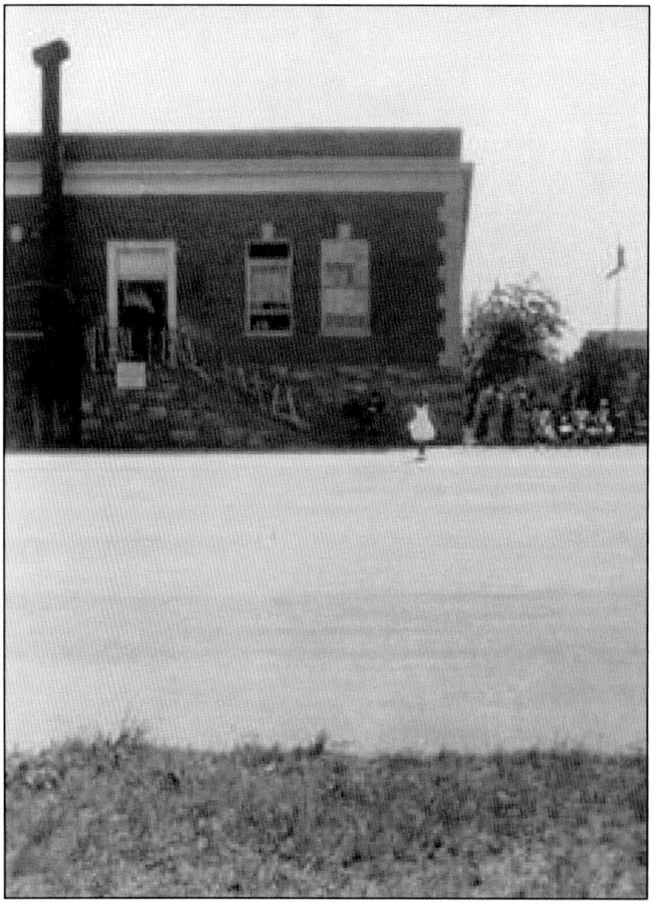

A New Kenilworth School. By the late 1920s, the Kenilworth School building was seriously dilapidated. It was vacated in 1931. In 1932, a contract was awarded for $54,698 to construct a one-story brick building on Forty-fourth Street. Still a whites-only facility, in 1949, parents were upset that trucks and cars traveling along a dirt road near the school would drive across the unfenced playground to reach the paved street leading to the dump entrance. Teachers were stationed around the perimeter of the playground at recess to keep students from wandering over to the dump area, often obscured by the smoke from the trash-burning fires. To the left are black children lined up at the rear of the school in the early 1950s to receive immunization, a rare instance in which they were permitted to enter. (Above, HSW; left, FM.)

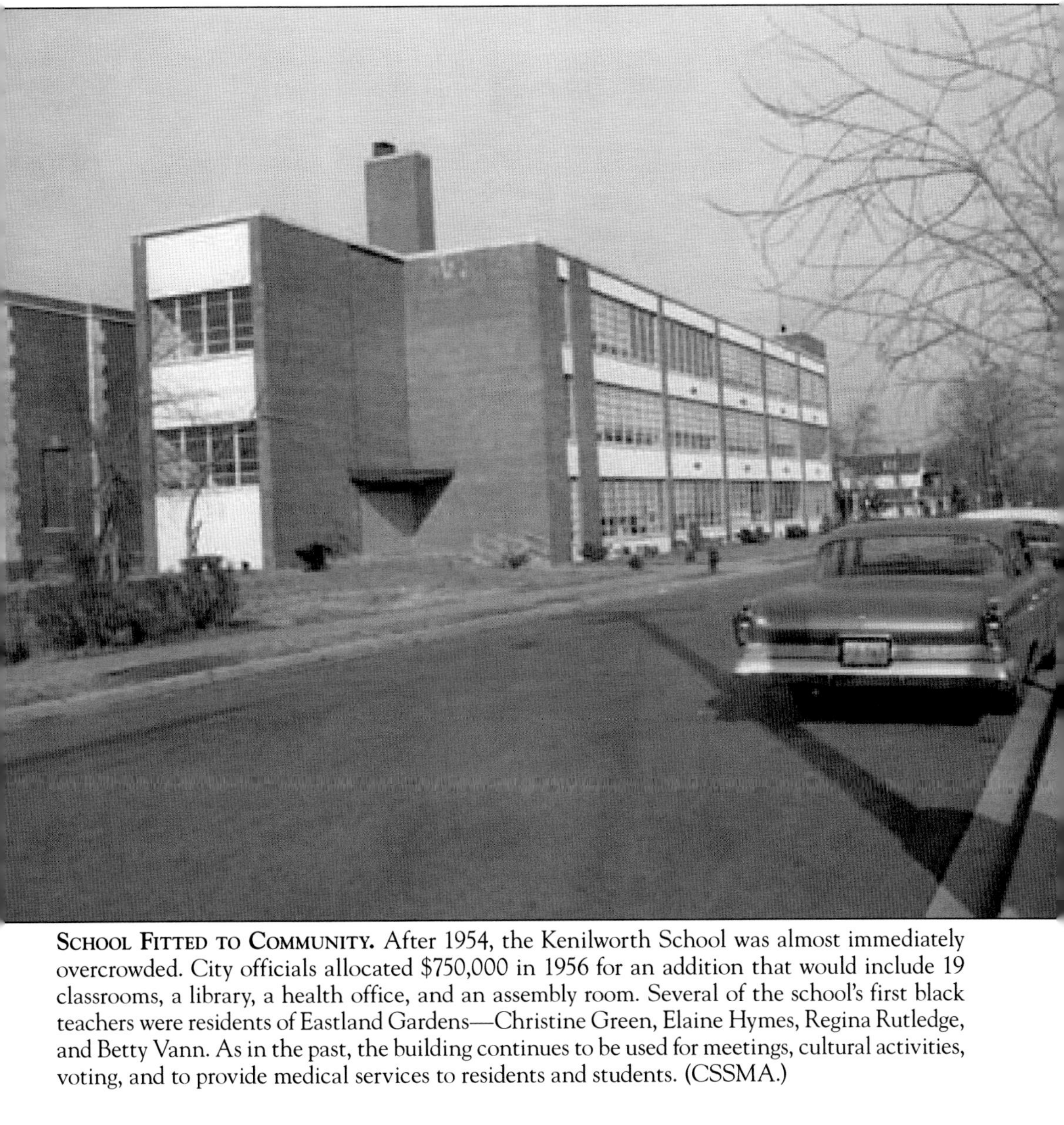

School Fitted to Community. After 1954, the Kenilworth School was almost immediately overcrowded. City officials allocated $750,000 in 1956 for an addition that would include 19 classrooms, a library, a health office, and an assembly room. Several of the school's first black teachers were residents of Eastland Gardens—Christine Green, Elaine Hymes, Regina Rutledge, and Betty Vann. As in the past, the building continues to be used for meetings, cultural activities, voting, and to provide medical services to residents and students. (CSSMA.)

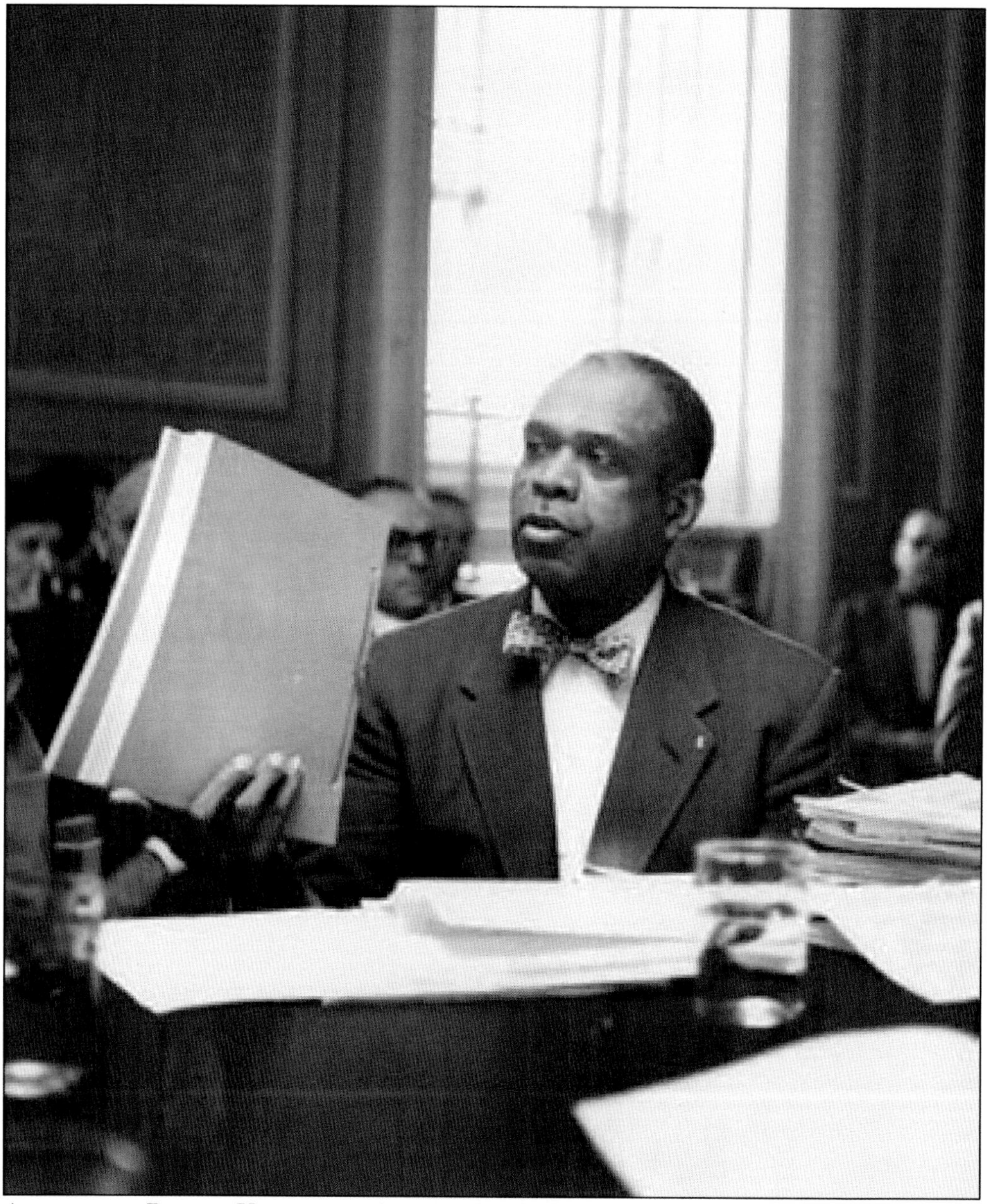

Attempts to Rename Kenilworth School. Residents requested that the neighborhood school be renamed after attorney George Hayes (1894–1968) in honor of his work on the landmark US Supreme Court school desegregation case *Brown v. Board of Education*. In 1955, Pres. Dwight D. Eisenhower appointed Hayes to the District of Columbia Public Utilities Commission, making him the first African American in nearly 100 years to serve in a municipal agency in Washington. In 1962, the District of Columbia Bar Association named Hayes to its board of directors, making him the first African American to hold office in that group. (MLK-W.)

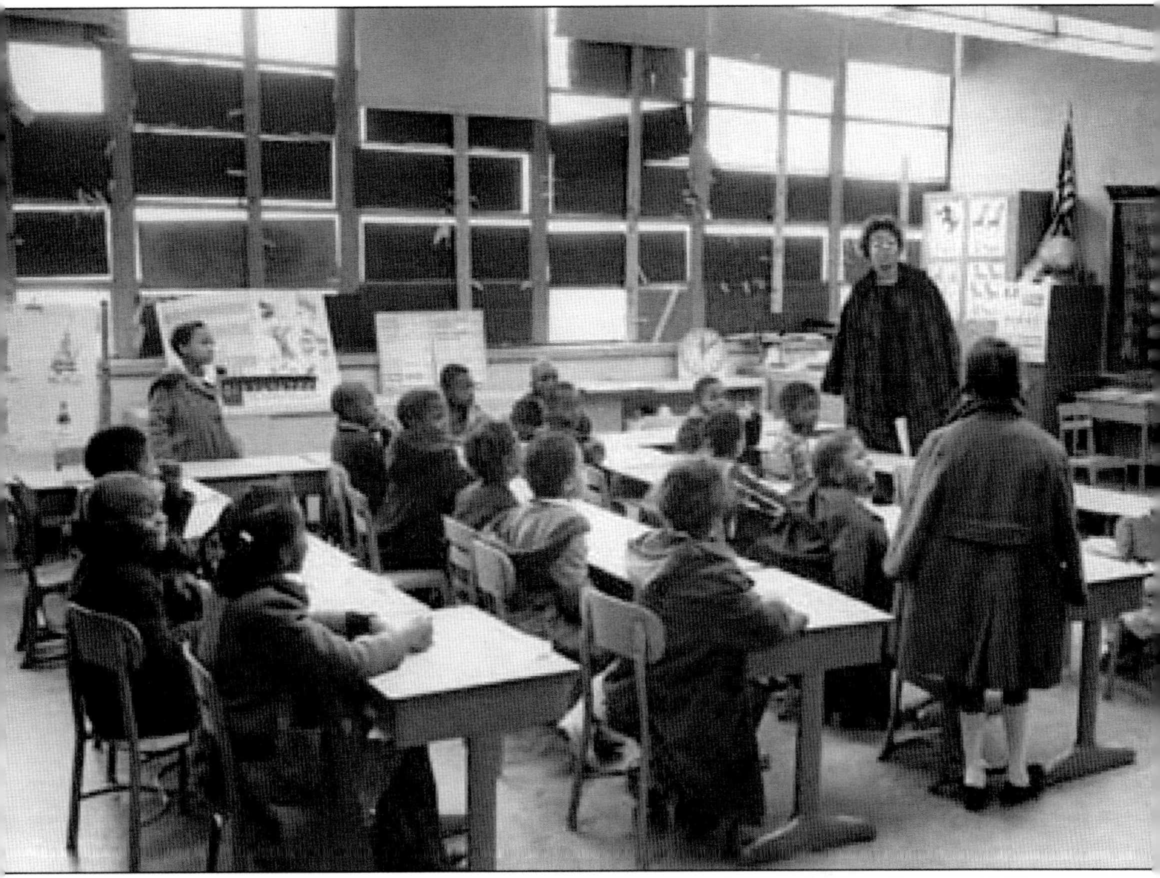

School in Disrepair. First-grade teacher Ruth Logan instructs her students in January 1968 at Kenilworth Elementary School as they wear their coats because of the cold air streaming through broken windows. The cold temperature, however, did not stop these children from getting an education. Parents sought relief from adverse environmental conditions and increasing deterioration and called for a meeting with school officials. (MLK-W.)

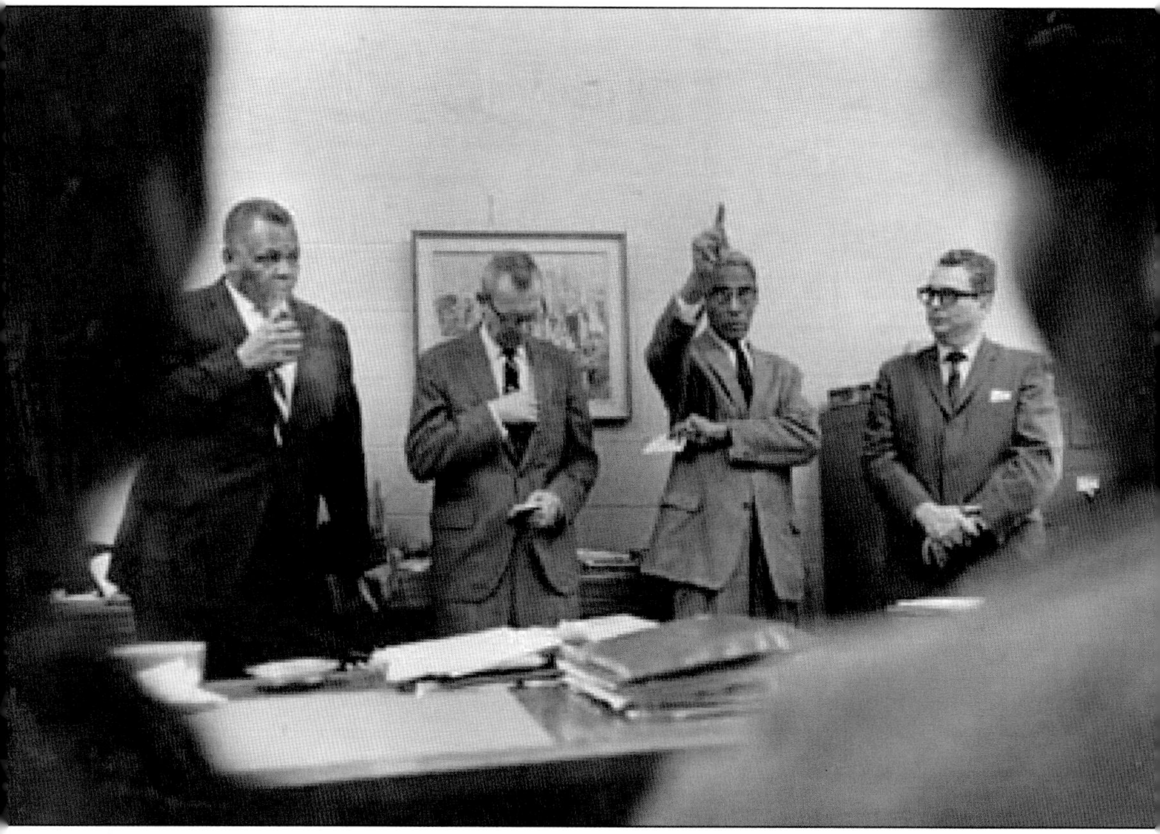

PARENT TEACHERS ASSOCIATION FORCE ACTION. Owen Davis, Parent Teacher Association head, pushed for government action at a meeting held with a representative from Mayor Walter Washington's office, the school superintendent, and the director of the buildings and grounds department. It was resolved that the replacement of the damaged windows at Kenilworth Elementary School would be a priority. Pictured are, from left to right, Owen Davis, head of PTA; James Blazer, director of buildings and grounds; Granville Woodson, assistant school superintendent for buildings and grounds; and Julian E. Dugas, director of the department of licenses and inspections. One outcome was that glaziers worked after school and into the evening to make the window repairs. (MLK-W.)

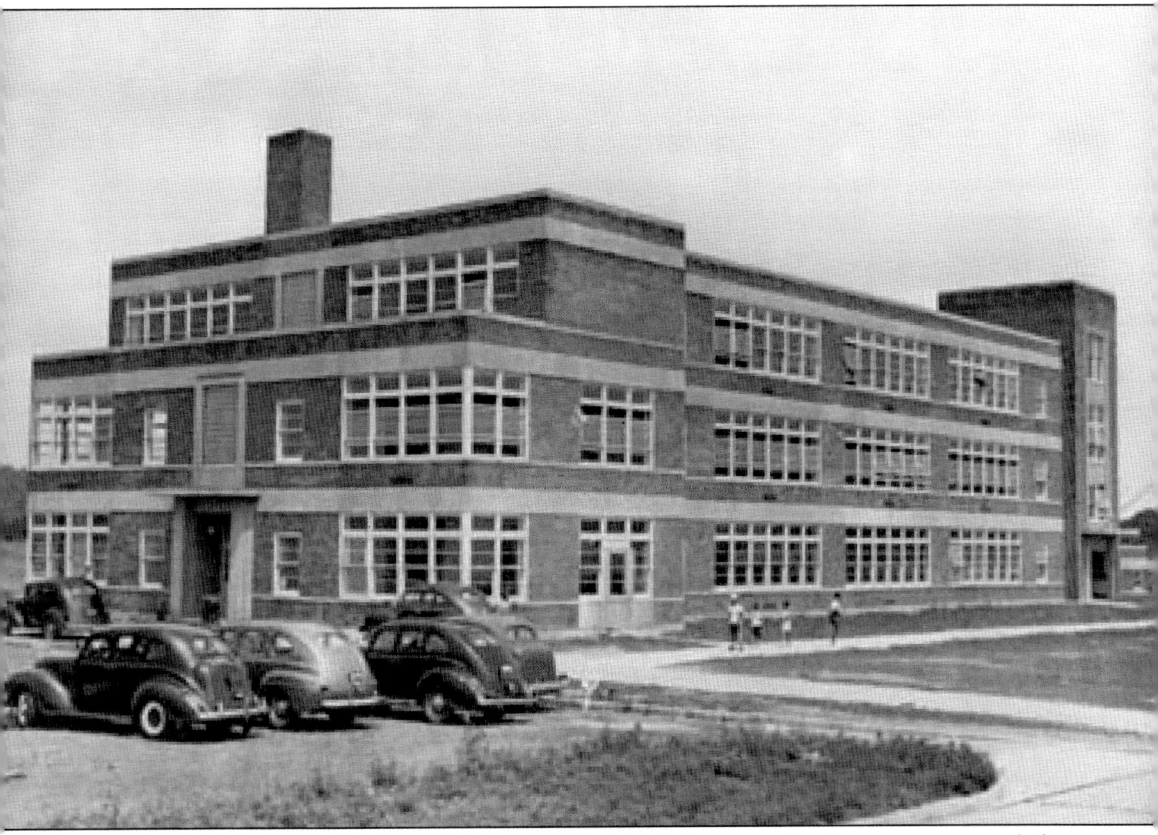

NEVAL THOMAS ELEMENTARY SCHOOL. Many African American schools were overcrowded, necessitating students to attend school in shifts. In the 1940s, the school board made the long-awaited announcement to build new schools for black students. Civic leaders and community groups lobbied to have the new buildings named after outstanding black leaders. Neval Holland Thomas was one of the names advanced by the EGCA. Thomas (1874–1930) had been an exemplary Dunbar history teacher and a National Association for the Advancement of Colored People official who had devoted his life to the fight for equality of opportunity for all. EGCA was successful—the new Neval H. Thomas Elementary School, with 24 rooms, opened in 1946 at 650 Anacostia Avenue in the nearby Parkside community. (CSSMA.)

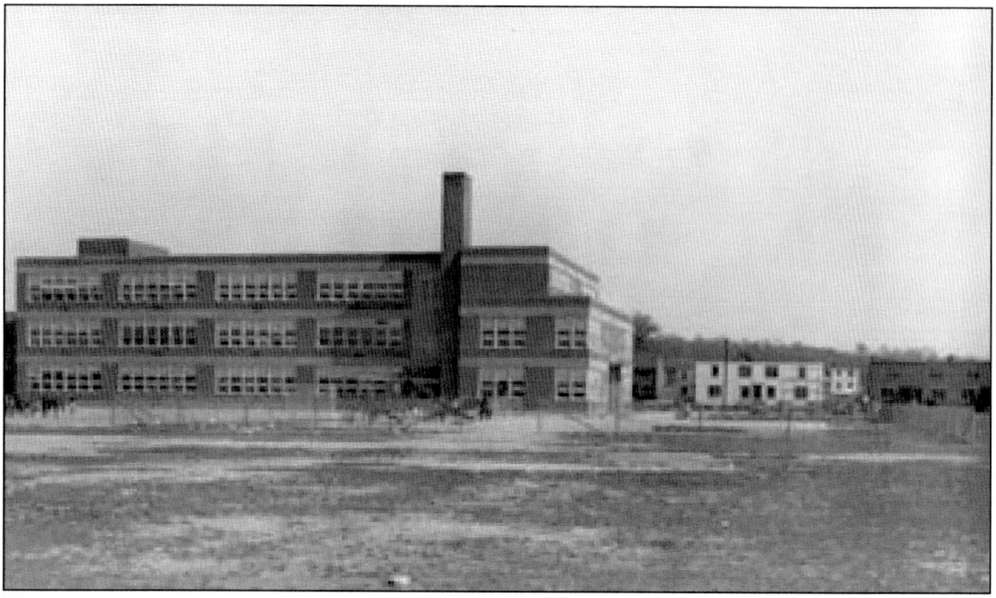

THOMAS MEETS COMMUNITY NEEDS. Many African American youth from River Terrace, Parkside, Mayfair Mansions, and Eastland Gardens were happy to have a brand new school in their community. Parents were relieved that children were no longer exposed to the dangers of crossing busy streets and railroad tracks, as evidenced by its proximity to Parkside apartments, seen above. The school quickly filled to capacity. In addition, junior high school students attended Thomas while awaiting the construction and opening of Kelly Miller Junior High. In spite of crowded classrooms, with outstanding and caring teachers employed at Thomas, the pupils' education did not suffer. (Both, CSSMA.)

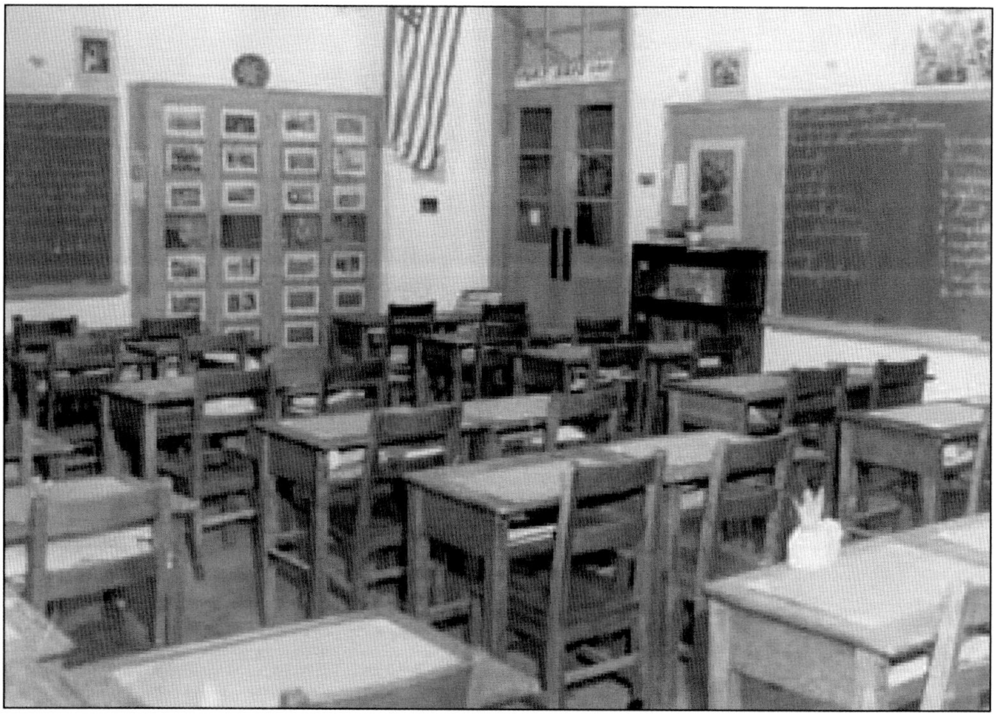

Seven

At Play in the Yards and Fields

Eastland Gardens was always the prime location for families with children because of the open spaces and opportunities for recreation, whether through play, organized sports, or gardening. Families found ways to involve their children in sports, like football, baseball, and cheerleading. Such activities became community projects as residents volunteered as coaches, donated money for uniforms, provided transportation, or cheered from the sidelines.

The Kenilworth-Parkside Recreation Center was built on top of the old municipal dump in the 1970s with the support of residents and the Eastland Gardens Civic Association. The center and park provided a convenient venue for a wide range of sports and recreational activities, including swimming in the outdoor pool and playing tennis. An updated football field and running track were added in 2007. Despite the new additions, the recreation center was rapidly deteriorating and outdated. In 2009, in response to residents' persistent lobbying, city officials razed the recreation center to make room for a new state-of-the-art facility, which has yet to be built.

The Boy Scouts and Girl Scouts were very popular in the neighborhood in the early years. Several of the adult residents served as troop leaders. In the 1970s, the Junior Rangers, a National Park Service program, was also popular due to a dynamic ranger, Walter McDowney, who taught participants about the natural wonders in their backyards. Many residents and civic leaders sponsored activities outside of the community, including trips to the US Capitol, to museums and galleries, and to cultural events. These activities gave Eastland Gardens youth (and adults) considerable freedom and positive guidance.

Kenilworth Aquatic Gardens attracted local and international visitors every year. Because of their proximity and interest, Eastland Gardens Flower Club members often participated as volunteers and exhibitors. The aquatic gardens's annual water lily festival in June is one such popular event and is supported by the Eastland Gardens community.

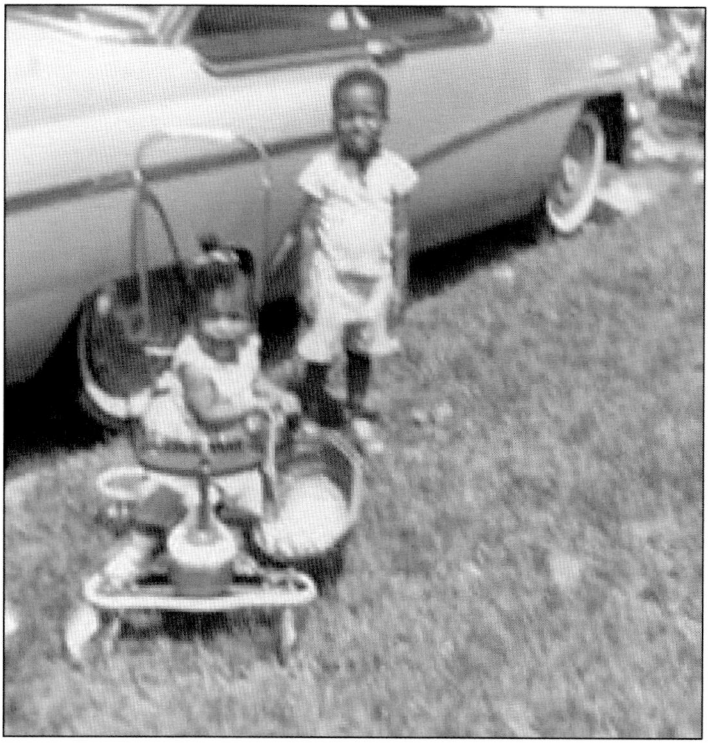

Wilkins Children. Justina Wilkins and her brother Matthews Leon Wilkins pose in the front of their home in 1962. The home, located in the 1200 block of Forty-fourth Street, remains in the family. As an adult, Justina became an active resident of the community and served as president of the EGCA. (JW.)

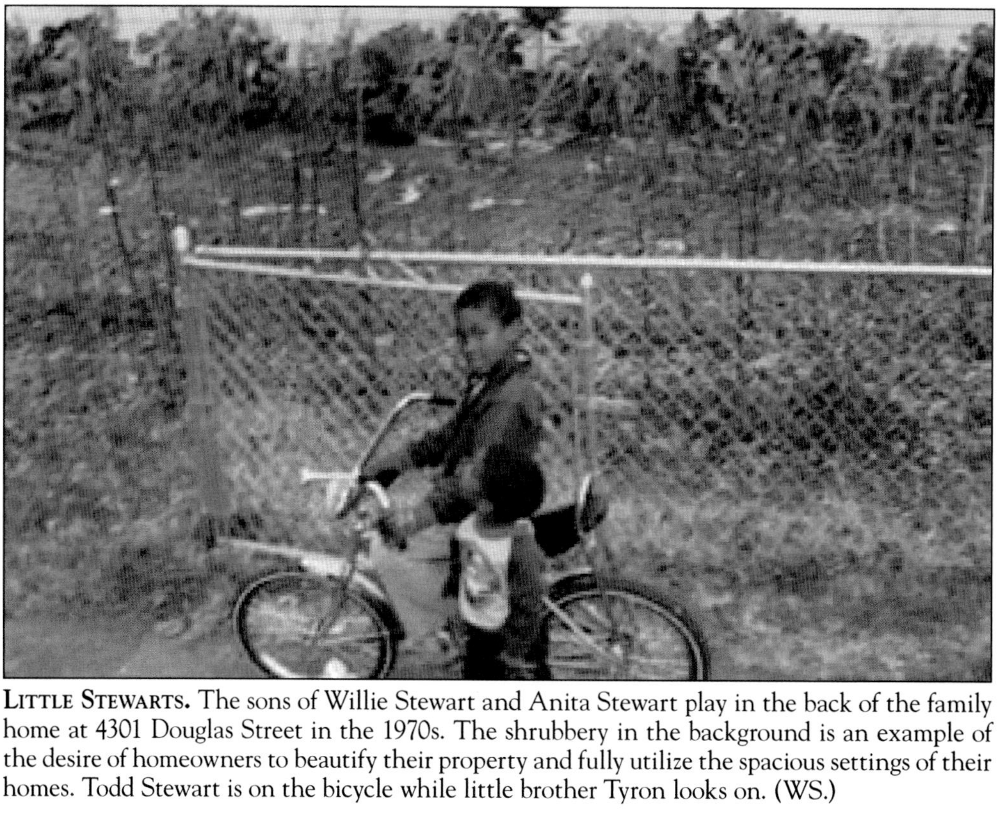

Little Stewarts. The sons of Willie Stewart and Anita Stewart play in the back of the family home at 4301 Douglas Street in the 1970s. The shrubbery in the background is an example of the desire of homeowners to beautify their property and fully utilize the spacious settings of their homes. Todd Stewart is on the bicycle while little brother Tyron looks on. (WS.)

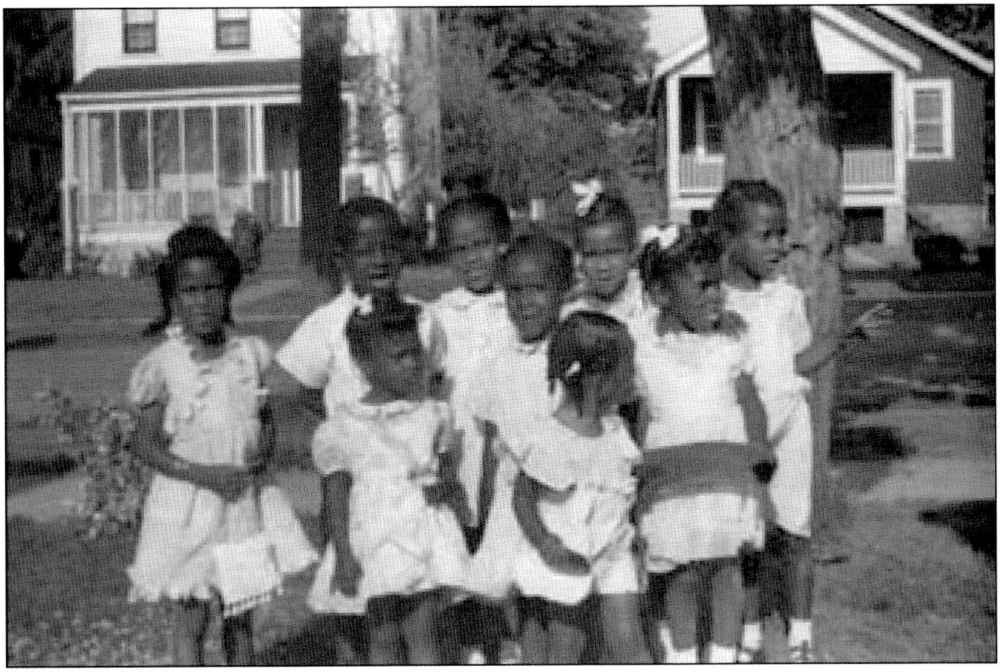

The Forty-second Place Crew. All dressed in their Sunday best on Easter Sunday in 1952, Charlita (Billingsley) McMillan and her "crew" pose for a photograph in front of one of the oldest streets in the tree-lined neighborhood. From left to right are (second row) a niece of Margaret Stevens, who moved onto the block in 1929; Robert Glover; Charlita (Billingsley) McMillan; Angela Cowan; and Terry Lee (Stevens) Freeman; (first row) unidentified, Carlotta Hardman, Marjorie Billingsley, and unidentified. (CM.)

Children at Play. In August 1969, these children on Forty-second Place stopped playing long enough to have their photograph taken. The trees provided shade for playing on hot summer days. Pictured are, from left to right, Arlett Freeman, unidentified, Harriet Baker, Monica Cowan, and Tom McMillan, a third-generation Eastland Gardens dweller. (CM.)

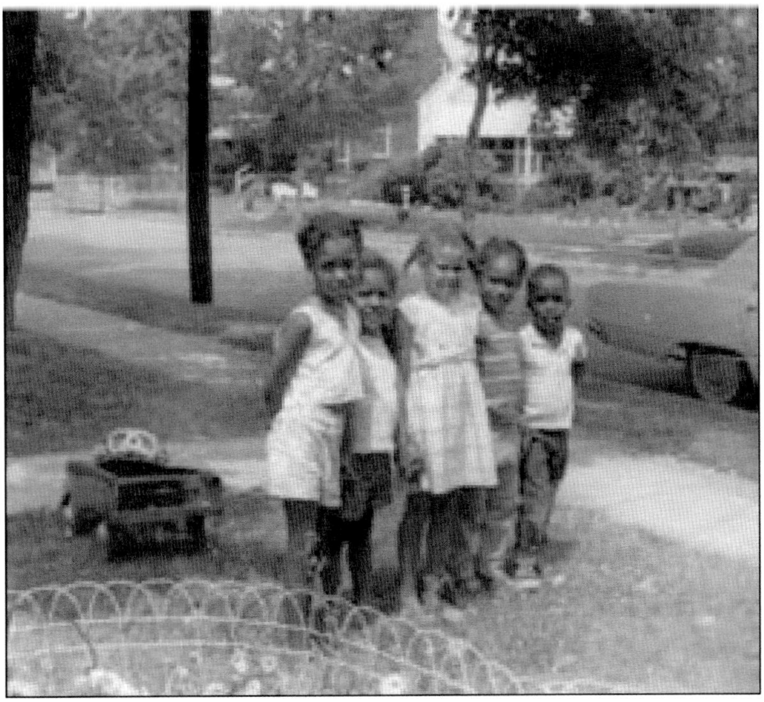

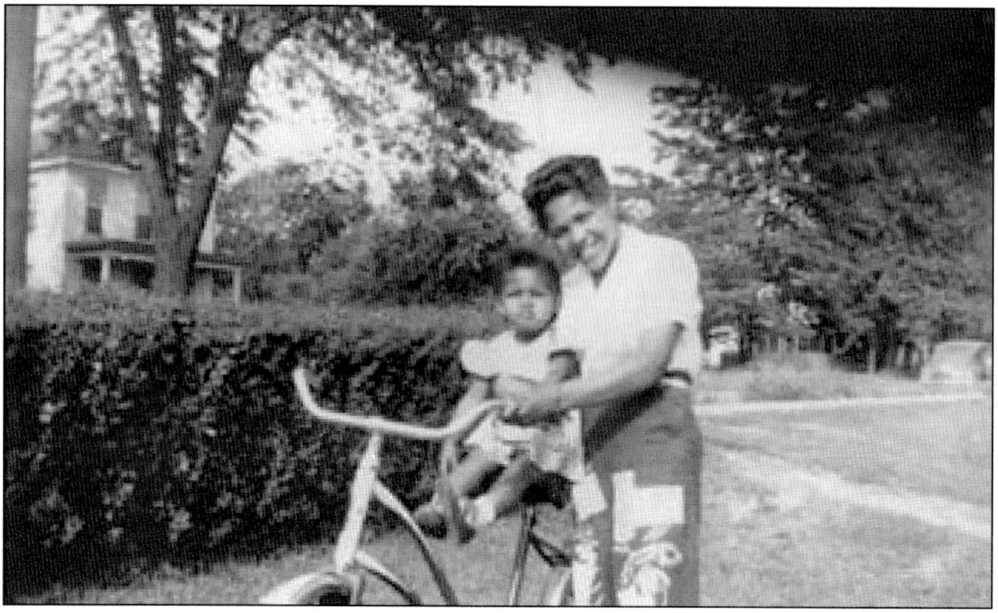

Fun on Douglas Street. Big sister Florence Canada holds little sister Bernetta "Sissy" (Matthews) Francis in the 1950s. Children in the community enjoyed riding bicycles along the wide streets and roller-skating on the paved sidewalks. Younger children, like Tyron Stewart, learned to ride their tricycles in their yards before being allowed on the sidewalks. (Above, FM; below, WS.)

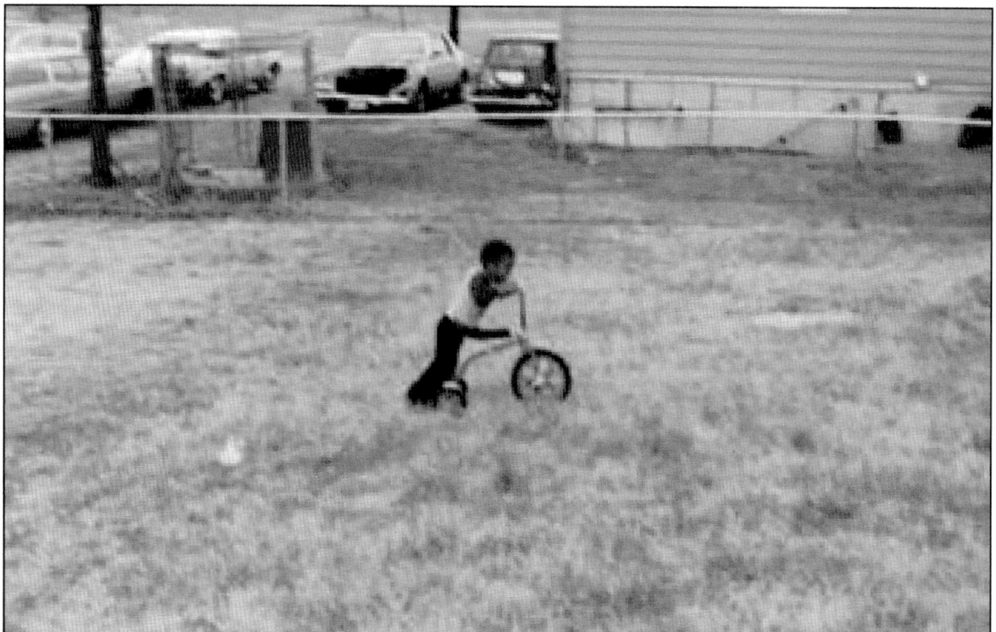

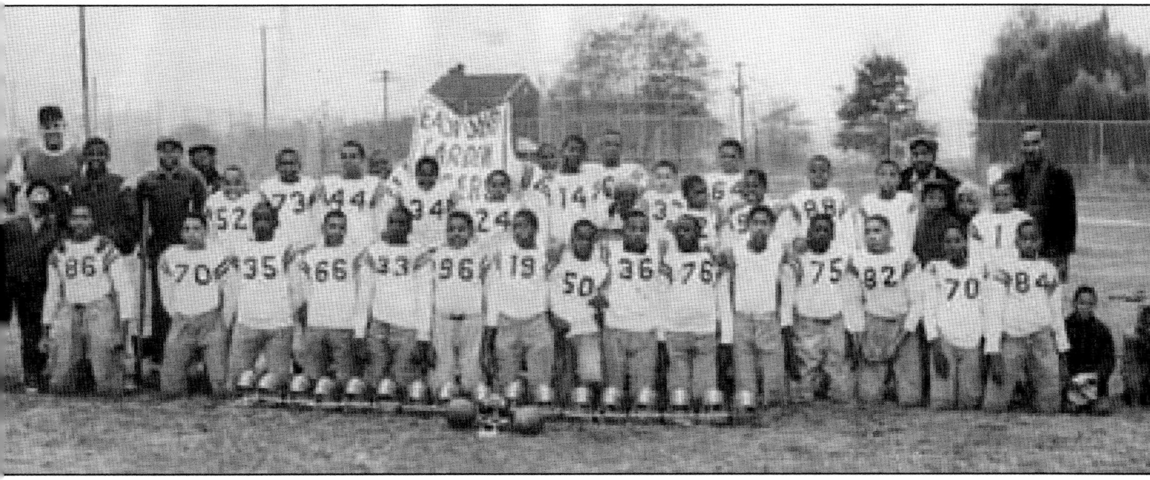

The Eastland Gardens Tigers Formed in 1962. Eastland Gardens's first youth football team was named the "Tigers." William White, seeing a need for organized sports teams for the neighborhood youth, formed a football team. This quickly became a community project. White was assisted in coaching by his brother Herbert White and other neighbors, such as Jake Glover, Claude Dawson, Cliff Glover, and Arnold George. The boys practiced at Kenilworth School grounds, and at night, neighbors would park their cars at the field and turn on the lights so the boys could see. Team uniforms and equipment were donated by resident Carol Swan, who was known by team members as the "Knight in Shining Armor." The Faxios would transport team members back and forth to games. (EW.)

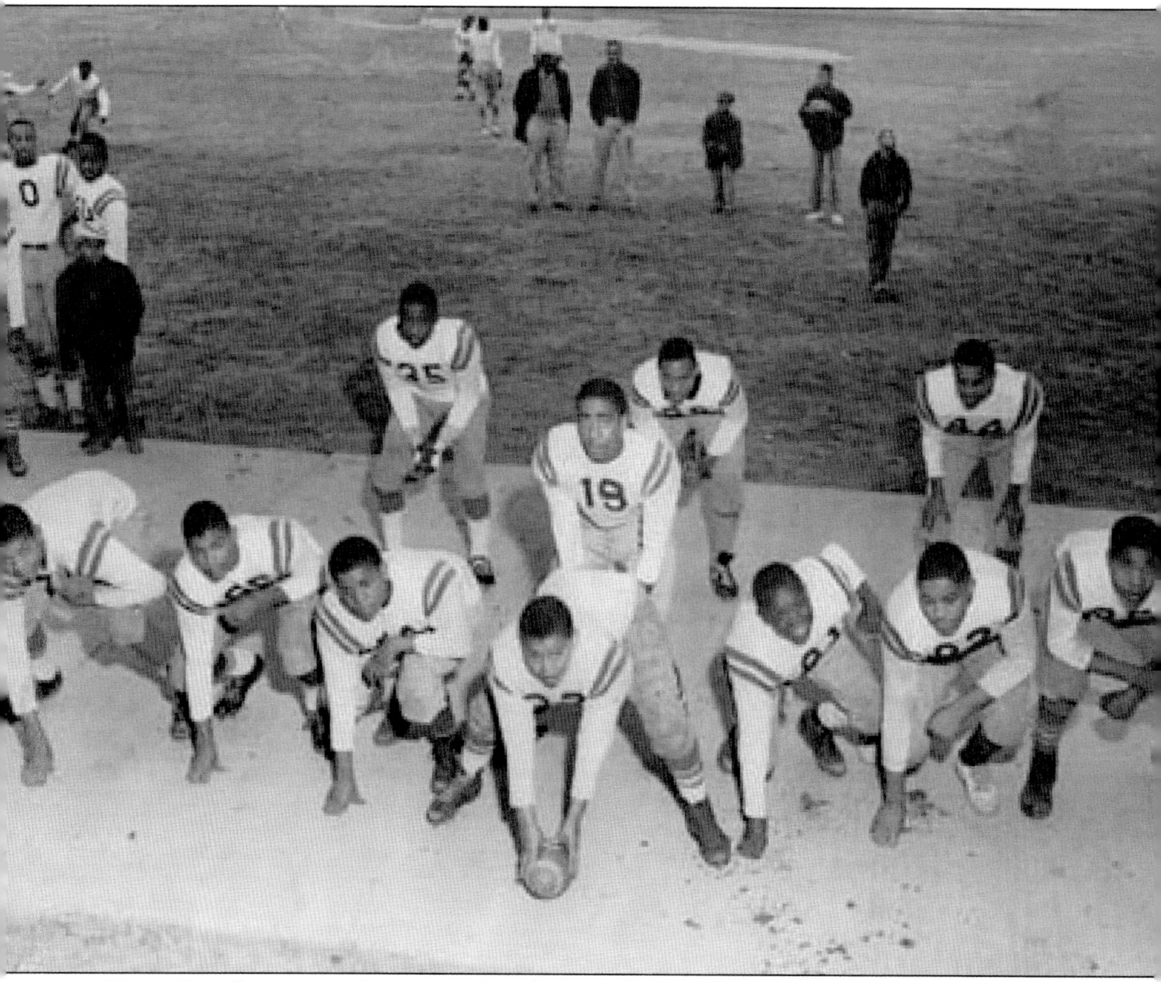

Three-Time Champions. Starting in 1964, the Tigers became three-time winners of the Metropolitan Police Boys Club Championships. Coach William White and his wife, Ethel, provided the annual football banquets at their home, generally in the form of a backyard barbecue. In the photograph above, hiking the ball is William White Jr.; No. 19 is Lloyd Edmonds at the quarterback position; directly behind Edmonds is Maurice Glover; at the back left is John Harry Walker, No. 25; and at the back right is Harland Hayes, No. 44. (LW.)

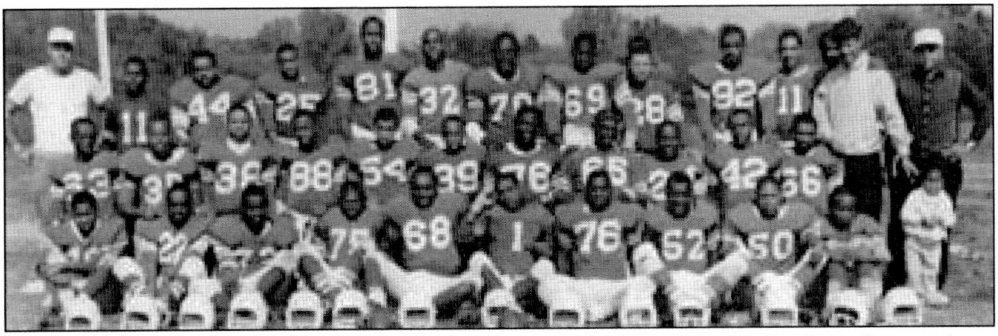

TIGERS IN 1966. As the team members approached high school age, Coach William White, on the far left, visited prospective high schools to encourage coaches to select Tigers players for their football teams. Here, the team is shown at Spingarn High School's field. On the far right are assistant coaches Charles Frazer and Herbert White, located on the end, standing behind his daughter Debbie White. (LW.)

CECIL TURNER, CHICAGO BEAR. One Eastland Gardens Tigers player, Cecil Turner, was recruited to play football for Spingarn High School under Coach Roper McNair. Turner went on to California Polytechnic State University where he received All-American honors in football and track and was considered one of the top-10 sprinters in the world. Passing up an opportunity to compete in the Olympics, Turner chose to play professional football for the Chicago Bears from 1968 to 1973. He set a number of records, including one in 1970 in the Pro Bowl where he tied for the most touchdowns on kick-off returns in one season—a record that still stands. (EW.)

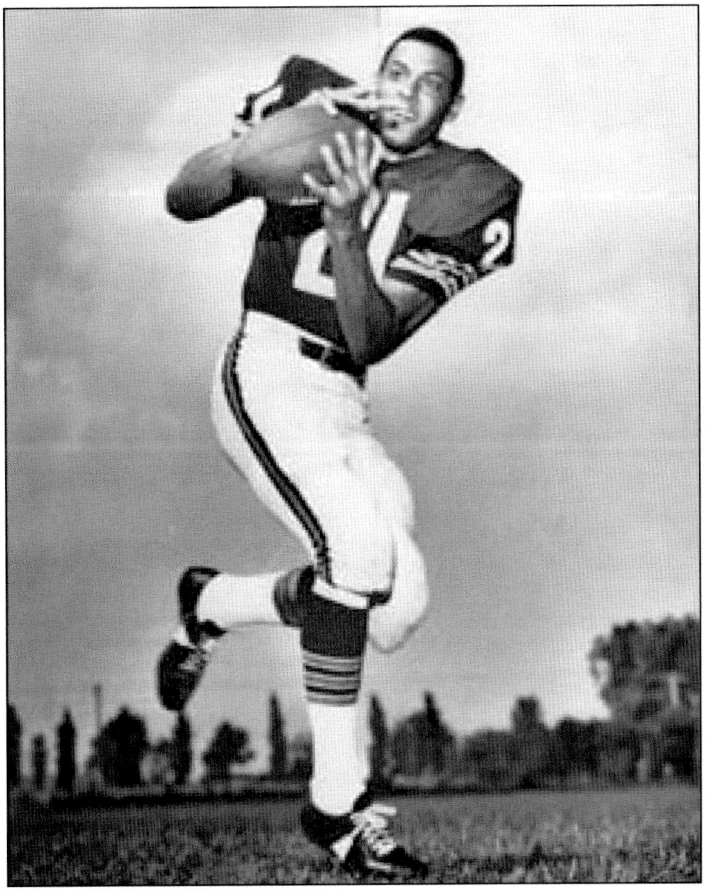

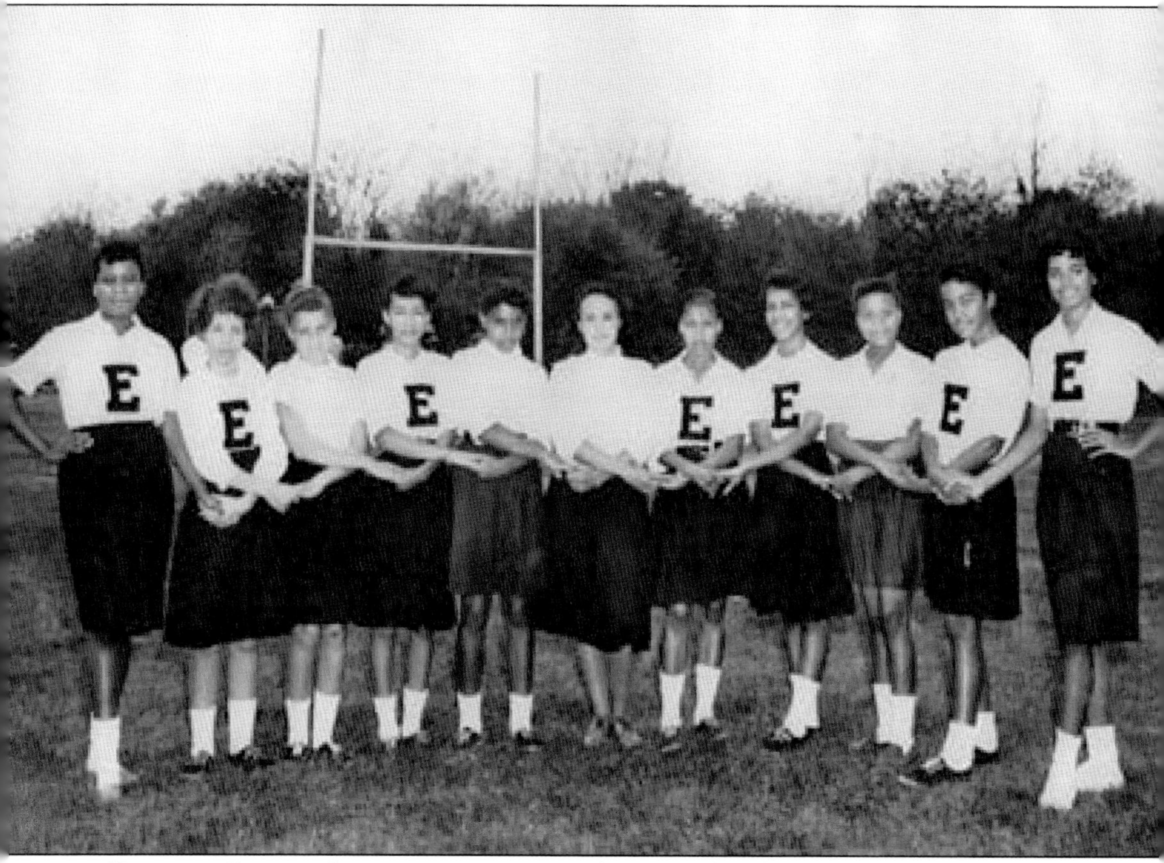

EASTLAND GARDENS CHEERLEADERS IN 1966. The 10-member cheerleading squad proudly rallied the Tigers players and spectators. With the assistance of their coordinator, Effie White, they purchased the fabric for their uniforms and designed and made their skirts. The "E" on their blouses represented "Eastland." On the football field are, from left to right, Carlotta Hardman, Diane Washington, Denise Washington, Angela Cowan, Sheryl Barkley, coordinator Ethel White, Doris Glover, Marjorie Billingsley, Christine Glover, Beryl Swan, and Jean Frazer. The cheerleaders were the second generation of Eastland Gardens dwellers. (LW.)

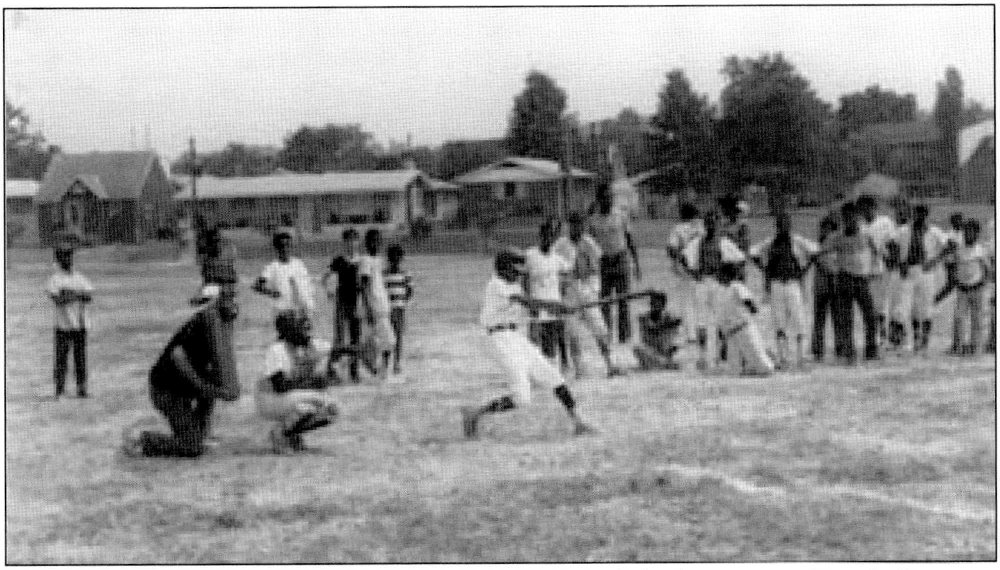

TEAM SPONSORED BY THE FLOWER CLUB. Spring marked the beginning of baseball season. Claude Dawson served as coach. The players looked forward to challenging teams from other neighborhoods. Here is a game in the 1970s where the team sponsored by the EGFC was pitted against the team from Kenilworth Courts. The game was played in Kenilworth Park against a backdrop of mid-century modern homes in Eastland Gardens. (DF.)

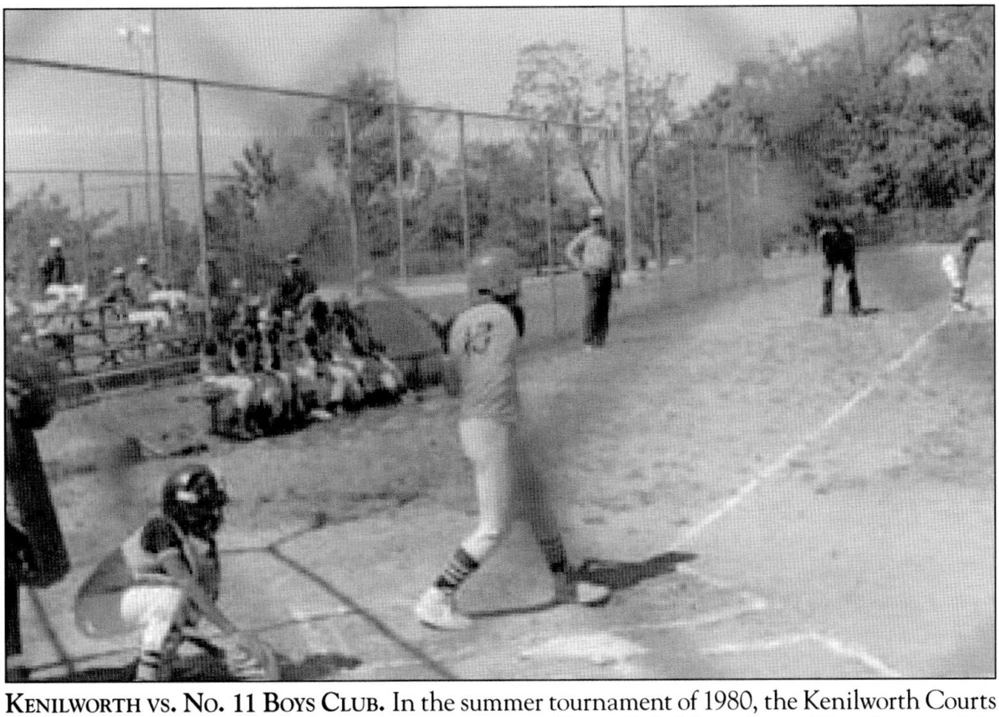

KENILWORTH VS. NO. 11 BOYS CLUB. In the summer tournament of 1980, the Kenilworth Courts team played against Southeast Washington's No. 11 Boys Club. Up to bat is Troy Stewart. His father, Willie Stewart, served as a volunteer coach, assisting Dwaine Glover, the director of the Kenilworth Recreation Center and coach of the team. Rhuedine Davis and other members of EGFC spearheaded fundraising to purchase uniforms for the team. (WS.)

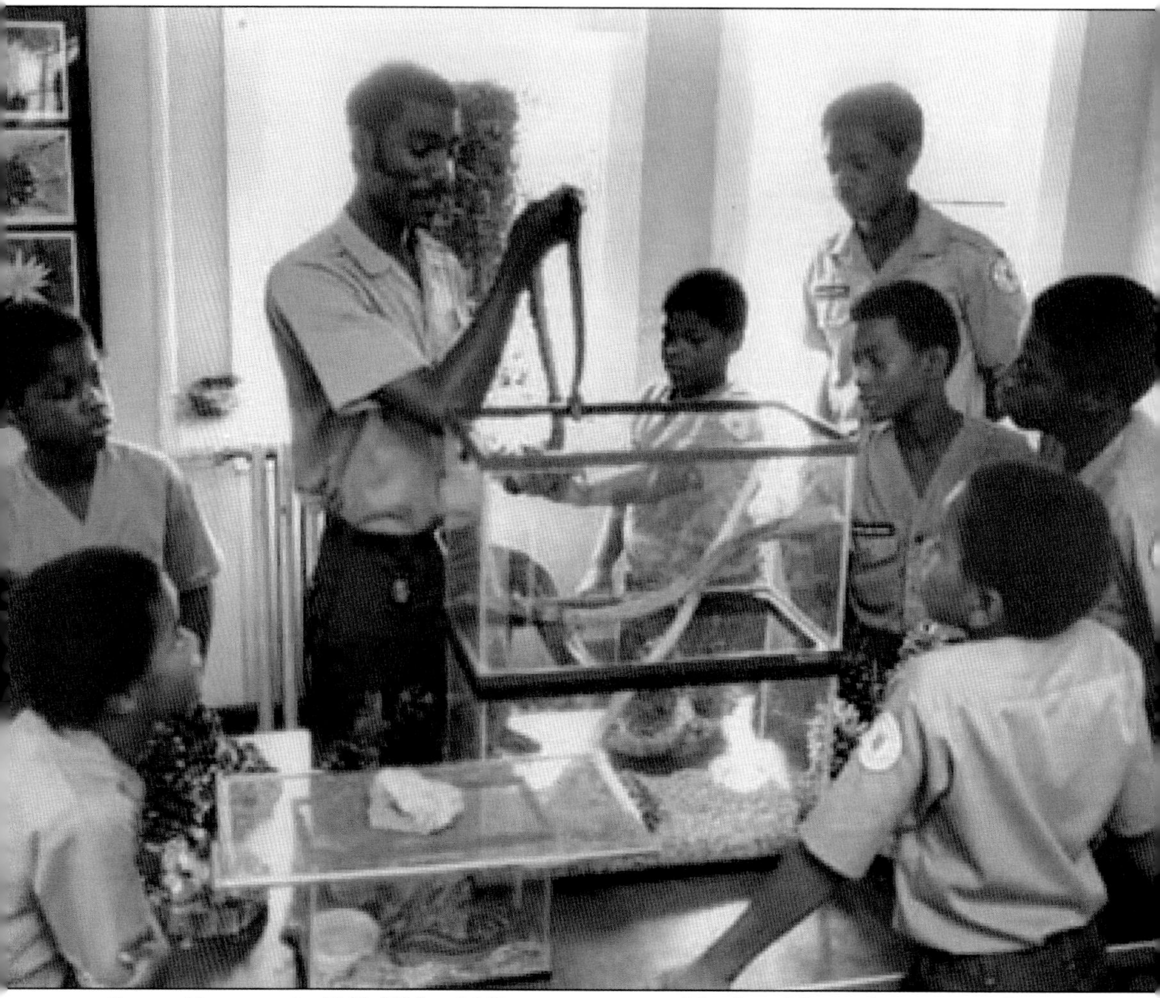

Junior Rangers. In 1968, Walter McDowney was one of the first African American park rangers in the National Park Service (NPS) system. He grew up in Kenilworth Courts and was encouraged by Rhuedine Davis to be a park ranger. He started the Junior Ranger club at the Kenilworth Aquatic Gardens. McDowney, with snake in hand, received several commendations for his work and knowledge. Here, he is teaching the boys about snakes from the surrounding habitat. Pictured are several members of the Junior Rangers, some of whom lived in the Paradise Parkside community. They are, from the left, counter clockwise, unidentified, David Hill, Kenneth Matthews, unidentified, Gary Smith, Tony Franklin, Allan Franklin, and Ranger McDowney. (DF.)

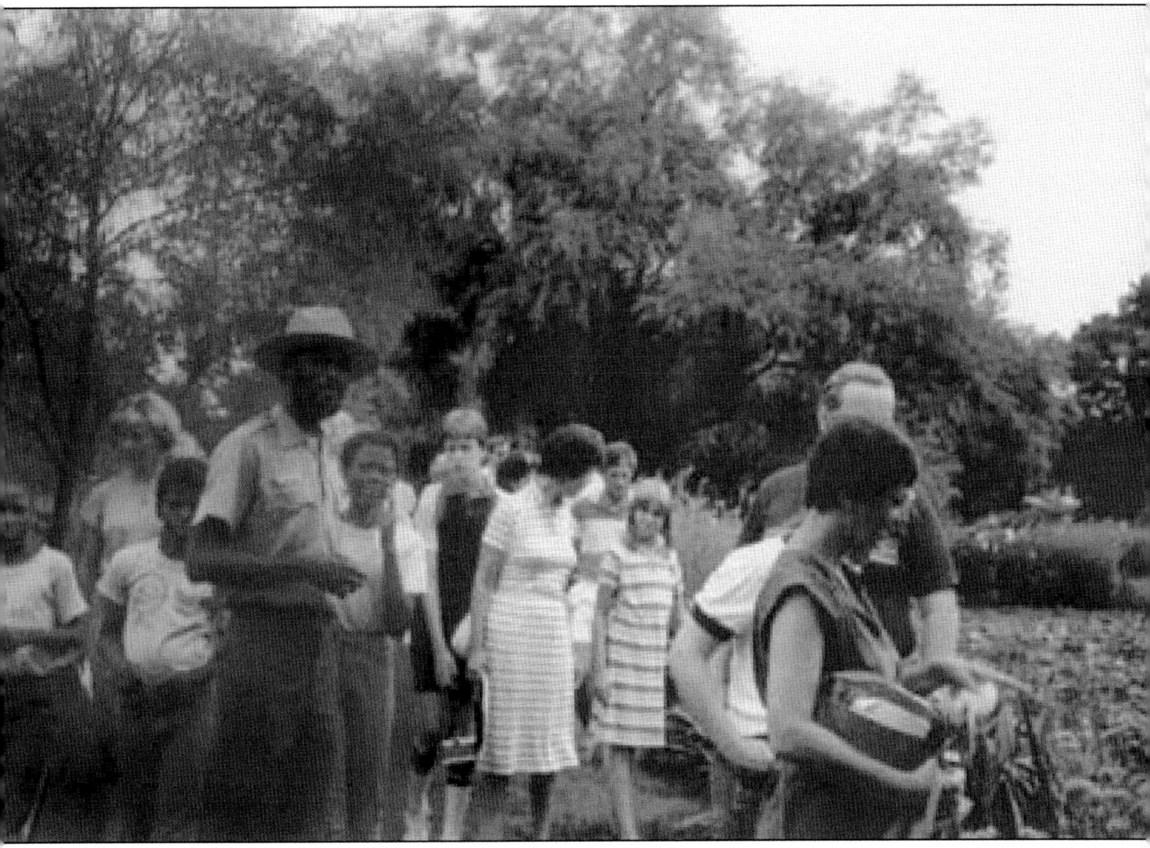

Summer at the Aquatic Gardens. Junior Park Rangers assist Ranger McDowney in the 1970s in guiding visitors through the Kenilworth Aquatic Gardens. This was a way to test their knowledge during summer camp. (DF.)

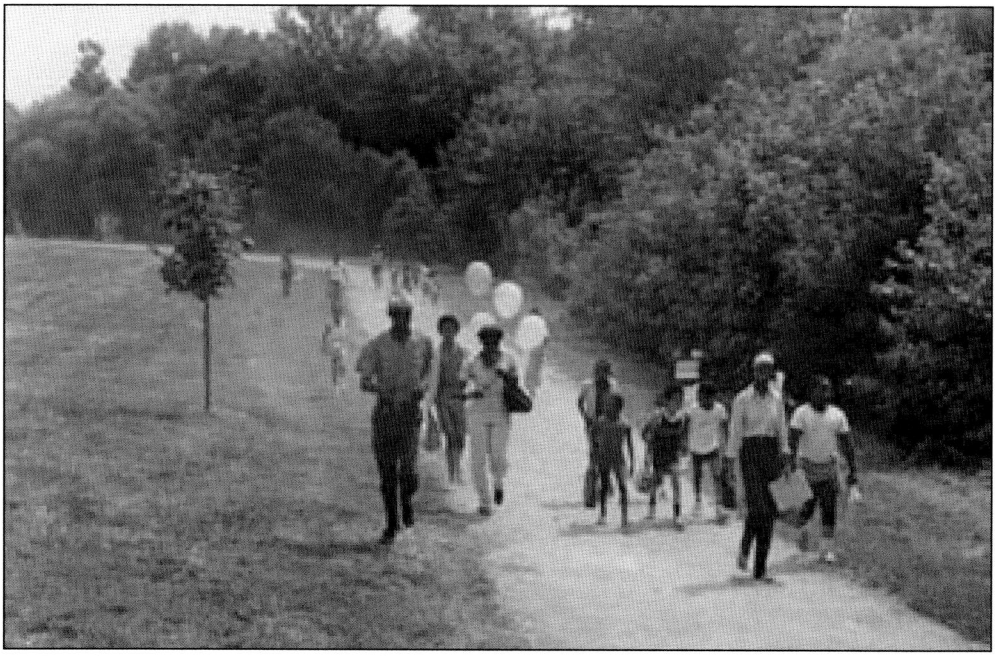

A New Athletic Field. Ranger Walter McDowney leads a group of participants to the opening of the athletic grounds at the back side of the community. This facility opened in 1977 and was cosponsored by the JC Penney Company. (NPS.)

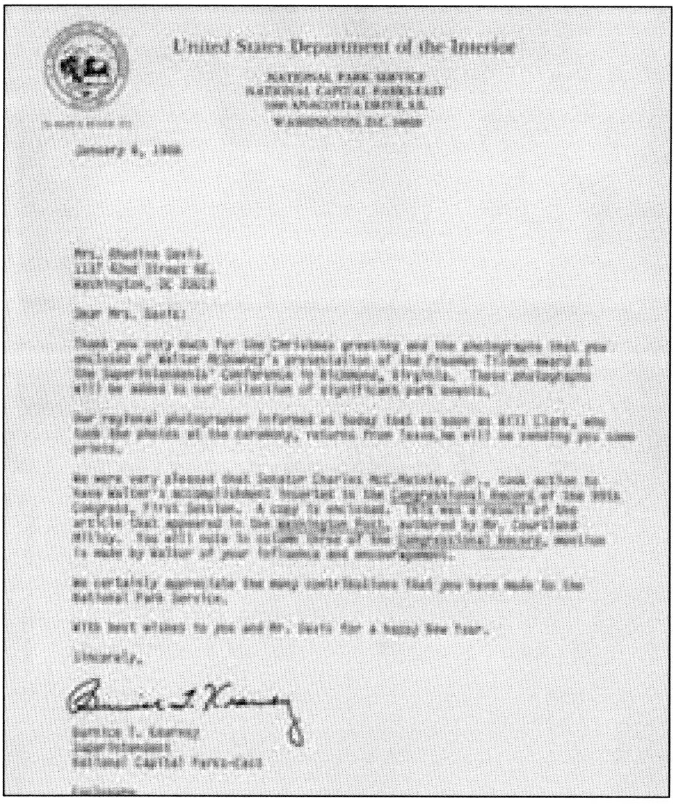

United States Department of the Interior

NATIONAL PARK SERVICE

NATIONAL CAPITAL PARKS-EAST

WASHINGTON, D.C.

Dear Mrs. Davis:

Senator Mathias Commends McDowney. Sen. Charles Mathias Jr. (R-MD, 1969–1987), a supporter of the civil rights movement and an advocate for Chesapeake Bay preservation, sent a letter in December 1985 to NPS regional director Jack Fish, commending the quality of McDowney's performance. Mathias submitted his remarks and an article about McDowney to the *Congressional Record* of the 99th Congress. A follow-up letter from Burnice T. Kearney, superintendent of National Capital Parks-East, to Rhuedine Davis highlights McDowney's accomplishments. McDowney currently works at Hains Point, a popular park in Washington, DC. (DF.)

Eight

"Where Nature and Know How Join Hands"

These words by resident Lillie Troublefield in 1981, on the occasion of the 50th anniversary of the Eastland Gardens Civic Association, described the long and visible history of civic activism in the community. This small, somewhat isolated neighborhood has made a huge impact primarily through two organizations: the Eastland Gardens Civic Association (EGCA) and Eastland Gardens Flower Club (EGFC). Through EGCA and EGFC, residents have exhibited exceptional leadership and unabashedly promoted love for their homes and neighborhood.

Community leaders such as Walter Robertson, Erman Clay, Clifford "Henry" Glover, Owen Davis, Rhuedine Davis, Wesley Collins Sr., Regina Rutledge, Hilda Banks, Herman Greene, Harold Chinn, and Louise Chinn all possessed the foresight, determination, adaptability, integrity, and social skills that made them good leaders. Residents from nearby communities were also leaders that greatly impacted Eastland Gardens. Kimi Gray (1945–2000), of Kenilworth Courts, chaired EGCA's youth activities committee in the early 1980s. Gray became a national public housing resident leader and formed a resident management corporation to purchase, manage, and develop Kenilworth Courts and Kenilworth-Parkside housing.

Among the many issues undertaken by the leadership was the infrastructure, which included streets and sidewalks; safety precautions for pedestrians crossing the railroad tracks, and later the freeway, resulting in the erection of an overpass; the naming of local schools; and the closing of the city dump. They fought against the location of public housing in their community but learned to work cooperatively with the residents of both Parkside Dwellings and Kenilworth Courts for the benefit of all three neighborhoods. When it was clear that they would not win the battle to keep their community from being divided by the construction of a freeway through its eastern edge, they participated in the design to reduce the negative impact.

A shining light in the leadership of Eastland Gardens and the surrounding neighborhoods in this section of Northeast Washington, however, was Rhuedine Davis. She had a vision for the community, which informed most of her activism. From cleanups of the aquatic gardens to services for senior citizens, she had ideas and the fortitude to pursue them to fruition. In the midst of all her activities, she was also something of the archivist of Eastland Gardens. It is from her files, records, and photographs compiled over the years that the majority of images and history in this book have been taken. Eastland Gardens owes her a tremendous debt of gratitude.

Since 1931, when the EGCA was founded, there has been a strong tradition of leadership that continues today. Eastland Garden's community leaders have consistently inspired and empowered their neighbors and other Washingtonians to make a difference in their communities.

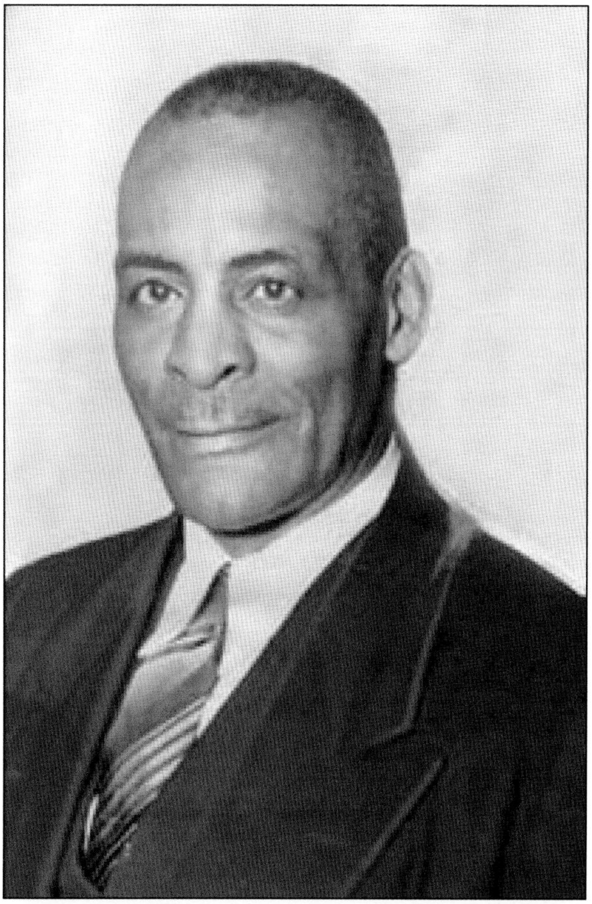

Walter Robertson. In 1931, Walter Robertson became the first president of the EGCA while working full-time at the US Veterans Bureau. Robertson led the association against a backdrop of slowly rising black homeownership and inadequate municipal services. During his tenure, Robertson brought positive changes to Eastland Gardens and increased black political influence within the local government. Robertson is also pictured below, in the center, with family and colleagues. (Left, AA; below, DF.)

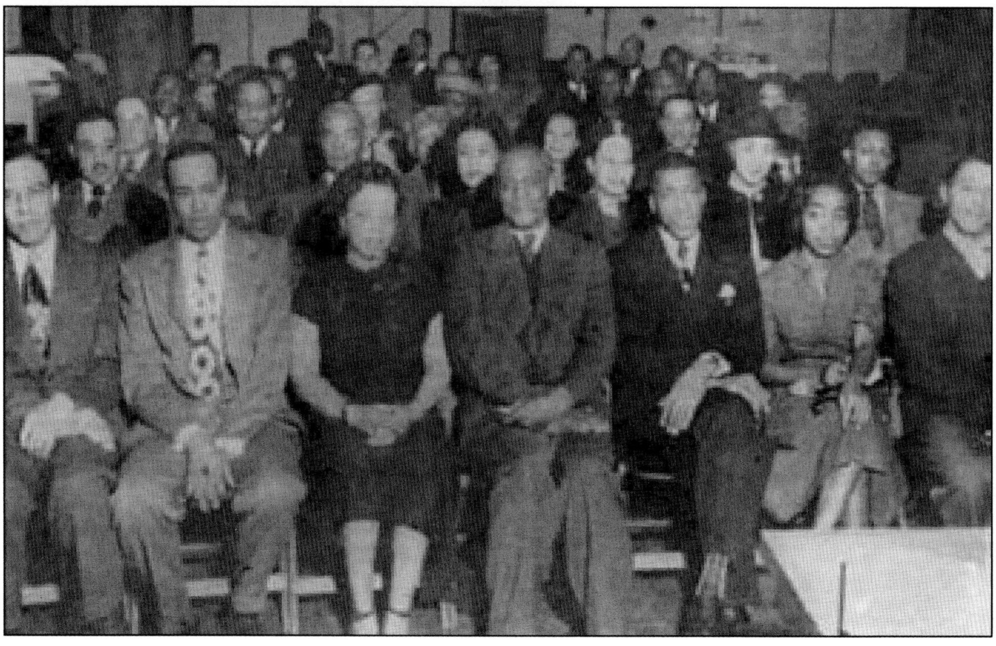

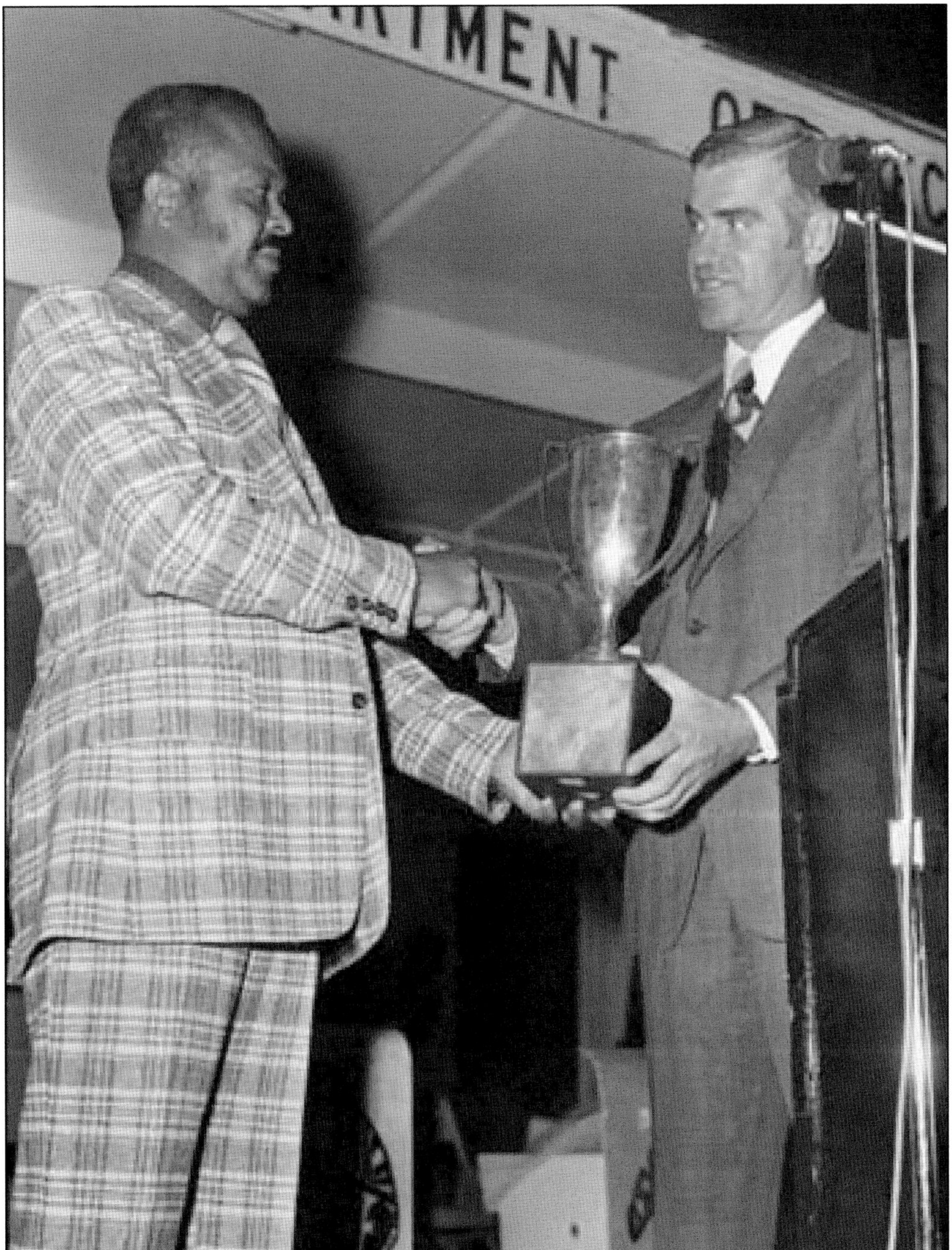

Wesley Collins. A native Washingtonian and a graduate of the prestigious Dunbar High School and Howard University, Wesley Collins (left) worked at the Federal Reserve System for 35 years. Collins served as EGCA president from 1977 to 1980 and was considered a great leader. He also served as president of the Far Northeast-Southeast Council of Civic Associations. Here, in 1972, Collins receives the Washington *Star-News* Cup on behalf of the Far Northeast-Southeast Council Civic Association for his role in helping to plan and design the Kenilworth corridor of Interstate 295. (MLK-W.)

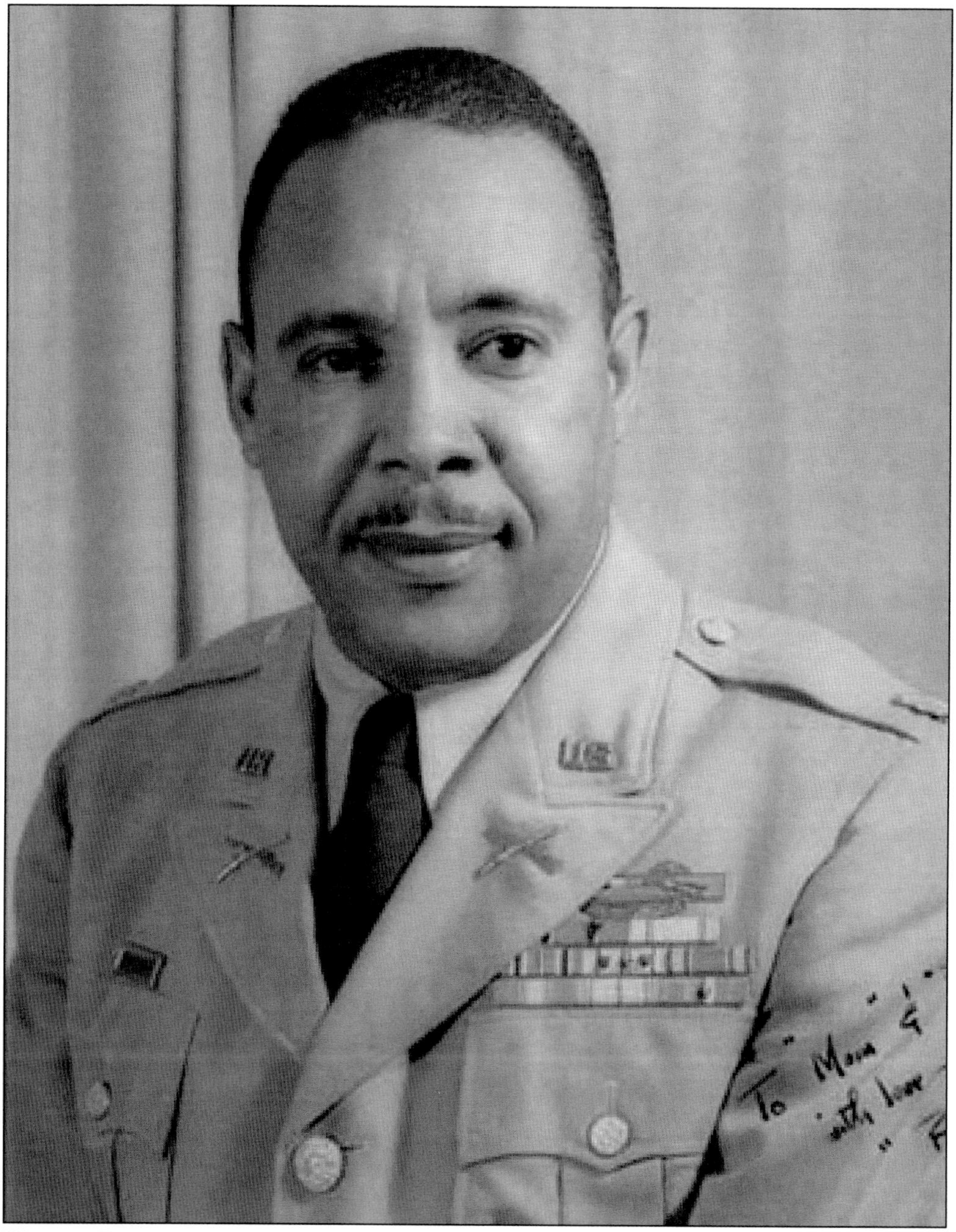

William Brooks. Native Washingtonian William Dandridge Brooks Jr. was a 1930 graduate of Dunbar High School and of Howard University from which he received a bachelor's degree in 1934 and a master's degree in 1936. He studied physics in a New York University doctorate program and, later, attended Robert H. Terrell School of Law at night. Brooks became one of the first African American patent examiners at the US Patent Office, where he worked from 1947 to 1950. For his service in the US Army during World War II and the Korean War, he received a Bronze Star medal for valor in combat and a Legion of Merit, respectively. Brooks volunteered in Eastland Gardens as a Boy Scouts leader from 1973 to 1990 and served on the National Capital Area Council of Boy Scouts. (FW.)

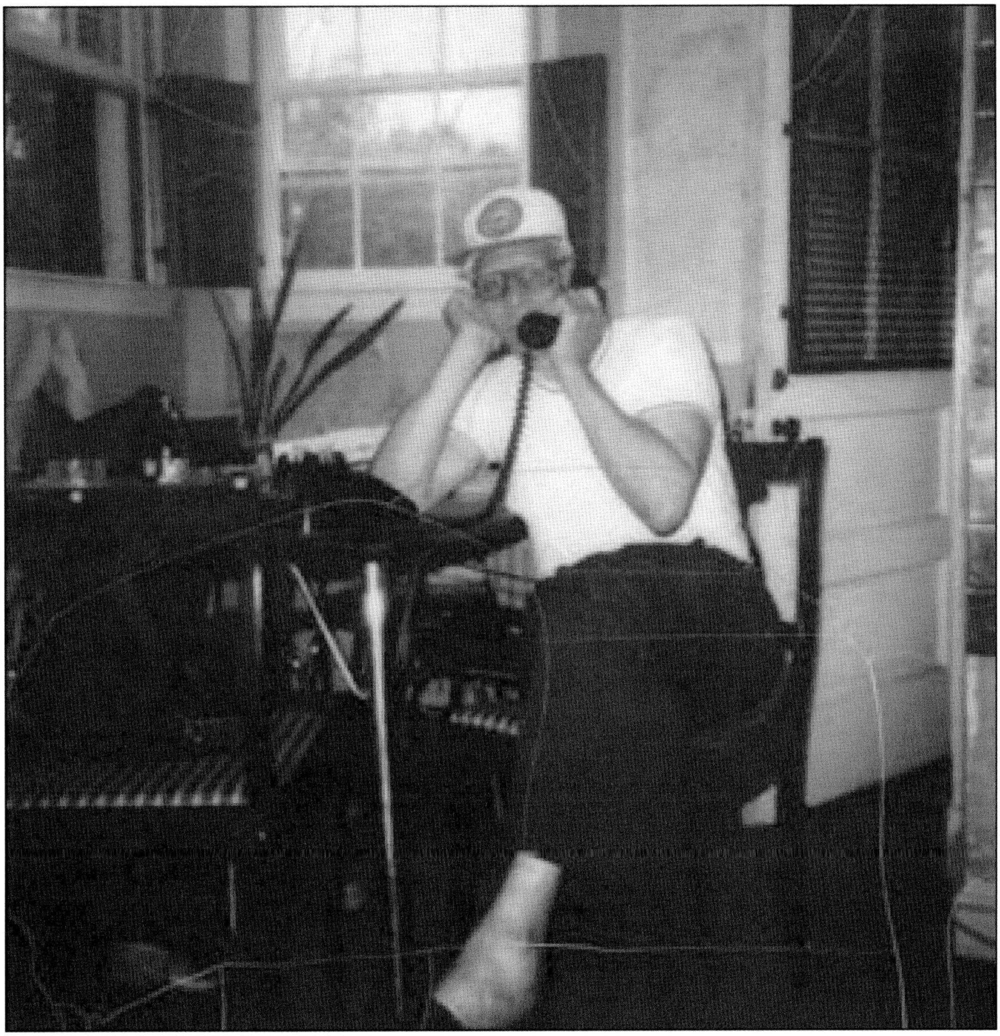

Harold Chinn, Education and Transportation Activist. As chairman of the education committee of the EGCA in 1953, Chinn testified before the District of Columbia Board of Education in favor of the proposed transfer of Kenilworth Elementary School to black students. He argued that the 135 children living near the school should not have to cross a dangerous railroad and dodge traffic to attend a school farther away that had overcrowded classrooms inhibiting effective learning. The same year, Chinn represented the EGCA before the district commission to protest the widening of Kenilworth Avenue to a six-lane highway and the proposed razing of 30 residences, local businesses, and churches, as well as the resulting reduction of tax revenue, stating that the losses were not worth the promise of convenience to motorists. (MC.)

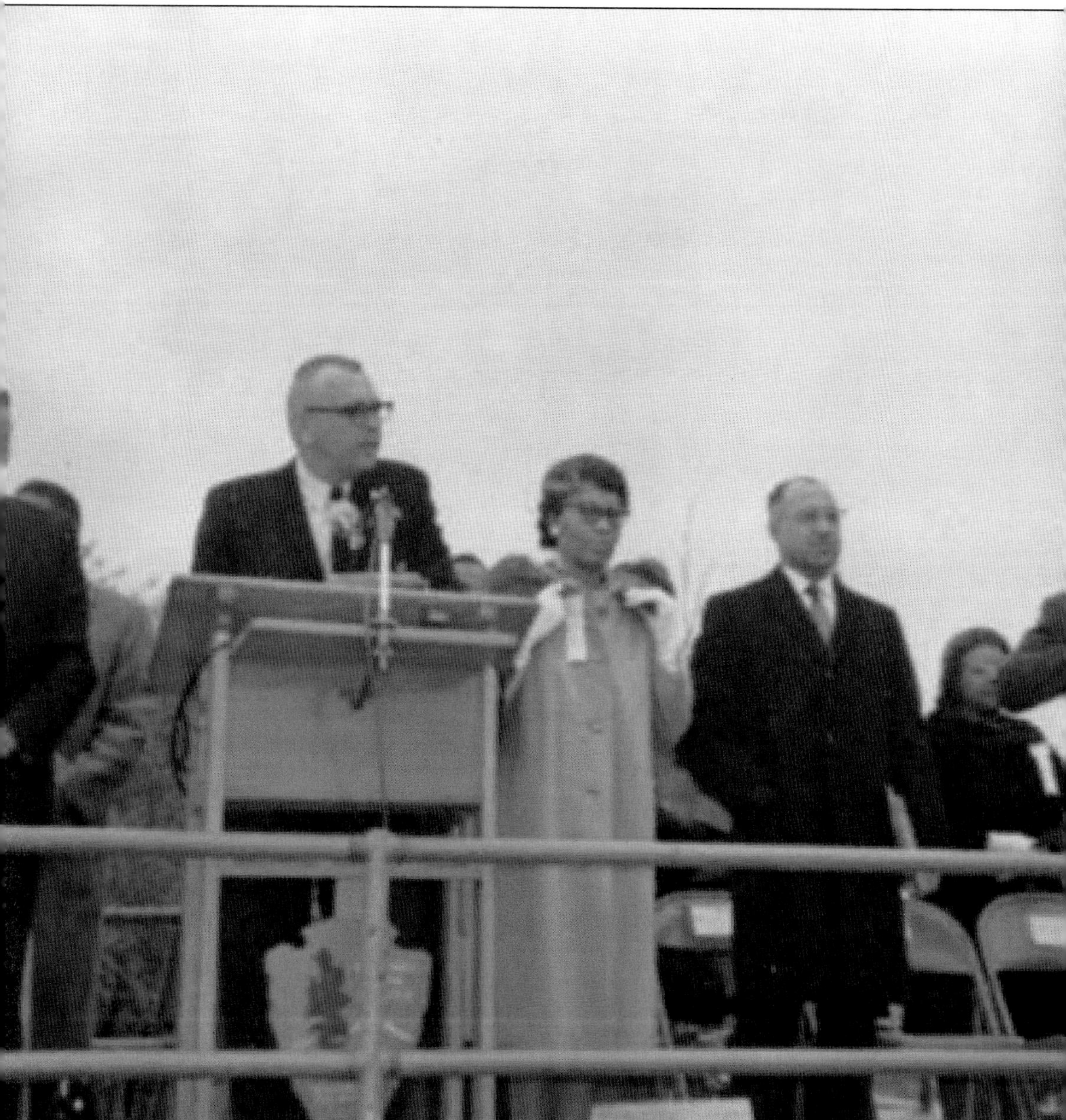

Wilbur C. Goodwin. Pictured on the right is Wilbur Goodwin, who lived on the 4200 block of Nash Street. An employee of the US Postal Service until retirement, he was active in the EGCA as president from 1967 to 1968. He chaired the inauguration ceremony for the unveiling of the Kenilworth-Parkside Park entrance, at which an NPS official is speaking above. As a community leader, Goodwin also protested the open burning of trash at the municipal dump on the site of the current park. His commitment to the beauty and maintenance of the entrance continued until his passing. (DF.)

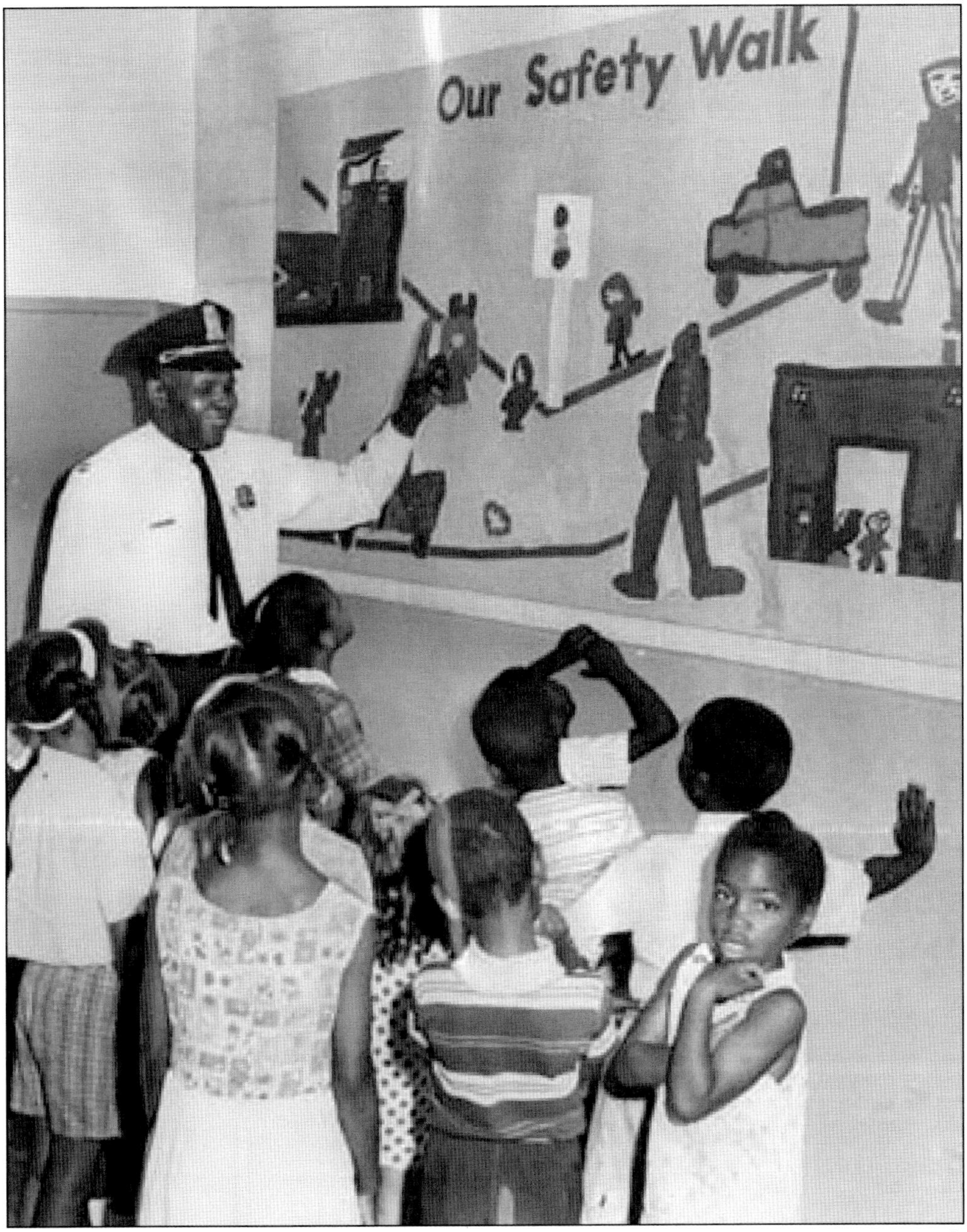

Capt. Owen Davis. As Captain Davis moved up in ranks, he never forgot community outreach and civic duties. In 1967, after being reassigned to the 11th Precinct, he visited Birney Elementary School on Nichols Avenue (now Martin Luther Jr. Avenue) and Sumner Road. He received thank-you notes from Birney students for a tour of the police station. Captain Davis always found ways to reach the youth of the city and to give back to the communities that loved and supported him. (MLK-W.)

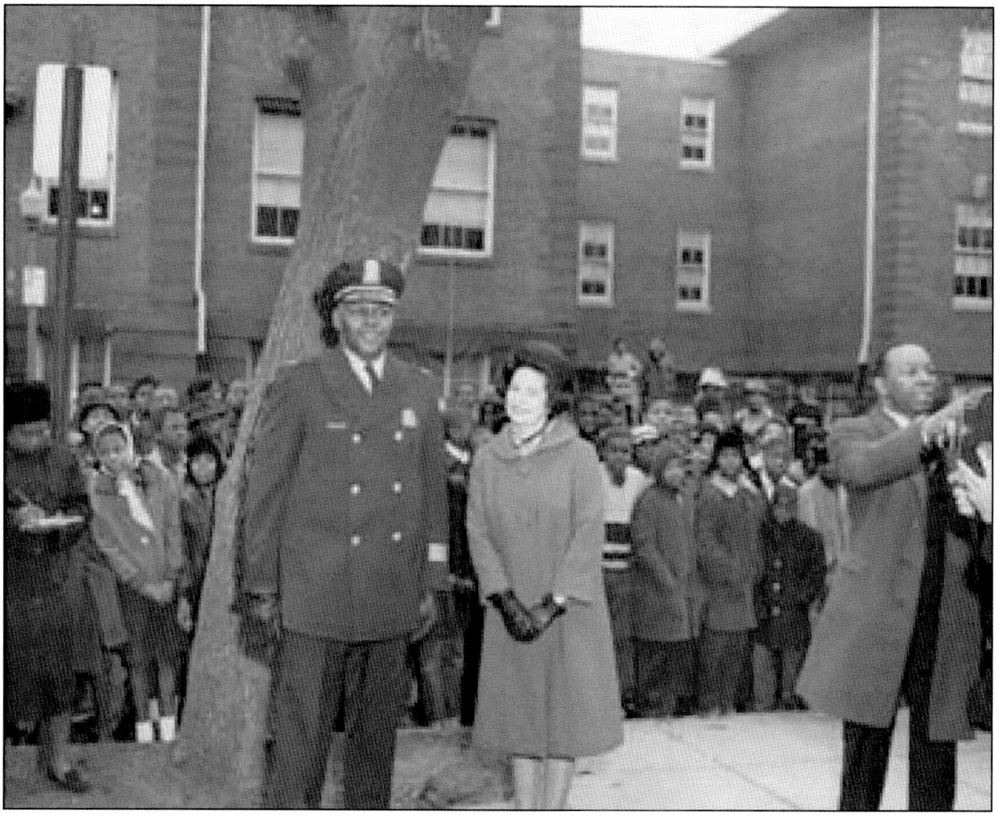

34 Years of Service. After serving 34 years with the police department, Capt. Owen Davis retired as deputy police chief in 1971. The police department had changed considerably during his tenure there. By the time of his retirement, more than one-third of the police force was black—the highest percentage of blacks in a metropolitan police department in the United States. He continued to be active in civic matters until his passing in 2007. One of the highlights of his career was his frequent assignments to accompany notables such as DC mayor Walter Washington, Martin Luther King Jr., First Lady Lady Bird Johnson, and Vice Pres. Hubert Humphrey. (Both, DF.)

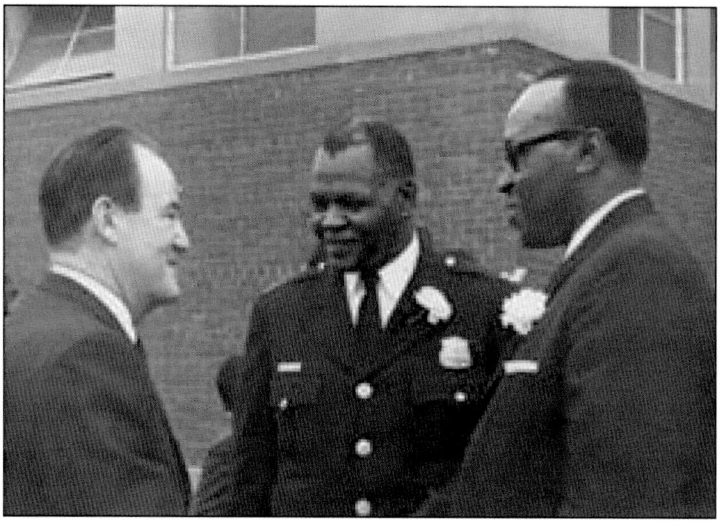

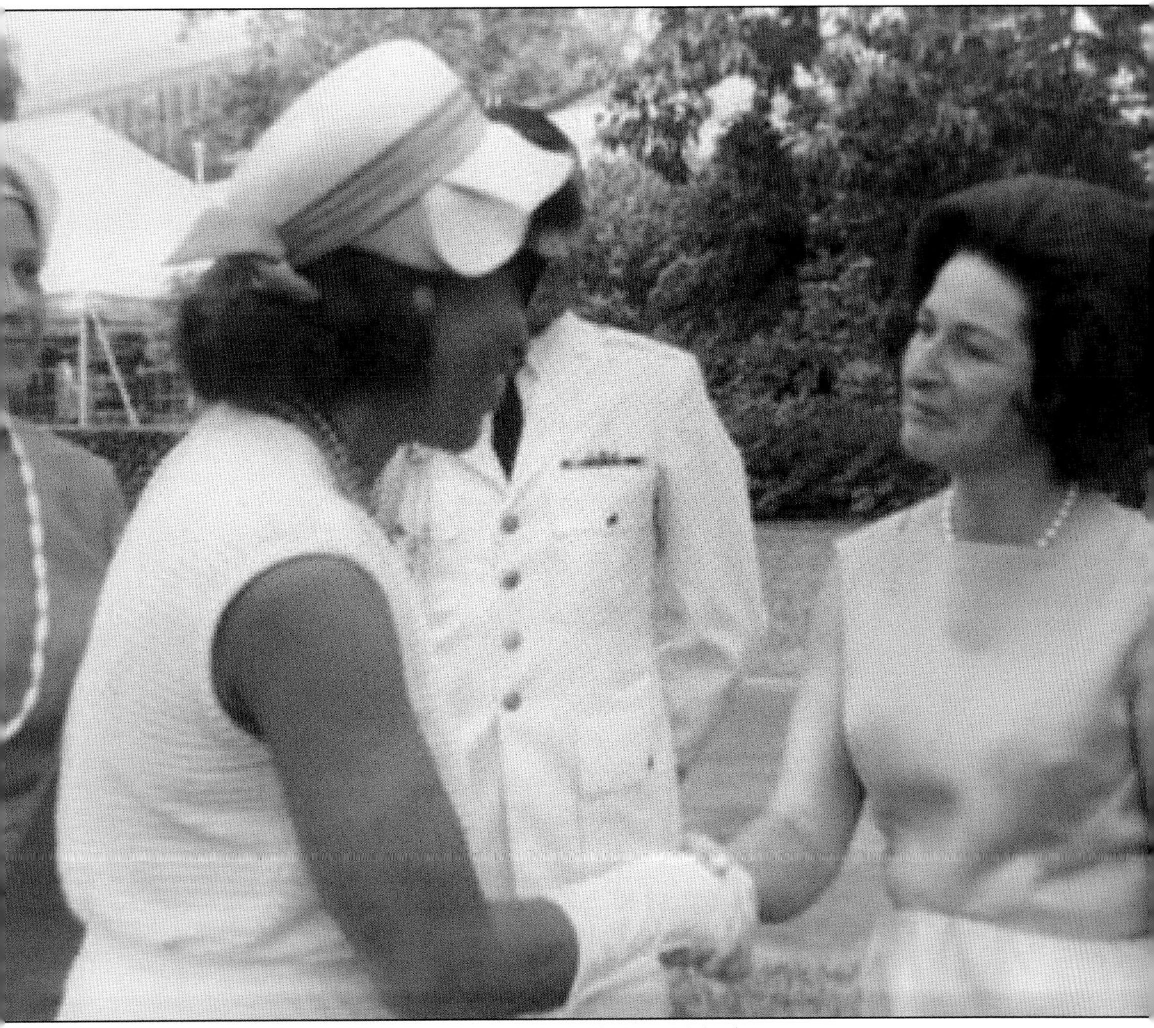

Davis Receives National Recognition. Honored in 1965 for her commitment to improving her community, Rheudine Davis received a Women Doer's award. The award was bestowed by Jane (Shields) Freeman, wife of secretary of agriculture Orville L. Freeman, during a tea commemorating Democratic Women's Day. Above, First Lady Johnson greets Davis at a White House reception for honorees of the First Lady's national beautification program. With her death in 2003, the community lost an indefatigable advocate. The EGFC continues her legacy by promoting neighborhood beautification and safeguarding the heritage of Eastland Gardens. (DF.)

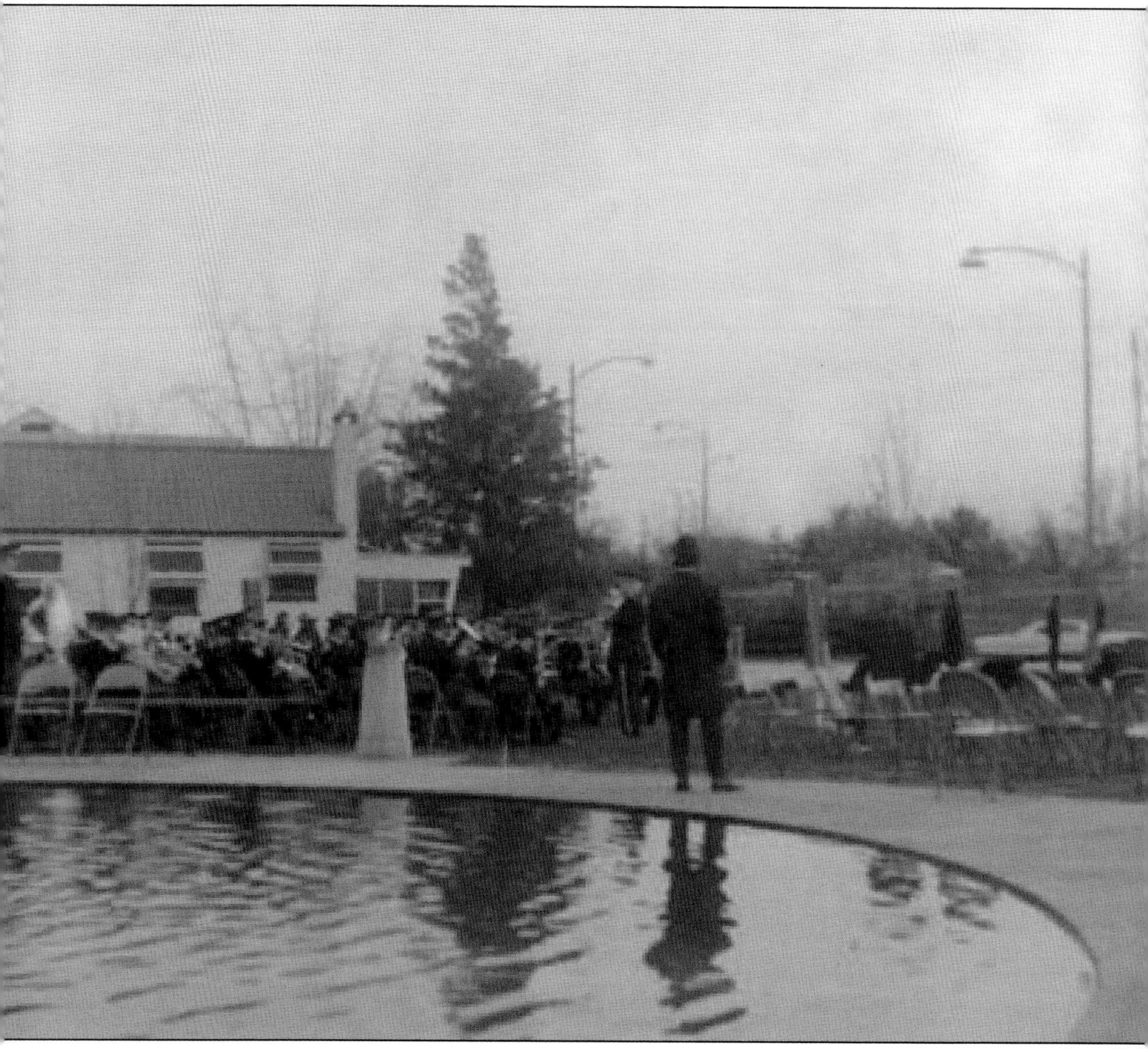

THE EASTLAND GARDENS FOUNTAIN. Pictured here in 1967, the fountain at the entrance of Eastland Gardens had been erected some years before. Few communities in Washington, DC, had fountains or similar features marking the gateway to a neighborhood. This was accomplished through the efforts of the flower club and the cooperation of the NPS. Events sometimes featured bands and very important guests. Although the fountain is no longer operable, the EGFC continues to use the site to host its annual Christmas-tree decorating and lighting ceremony. (CM.)

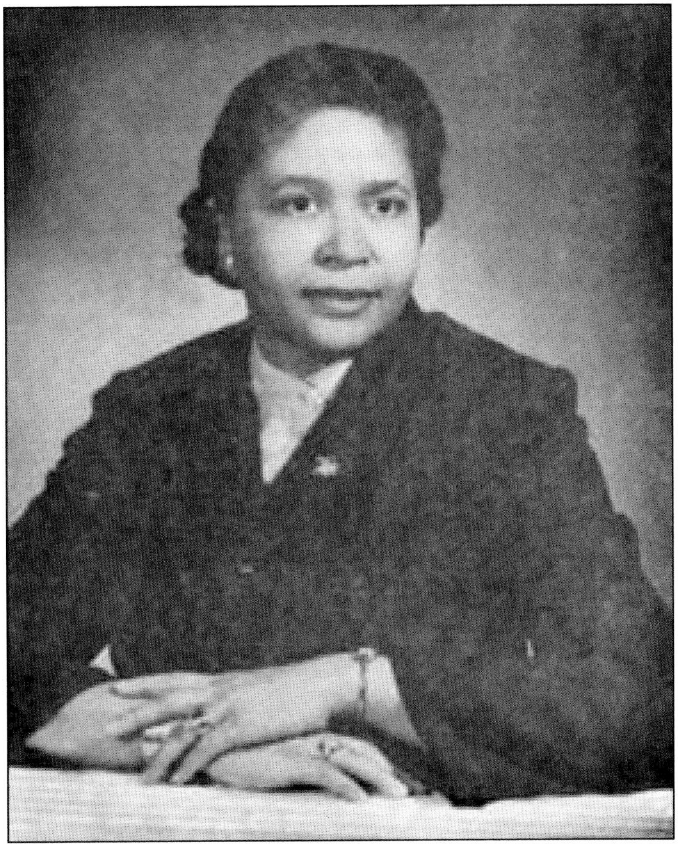

Hilda Banks. Hilda Banks and her husband, Theodore Banks, moved into their home in Eastland Gardens in the 1960s. By 1965, she had become an active member of the flower club and, by 1981, she was serving as its president. She once wrote of Eastland Gardens, "you cheered me when I won blue ribbons, participated in garden tours, and gave love and support to me as activities chairperson with KEMP Seniors, the annual Mount Airy Baptist Church Choir's Benefit Recital (initiated by my late husband, Theodore Banks), and other events too numerous to list. For this, I am extremely grateful." (Both, DF.)

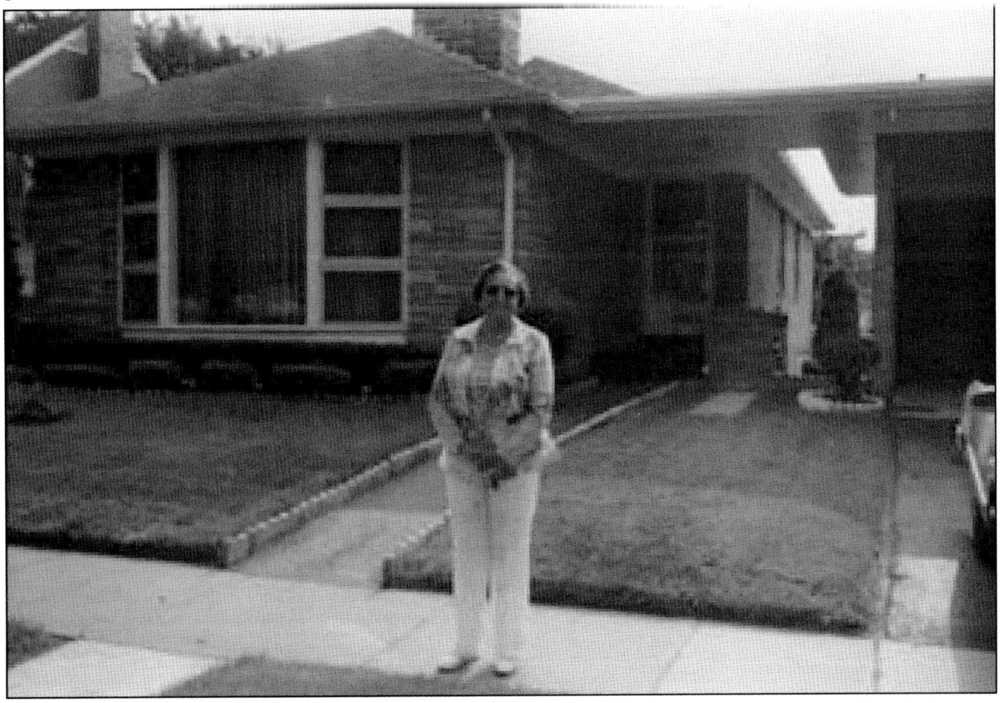

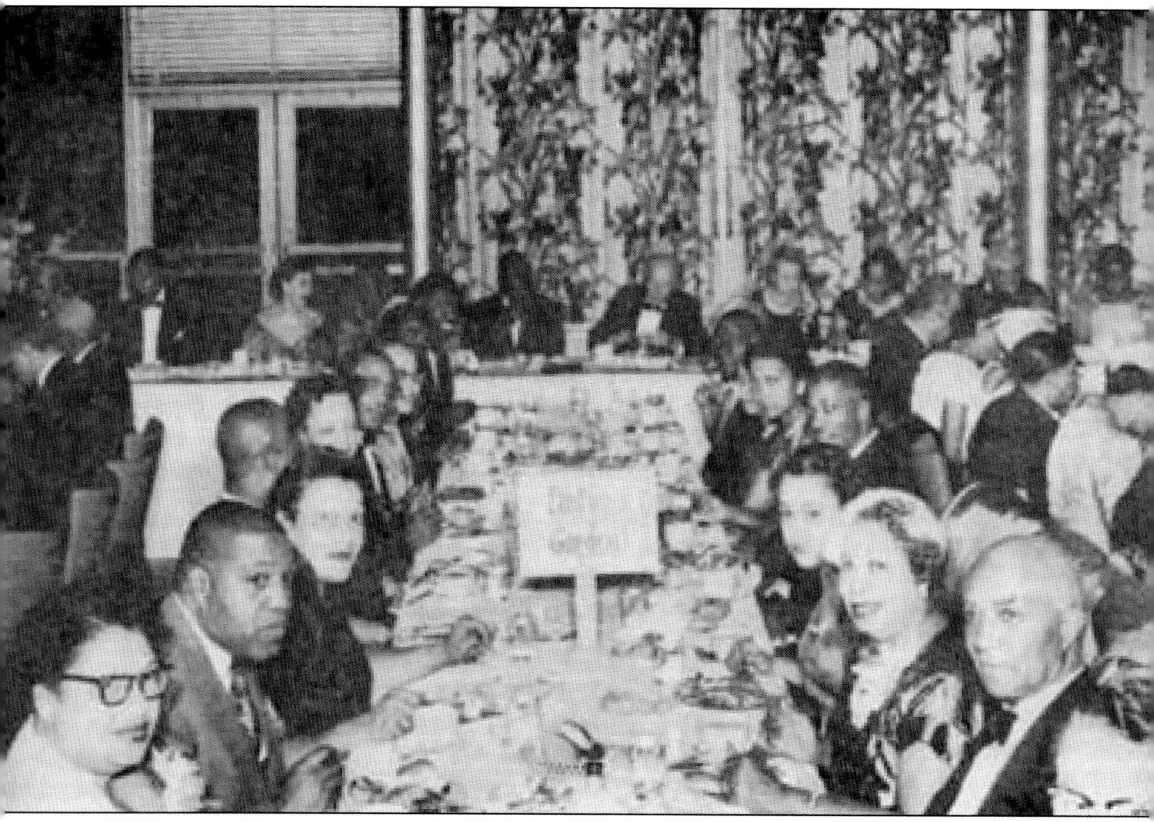

25 Years of Neighborliness. In 1956, the EGCA celebrated 25 years of activism in Eastland Gardens and in civic participation in Washington, DC. Here, at a banquet held in the recreation hall of Metropolitan Baptist Church in Northwest Washington, EGCA members enjoy a repast and fellowship with one another. EGCA was active in the Federation of Civic Associations, which was formed in 1910 after black neighborhood groups were rejected by the Federation of Citizens Associations. The federation lent support to the EGCA in many of its concerns. (PA.)

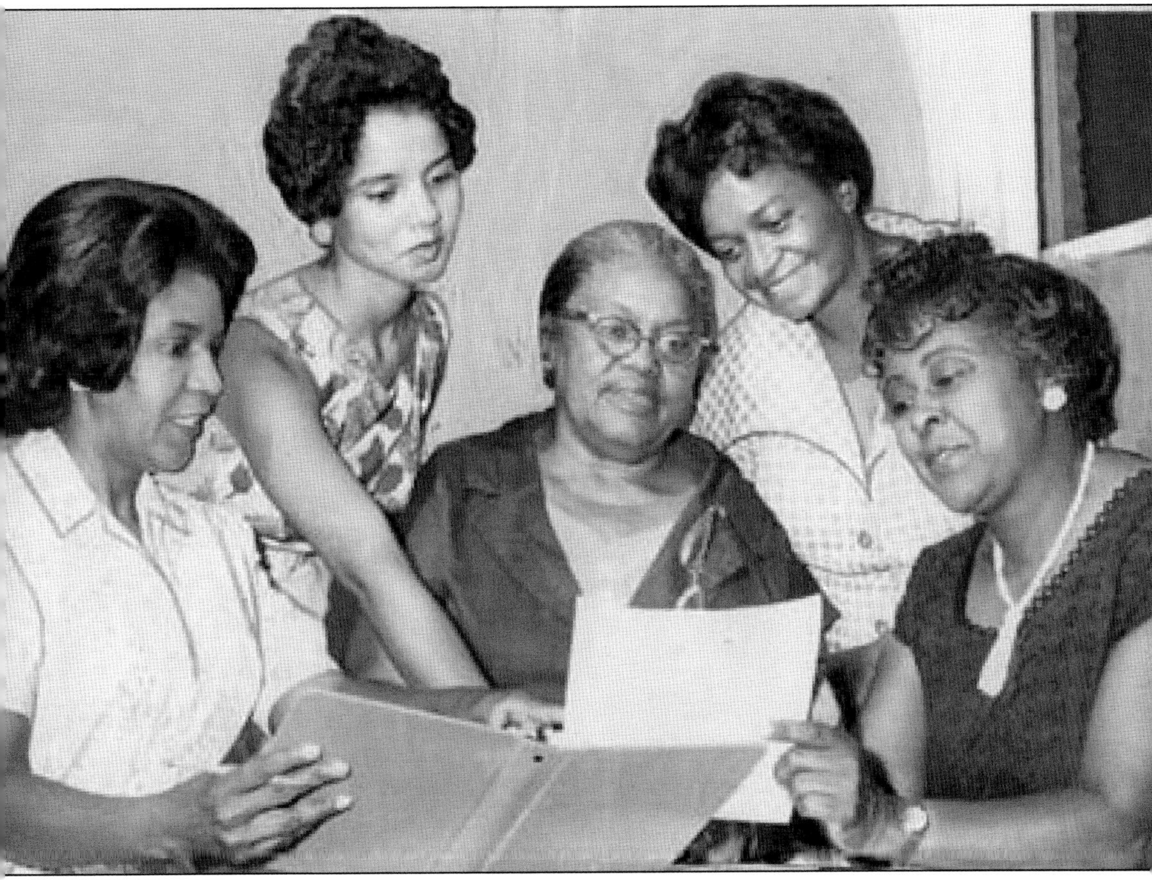

Event Planning in 1963. Members of the EGFC plan for their benefit luncheon and fashion show. Pictured in the *Afro-American* newspaper are residents and committee members. Those pictured are, from left to right, Michelle Coleman; Priscilla Mayfield; Hattie G. Robinson; America Nelson, chair of the event; and Rebecca Cole, EGFC president. The occasion was highly anticipated and raised a substantial amount of funds for the club. (AA.)

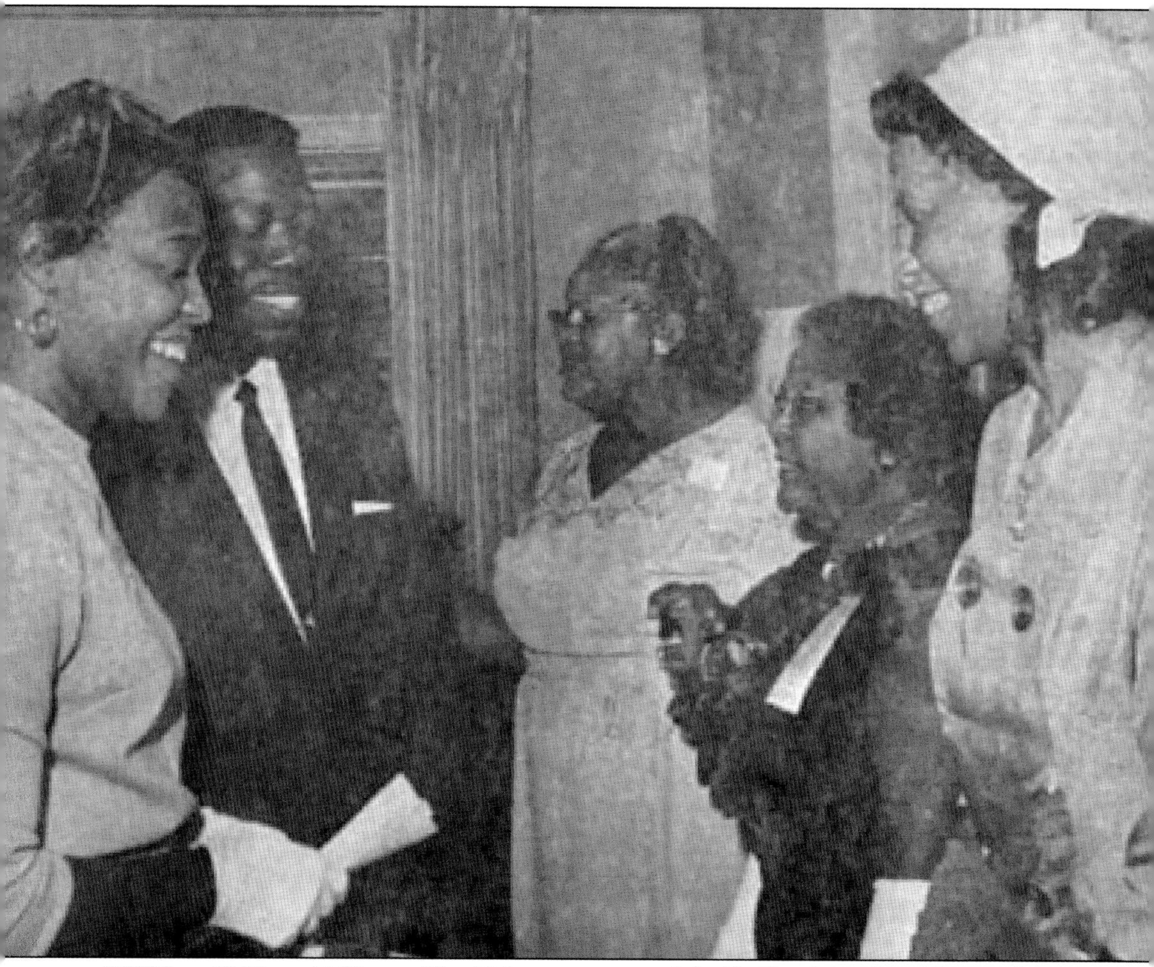

EGFC in 1968 at 10 Years. The 10th anniversary of the Eastland Gardens Flower Club was held in the home of Maj. Peter L. Robinson and Hattie Robinson at 4110 Meade Street. Hattie was the EGFC president. Pictured are, from left to right, Oscar Chapman and Rose Chapman of 4008 Lee Street; Hattie Robinson; Rebecca Cole, president from 1959 to 1965; and Rhuedine Davis, founder and first president. The EGFC was just one of numerous neighborhood garden clubs in the city. Members often belonged to more than one club and attended other club events. (DF.)

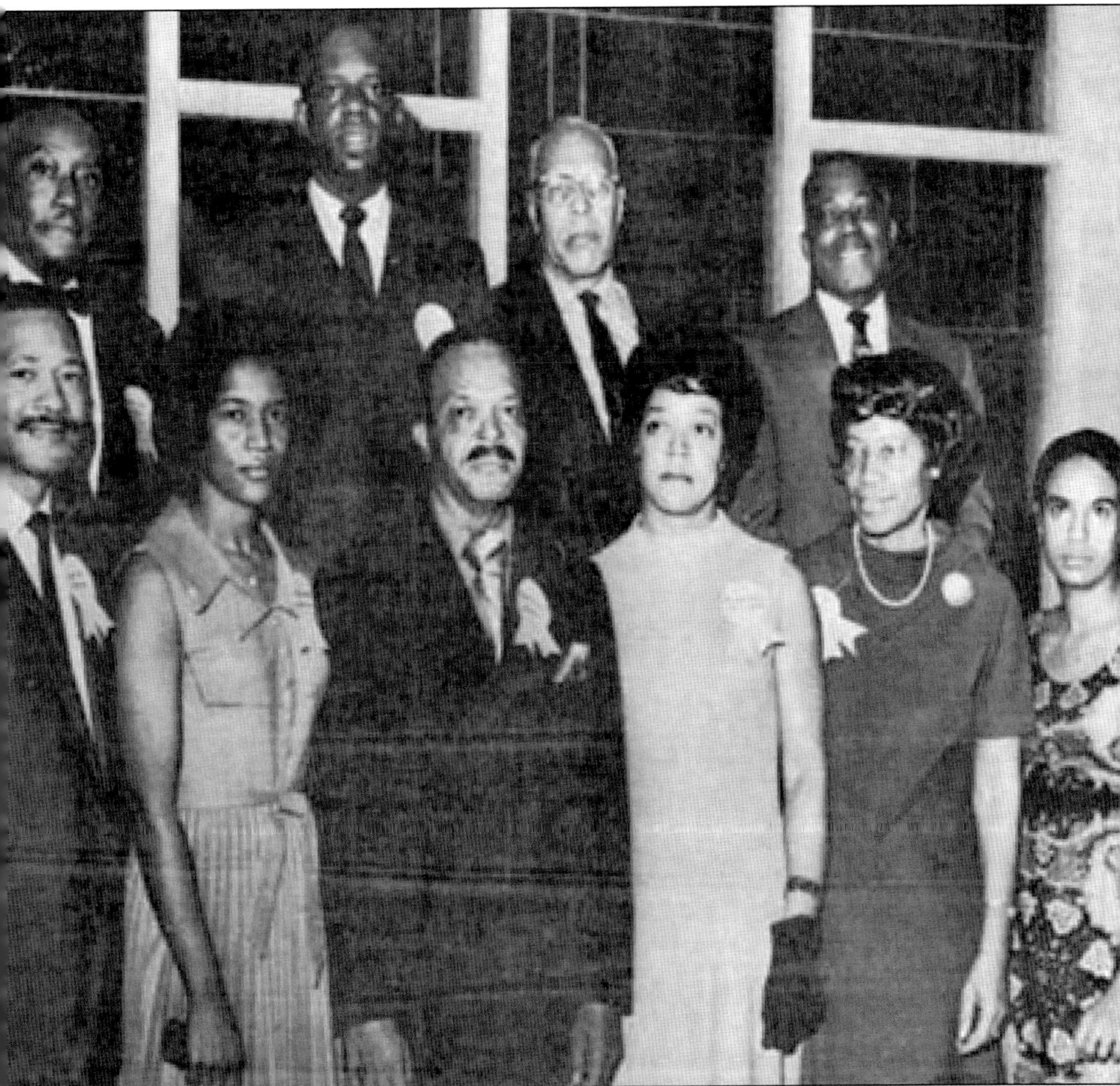

Installation of New Officers, 1970. EGCA officers are pictured here at their installation to two-year terms. The ceremony and reception were held at the Zion Baptist Church at 1234 Kenilworth Avenue. Those pictured are, from left to right, (first row) Alvin Hill, Barbara Blackwear, Wesley B. Collins, Nella Garner, Rheudine Davis, and Claudia Dawson; (second row) Mason George, John Attaway, Harold Chinn, and Baker Sabb. The civic association has been active in community affairs since 1931, serving as a watchdog to ensure the neighborhood and residents received equitable public services. (AA.)

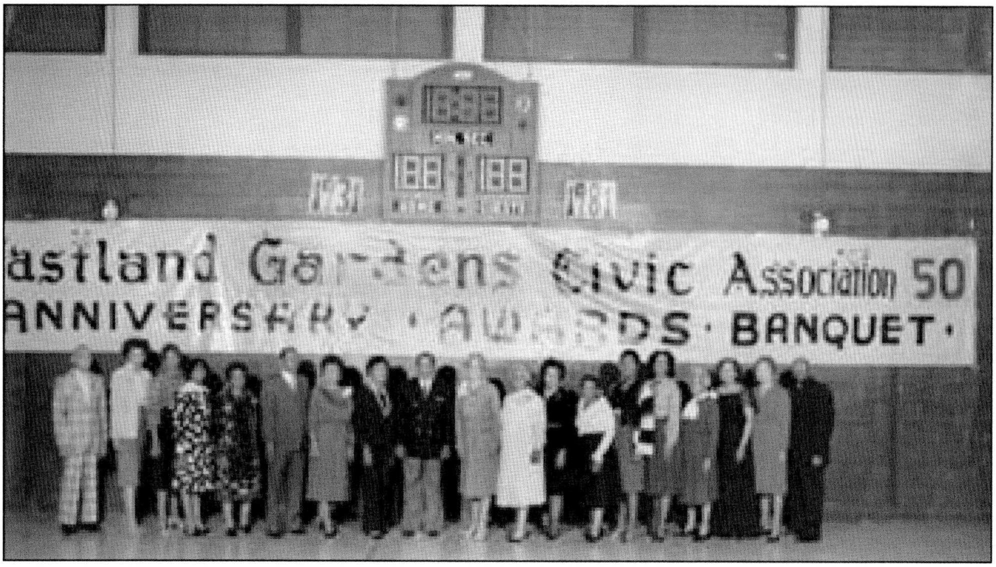

Celebration of 50 Years. EGCA members gathered in 1981 to plan the golden anniversary celebration. Included in the photograph below are, from left to right, (first row) Lois Strauss; Emma Swann; America Nelson; Rhuedine Davis, chair; Katie Johnson; Norvel Overall; Regina Rutledge; and Martha Green; (second row) William D. Strauss; Erman Clay, president; and Walter Overall. (Above, PA; below, DF.)

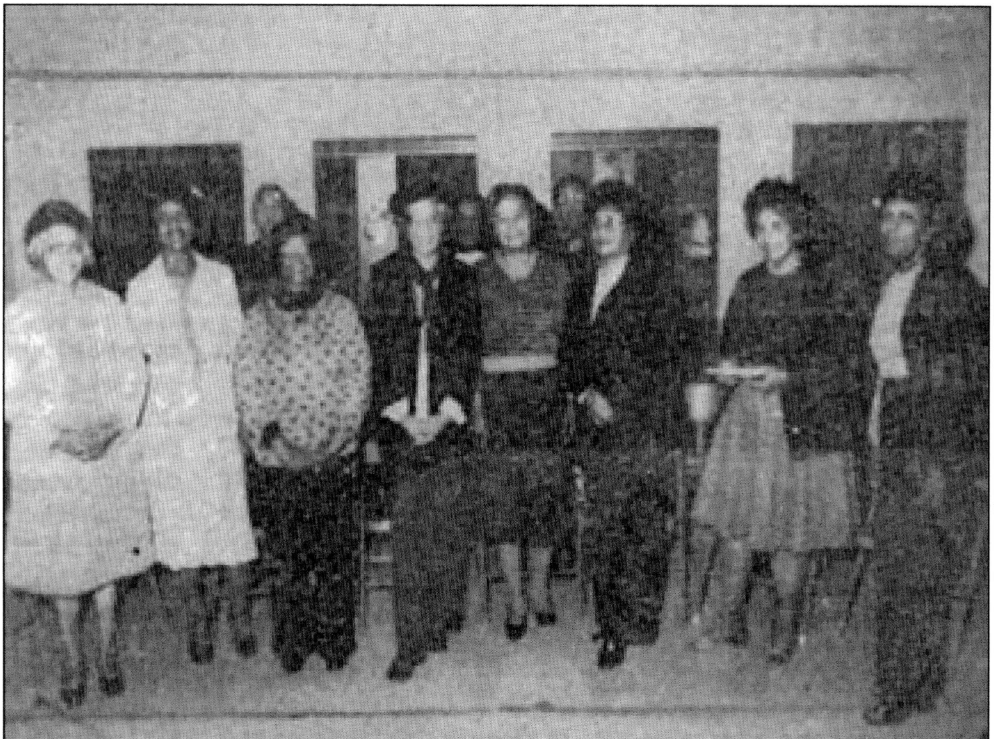

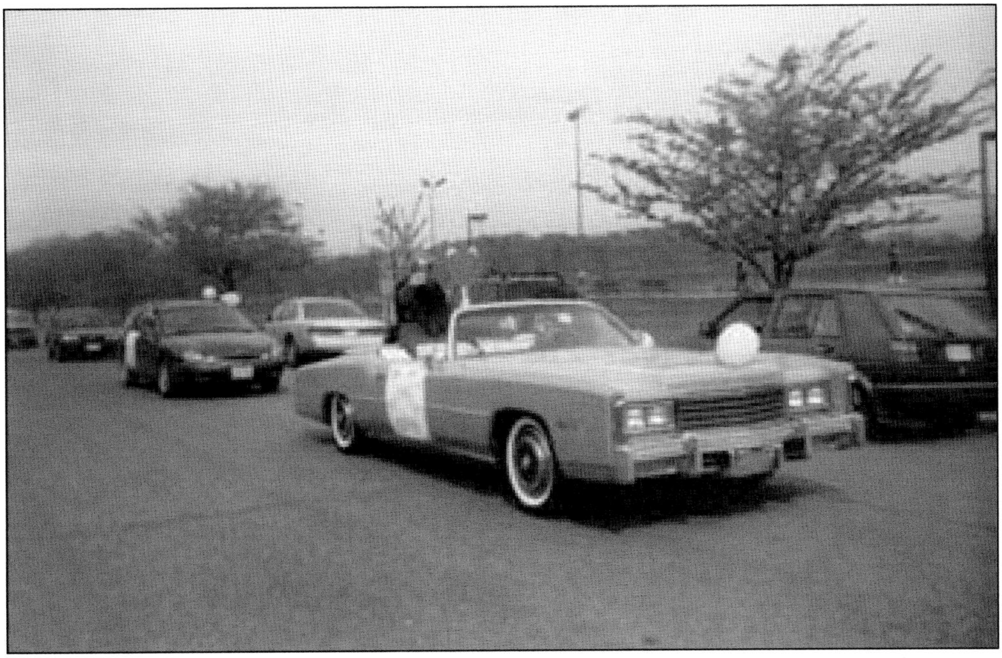

COMMUNITY PARADES. The annual spring parade was organized by Parkside, Kenilworth Courts, and Eastland Gardens Civic Associations and took place along Anacostia Avenue. The parade included school marching bands and representatives of organizations, including the EGFC and the KEMP Senior Citizens Club, which is a nutrition and social program organized in 1974 by Rhuedine Davis. Seated atop the Cadillac is Delores Crim-Neal, EGFC president. Pictured below, KEMP members were represented by Rebecca Cole, with a sign in her hand, and her driver. (Both, CJ.)

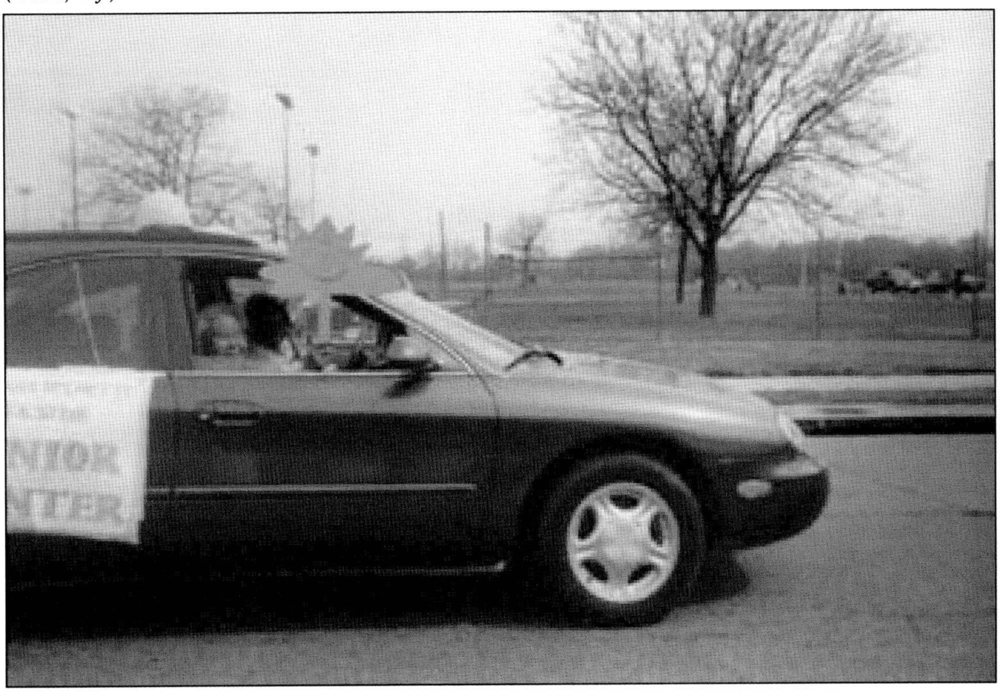

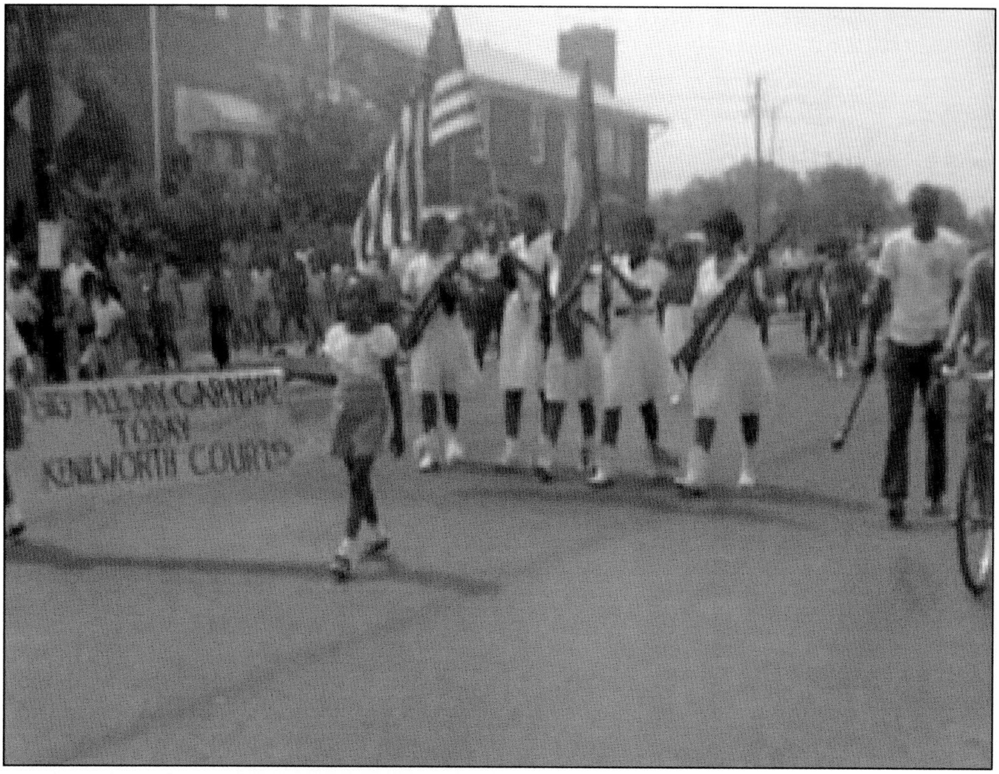

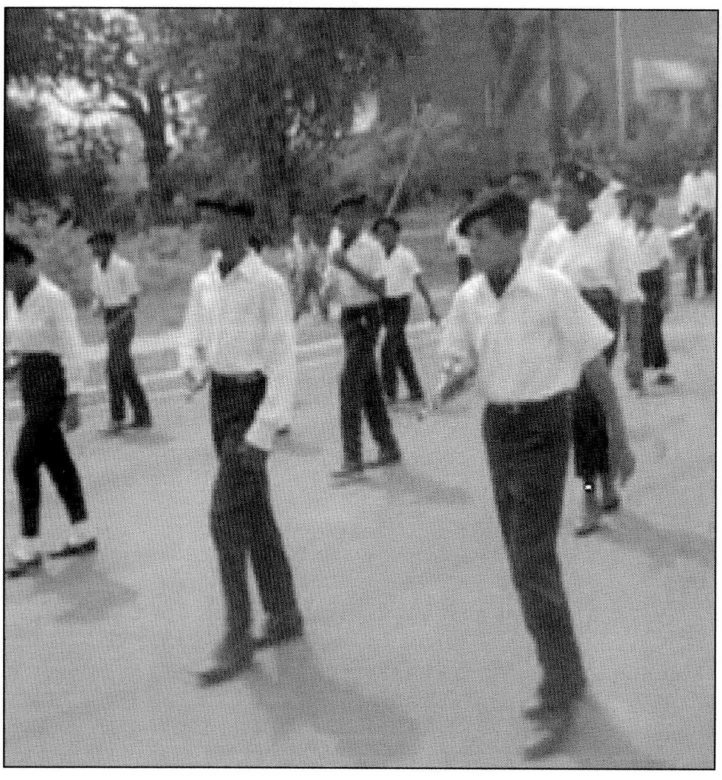

YOUTH MARCHERS. Community unity is exhibited here as the youth march through Eastland Gardens in the 1980s. The young representatives of Eastland Gardens and nearby Kenilworth Courts proudly strut down Forty-fourth Street heralding the "All Day Carnival," sponsored jointly by both neighborhoods. As they proudly displayed their skill and technique for marching in unified precision, strong ties between the local communities were nurtured and displayed. (Both, JW.)

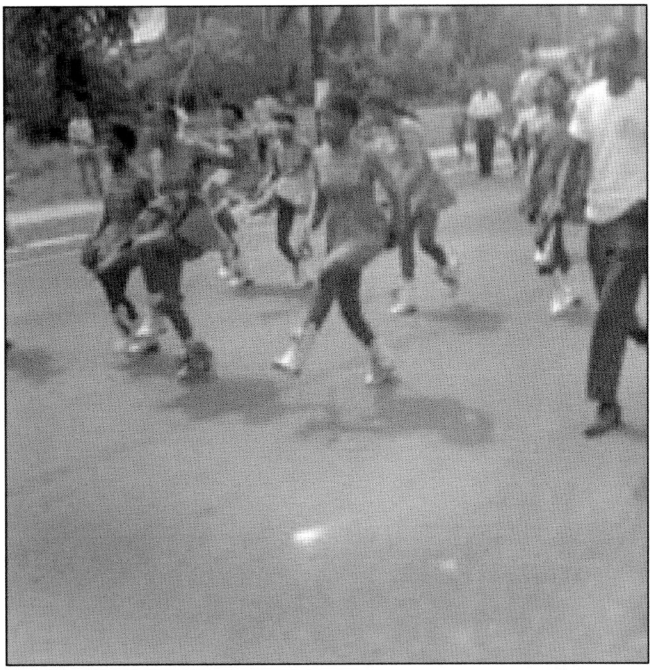

Marching Squads, a Tradition. In the same parade, a drill team marches down Forty-fourth Street in one of several celebrations the community was known to hold. Girls from the neighborhood were eager to join the high-stepping team. This was a way for local youth to display citizenship and to give back to their community. (JW.)

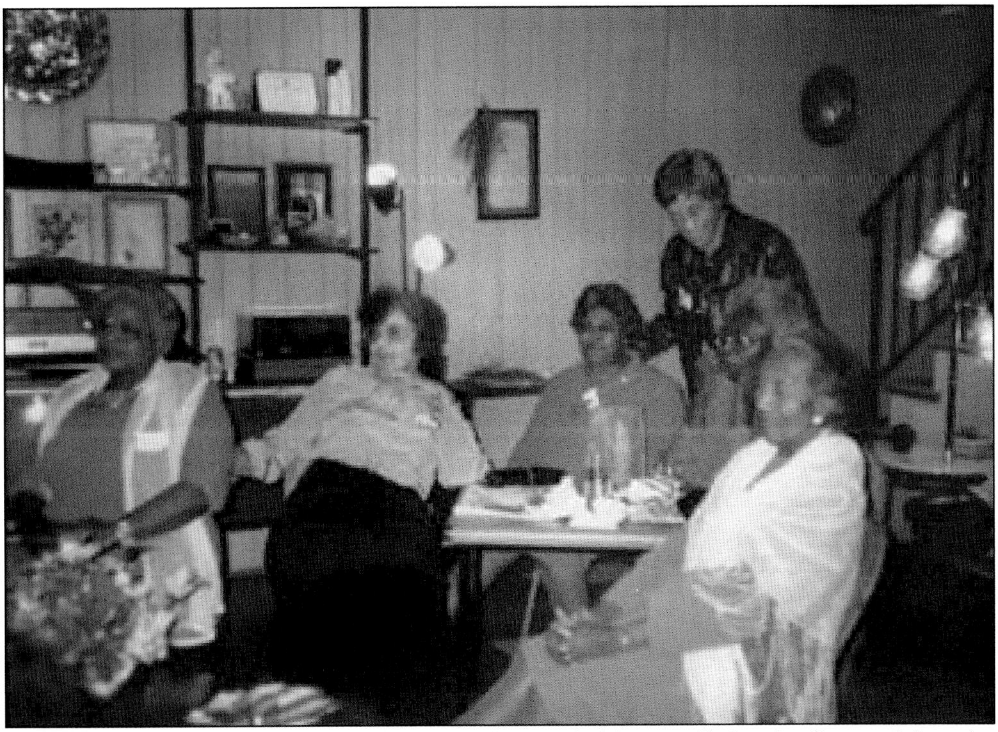

Annual Christmas Party. Another special event held annually by the flower club is the Christmas celebration, which is generally hosted in a member's home. In this photograph, the party was conducted at the home of Erman Clay and Vanetta Clay. Enjoying the festivities are, from left to right, Grace Connolly, Minnie Woodson, Rebecca Cole, Rheudine Davis, and two unidentified members. (DF.)

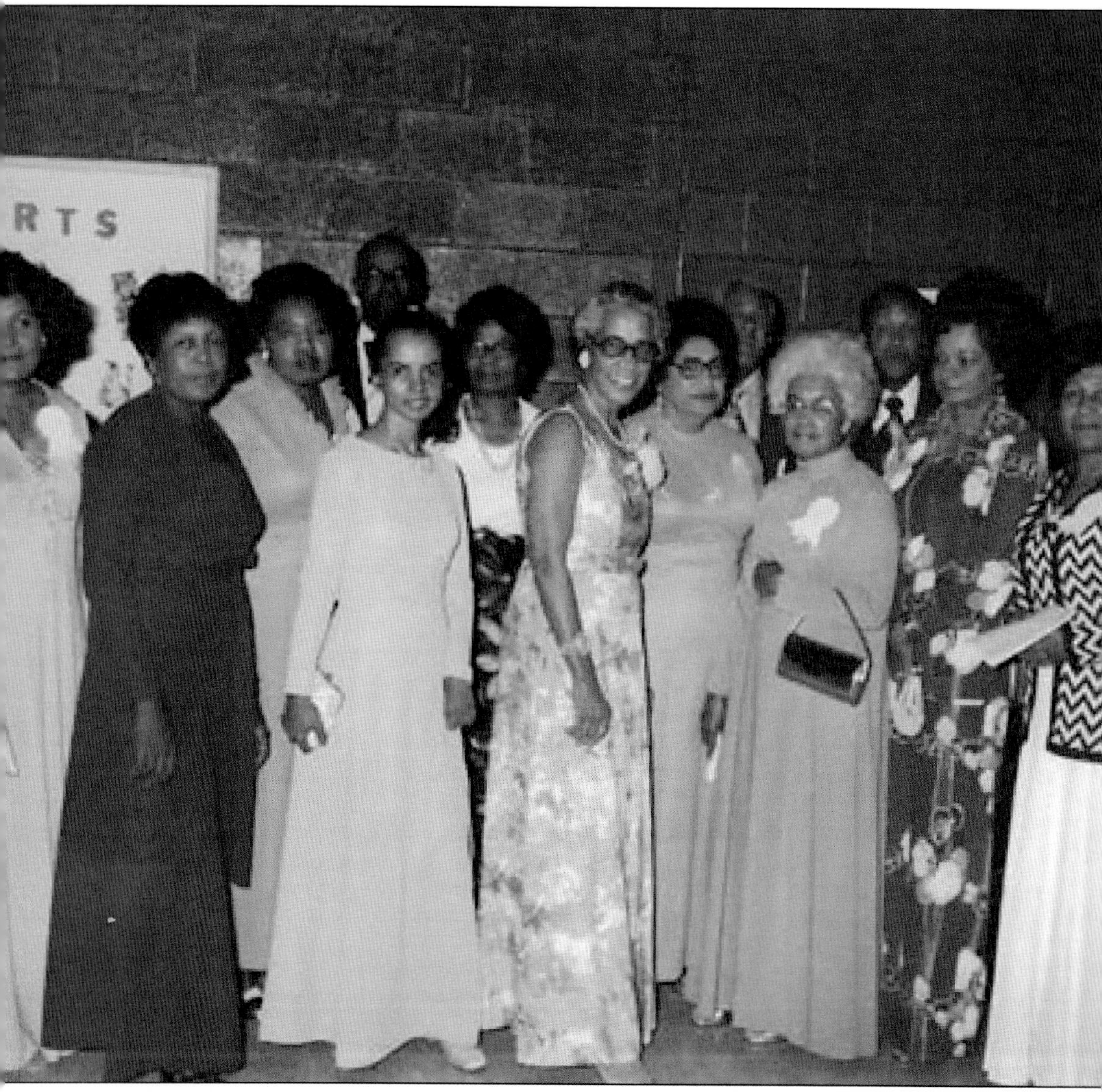

The Flower Club's Annual Ball. The annual gala of the EGFC not only raised money for the organization but also provided an opportunity for members to dress up and have fun with their neighbors. As in most years, the special event was held at the recreation center, which had been transformed for the night. Here are some of the ladies of the flower club with their husbands at a 1980s gala. Those pictured are, from left to right, Katie Lacey Johnson, Martha Green, Lillian Barham, three unidentified people, Rhuedine Davis, Roxie Fowler, Virginia Brown, Walter Overall, Vanetta Clay, and Norvel Overall. (DF.)

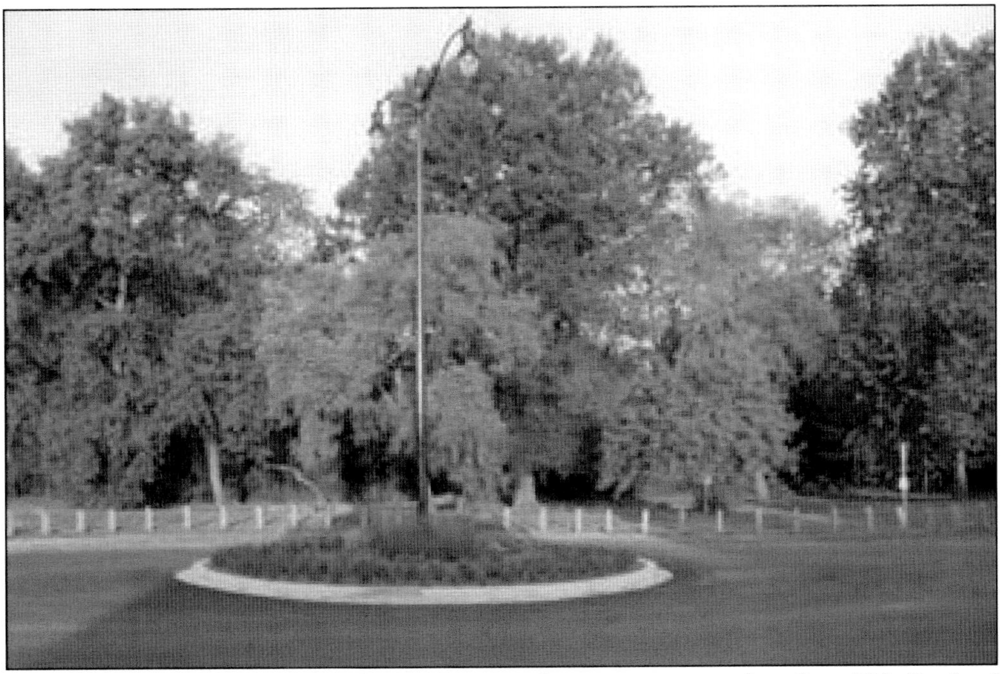

EASTLAND GARDENS'S TREES. Working to improve the environment and quality of life, Eastland Gardens's trees are on the job 24 hours, every day. The neighborhood was defined by its trees. Aside from the obvious aesthetic benefits, trees within the urban forest improve air, protect water, save energy, and promote economic sustainability. The trees at the entrance on Lee Street bring shady relief on hot sunny days, making it a delightful place to be. (JB.)

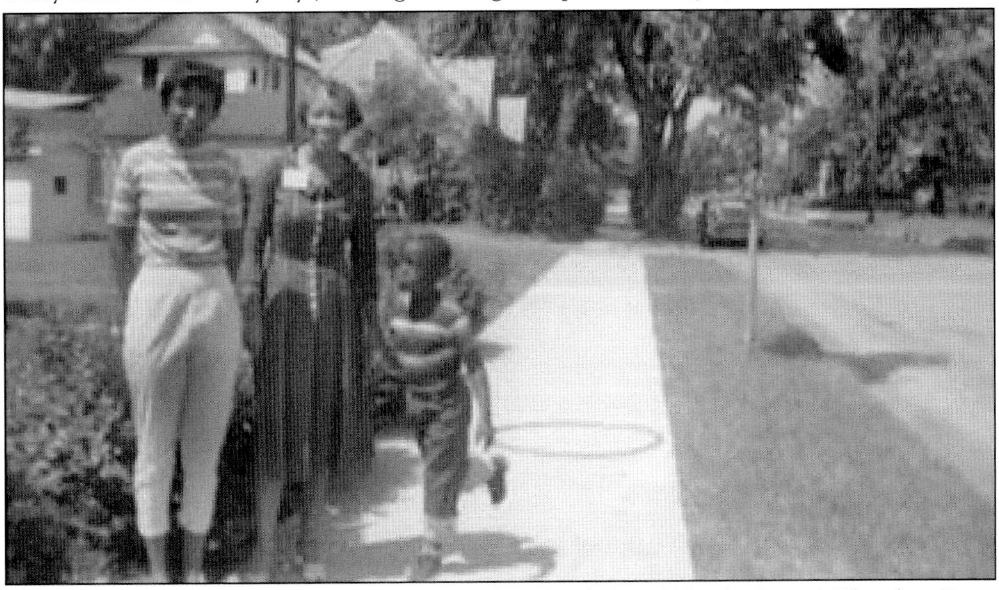

A NORTHEAST WASHINGTON PARADISE. Pictured are family friend Natalie Stroud, Rhuedine Davis (center), and her son Alan Davis, with a view of the community Davis worked so hard to protect. This 1950s scene is composed of lush trees, manicured and landscaped lawns, stylish housing, paved streets, and sidewalks. This suburban scene is their community—within the city limits of Washington, DC, where they are residents, owners, and leaders. (DF.)